BEYOND ARISTOPHANES

AMERICAN PHILOLOGICAL ASSOCIATION
American Classical Studies

Series Editor

David L. Blank

Number 38

BEYOND ARISTOPHANES
Transition and Diversity in Greek Comedy

edited by
Gregory W. Dobrov

Gregory W. Dobrov

BEYOND ARISTOPHANES
Transition and Diversity in Greek Comedy

Scholars Press
Atlanta, Georgia

BEYOND ARISTOPHANES

edited by
Gregory W. Dobrov

© 1995
The American Philological Association

Library of Congress Cataloging in Publication Data
Beyond Aristophanes : transition and diversity in Greek comedy /
[edited by] Gregory W. Dobrov.
    p. cm. — (Monograph series / American Philological
Association ; no. 38)
  Includes bibliographical references (p.) and index.
  ISBN 0-7885-0139-9 (acid-free paper). — ISBN 0-7885-0140-2 (pbk. :
acid-free paper)
  1. Greek drama (Comedy)—History and criticism. 2. Aristophanes—
Criticism and interpretation. I. Dobrov, Gregory W., 1957– .
II. American Philological Association. III. Series: Monograph
series (American Philological Association) ; no. 38.
PA3161.B4 1995
882'.0109—dc20   95-23502
                                           CIP

Printed in the United States of America
on acid-free paper

For Mara
(who laughs at most of my jokes)
on the occasion of our anniversaries:
the tenth, of marriage,
and twenty-fifth, of friendship

Contents

Introduction	ix
Acknowledgments	xv
Myth, Parody, and Comic Plots: The Birth of Gods and Middle Comedy *Heinz-Günther Nesselrath*	1
The Fabrication of Comic Illusion *Niall W. Slater*	29
The Poet's Voice in the Evolution of Dramatic Dialogism *Gregory W. Dobrov*	47
The Continuity of the Chorus in Fourth-Century Attic Comedy *Kenneth S. Rothwell, Jr.*	99
Plato Comicus and the Evolution of Greek Comedy *Ralph M. Rosen*	119
The Maculate Music: Gender, Genre and the *Chiron* of Pherecrates *Gregory W. Dobrov and Eduardo Urios-Aparisi*	139
Beyond Aristophanes *Jeffrey Henderson*	175
Bibliography	185
Index Locorum	205

Transition and Diversity In Greek Comedy
Editor's Introduction

> Old Comedy was destroyed by the political downfall. Thalia's heart was broken, and though she recovered her poise she never regained her spirits.
>
> —Gilbert Norwood

From its official introduction to the Athenian City Dionysia through a continued life in Roman adaptations, the commedia dell'arte, Molière and beyond, comedy has endured as the most vital literary genre to emerge from Classical antiquity. Longevity and variety are qualities that make this branch of literary history especially attractive and, at the same time, demanding. Aristophanes in particular continues to attract those with a penchant for complexity and paradox. What sort of experience was this thing called κωμῳδία? Consistently funny and entertaining, no doubt; rich and diverse, indeed, as even a sampling of fragments will reveal; and *always* a challenge to our grasp of Greek language, politics, and social history. A performance such as *Acharnians* simultaneously involved buffoonery played across an elaborate formal structure; a simple plot articulated by a complex text; fantasy improvised from history; humor made of crisis; sociopolitical ideas dressed in carnival garb; "unserious" poetry intimately bound up with its most "serious" kin; rustic naïveté masking acute self-consciousness; a discourse so diverse as to be the antithesis of style. Even when speaking strictly of Athenian Comedy, moreover, we stretch a rubric to the breaking point by including the very different theaters of Cratinus, Pherecrates, Eubulus, and Menander. Plato's anecdotal choice of Aristophanes as the best textbook on Athenian affairs and the Hellenistic scholar's "Menander! Life! Which of you imitated the other?" are eloquent expressions of this breadth and diversity.

One of the great challenges to the students of Greek theater history involves the "what," "how," and "why" of comedy's evolution over the better part of three centuries—What evolved into what? Are we to regard the trajectory from putative ritual origins to New Comedy as the progress towards a *telos* similar to that achieved by tragedy in Aristotle's view (Poetics 1449a14-15), or is the evolution more complex, less linear? How did Greek Comedy change, e.g., how many phases do we discern in its evolution? What exactly happened to the chorus, parabasis, obscenity, and fantasy in the fourth century? What forces drove this evolution in the first place? Why, for example, did the style defined by Aristophanes in the 420's become extinct, enjoying neither revival nor imitation, while there is evidence to the contrary for later plays such as *Thesmophoriazusae* and *Frogs*? Do we seek the explanation in extra-dramatic reality, i.e. in the sociopolitical evolution of the polis, or is this an aesthetic issue having more to do with the intangible tastes of playwright and public? Any one of these questions naturally leads to the others in a way that suggests a holistic approach to the genre beyond the comfortable limits of the canon. The reality, of course, was far richer than our record where hundreds of names, play-titles, and anecdotes linger to remind us of how little we know. This faint glow from the edge of the literary universe suggests that we have much more research to do on comedy's origins, diversity, complexity and vital connection with its artistic, social, and political contexts. This holistic imperative is quickly humbled, however, by the inadequacy of our evidence. The work of all playwrights other than Aristophanes and Menander is represented only by fragments few of which satisfyingly relate what we might call a scene. Until recently, moreover, students of the genre have had to content themselves with editions of these fragments that had not been successfully updated for a hundred years or more. This situation has conspired at various times with the lack of an adequate critical text of Aristophanes and the ongoing discovery of Menander to present formidable obstacles to progress in the field.

With the publication of Kassel and Austin's masterly *Poetae Comici Graeci* (in progress since 1983), the study of ancient Greek Comedy is finally being put on a much sounder basis. The excellence and breadth of *PCG* is facilitating and inspiring new research into the history of the genre. Works such as Heinz-Günther Nesselrath's *Die attische Mittlere Komödie* and Jeffrey Rusten's *Birth of Comedy* (to say nothing of numerous articles and dissertations) are filling a long-standing need for reevaluation and presentation of the texts bearing on the evolution of Athenian Comedy from Cratinus to Menander. Earlier contributions to this field such as August Meineke's *Historia critica* (1839) and Gilbert Norwood's *Greek Comedy* (1931) are especially out of date with respect to New Comedy and its relation to earlier evolutionary stages. An encouraging development in the field is a movement toward an integrated approach that embraces both mainstream and periphery, a trend quite obviously stimulated by Kassel and Austin's comprehensive edition of the fragments that is as accurate as it is rich in textual and bibliographical detail. As we look forward to the *PCG* volumes of Menander and Aristophanes, we are invited to reopen an important chapter of Greek literary history and to examine its underlying assumptions.

This collection has its origins in the 1992 Annual Meeting of the American Philological Association in New Orleans where the contributors met to participate in a panel session on the evolution of Athenian Comedy. New Orleans, known by many names including "The Big Easy" and "The City That Care Forgot," furnished an ideal setting for our celebration of comedy and the first decade of *PCG*. The present volume is an expanded version of that session and is devoted to the most important changes—in theme, language, structure, style, and production—that characterize the transformation of Athenian Comedy from the mid-fifth through the fourth century.

Nesselrath's definitive *Mittlere Komödie* suggests a valuable corrective to the famous purple patch describing the first half of the fourth century as wasteland between "the excitingly varied landscape of Old Comedy and the City of Menander" (Norwood, *Greek Comedy* 38, see p. 175, below). It is precisely in the Middle Comic period that the genre underwent its most rapid and profound transformation. The privilege traditionally accorded the political Aristophanes and the remains of Menander, while no doubt justified, does much to distort our "big picture" of comedy's development. It is important to remember that the competitors of the young Aristophanes included Plato

Comicus, Eupolis and Pherecrates, playwrights whose work was often quite different in subject and style. As an older man, on the other hand, Aristophanes was part of a vital and complex literary scene that abandoned the fashions of the late fifth century. This Middle Comedy exhibited many features, however, that distinguished it from the stagecraft of Diphilus and Menander. Having a sharper picture of the sources for this period and a superior text of the fragments themselves, we are in a better position to address a number of leading questions concerning the various elements of comedy and their evolution. The leading figures, especially Aristophanes, continue to hold the limelight as the scholarly industry intensifies its research into every aspect of the genre. Herein we find a natural framework for a volume devoted to the remains of Greek Comedy around and beyond the canon. Each essay explores a specific parameter with an emphasis on transition and diversity.

Myth and parody in the plots of post-Aristophanic comedy are the subject of Heinz-Günther Nesselrath's paper. Middle Comedy plays based on a divine birth constitute a unique subgroup which exhibits a complex moment in the genre's development, as various influences converge. The shift in style, according to Nesselrath, has a close affinity with the satyr-play (less the satyrs). The Θεῶν γοναί theme enjoyed a heyday of at least thirteen or fourteen years during which comedy expanded its range to admit the influence of didactic epic, the Homeric hymns, and folktales. Janus-like, these plays look simultaneously back to an archaic heritage rich with divine mythology, forward to the family themes of New Comedy, and beyond to Callimachus and Lucian. The Θεῶν γοναί fad tests our assumptions about the function of parody and myth in the evolution of comic dramaturgy.

Niall Slater takes up a central issue of the aesthetics of the comic performance in seeking to explain the gradual move away from the non-illusory and metatheatrical performance of Old Comedy to the highly developed illusion and apolitical mannerism of New Comedy. It is not the influence of tragedy, Slater arugues, but rather a diverse and internationalized audience that created a demand for a standardized and portable product. This emphasis on the viability of a comic performance outside Athens is rich with implications for characterization, plot, topicality, metatheater, chorus, and theater architecture in the fourth century. Slater's argument aligns discussions of each of these elements in a coherent account of the largely circumstantial "triumph of illusion" on the New Comic stage.

My essay is concerned with the poet's voice in the evolution from Old to New Comedy. Distinguishing features of Aristophanes' political satires are "polyphony," "discourse irony," and "improvisation" whereby the poet makes of his stage figures a complex poem in which his own persona and voice are prominent elements. A review of comic harangues spanning the century from *Acharnians* to *Dyscolus* reveals a gradual withdrawl of the poet (as quasi-fictional persona/presence) from the world and language of his play. With the evolution of comedy through the Middle period, the three dimensions of poet-players-spectators are reduced to two in the plane of a more rigid dramatic illusion. The transition from the archaic poetics of the Old Comic competition to the realistic dialogism of Menander marks a fundamental shift in the theory of the comic towards "the probable" (Aristotle's τὸ εἰκός), a concept bound up with the simultaneous development of dramatic illusion, mannerism and an international market.

Kenneth Rothwell confronts the commonly assumed link between choral drama and civic solidarity. From a careful review of the sociopolitical context of dramatic production in the fourth century, he concludes that contrary to the largely unexamined *communis opinio*, it was owing precisely to the stability of the Athenian democracy that the polis could afford to abandon the chorus and to rely on drama made up exclusively of individuals in dialogue and debate. Rothwell's discussion of the chorus and its place in the evolution of Greek Comedy complicates the received view by allowing for greater diversity within various periods and by questioning the assumption that dramatic form was critically dependent on Athenian politics. If comic playwrights decided to write plays whose plots depended on individual characters and excluded choruses from their action—he argues—that was a conscious choice on their part.

Ralph Rosen's paper and my joint effort with Eduardo Urios-Aparisi treat the difficult issues of poet, sub-genre, and synchronic diversity by examining the places in the evolutionary scheme of Plato Comicus and Pherecrates, respectively. Although chronologically contemporary with Aristophanes, the work of Plato anticipates Middle Comedy in certain respects. In a detailed discussion of important fragments, Rosen questions both the linear concept of literary evolution as well as a narrow approach to generic categories with respect to plot, political satire, and invective.

The paper co-authored by myself and Urios-Aparisi complements Rosen's discussion by first reviewing the traditional claims about Pherecrates and his craft. Our hypothesis that Μουσική, the main speaker of the famous *Chiron* fragment (155 K.-A.), was presented as a hetaira leads to a reconsideration of *Chiron* in the context of comedy's evolving response to the new music and dithyramb. Though rooted in Old Comic agonistic ribaldry, the suggestive allegory in which Music's (female) body is prostituted to various clients, such as Cinesias and Timotheus, looks forward to the progressive theatrical assimilation of the dithyramb in Middle Comedy (e.g. the parodos of Aristophanes' *Wealth*). Comedy's reception of the new dithyramb evolves from a mode of overt criticism to one of mimesis and incorporation.

In keeping with the format of the original session, Jeffrey Henderson responds to each contribution, posing questions and suggesting directions for further research. This conclusion is essential to the spirit of our collective effort in that it looks toward the future. It is our hope that these essays will kindle interest and point to further work that remains to be done in this stimulating field.

Los Altos-New Orleans-Ann Arbor

Acknowledgments

It is a pleasure to acknowledge the fellowship and support provided by the Institute for the Humanities at my home base, the University of Michigan, Ann Arbor. To the director, James Winn, the Institute's expert staff, and the fellows of 1994-95, especially Sabine MacCormack, my warmest thanks. I am pleased to acknowledge David Blank, editor of the American Classical Studies Monograph Series, the three anonymous readers, and Thomas K. Hubbard (the fourth, not-so-anonymous reader) for their efforts in evaluating our book. My thanks also to those who worked on various editorial tasks, Robert Sklenar, Pedar Foss, Emily Tse, and Eduardo Urios-Aparisi. The encouragement and advice of Jeff Henderson, Niall Slater, and Ralph Rosen made the passage from panel proposal to monograph truly rewarding and worthwhile. Heartfelt thanks to Eva Wampuszyc, my publications assistant at the Institute for the Humanities, for her alacrity, creativity, and hard work. Finally, I owe a special debt of gratitude to Heinz-Günther Nesselrath for his many contributions to this project from our preliminary discussions (Köln to Syracuse) of the New Orleans symposium to his several sojourns in Ann Arbor.

I alone am to blame for the cover illustration of the dance through time by an impossible chorus—black-figure knight, Getty bird, padded dancer (stone relief), and *miles gloriosus* (S. Agata "Antigone").

Myth, Parody, and Comic Plots: The Birth of Gods and Middle Comedy

Heinz-Günther Nesselrath

I

Greek myth has developed a number of intriguing stories about the birth of various gods of the Olympic pantheon, and Greek literature dealt with these stories from archaic times well into the Imperial Age. Already in the so-called *Homeric Hymns* a number of divine births are either briefly alluded to or presented in some detail;[1] the most delightful of these hymns tells about the newborn Hermes already wheeling, dealing and stealing, with the adult deities being apparently no match for the little villain.[2] In Hellenistic times, Callimachean hymns retell the story of Leto giving birth to Apollo and give us the charming picture of little Artemis grabbing for Zeus' mighty beard;[3] and in the second century AD, the Syrian satirist Lucian devoted several of his entertaining *Dialogues of the Gods* to kindred themes.[4] These are

---

[1] All in all, the number of places in the Homeric Hymns where there is talk about a divine birth is considerable: see the *Hymn to Dionysus* (I) 6-8; *Hymn to Apollo* (III) 14-18, 25-139, and 305-354 (Hera, angry about Zeus bringing forth Athena, all by herself brings Typhon into the world); *Hymn to Hermes* (IV) 3-end; *Hymn to Aphrodite* (VI) 2-18; of the lesser Homeric Hymns see the eighteenth (Hermes), lines 3-9; the nineteenth (Pan), lines 28-47; the twenty-eighth (Athena), lines 4-16; the thirty-first (Helius), lines 2-7; and the thirty-second (Selene), lines 14-16.

[2] *Hymn to Hermes*, lines 3-end.

[3] Callimachus, *Hymn to Delos* 55-274; *Hymn to Artemis* 4-28.

[4] Lucian, *Dialogues of the Gods* 2 [22], 11 [7], 12 [9], 13 [8]; compare also 18 [16] and *Dialogues of the Sea Gods* 9 [10]. It is a moot question whether Lucian might have taken some of these mythical births from the comic plays that are the subject of this paper. There is no real solid evidence for this, and thus it is safer to assume that he was very well able to work up

the still extant areas of Greek literature where even today we can enjoy the entertaining and ingenious literary treatment of these myths. There once was, however, yet another literary branch which—at least for a while—took over this kind of story after it had detected its comic (and sometimes farcical) potential and developed it into something like a specialty of its own: Attic Comedy. During a period of about three or four decades (starting probably around 410 BC), at least thirteen or fourteen plays (and maybe more, of which no trace remains today) appeared on stage, all of which dramatized a story-line that was somehow woven around the birth of a god.

Such a concentration of similar themes would be notable at any time, but it is even more remarkable for the period just mentioned, because it is in these very decades that momentous changes took place in the development of Greek comedy as a whole: Old Comedy reached its final stage about or soon after 410 BC,[5] and by 380, some of its most characteristic features either had already been discarded or were about to be (chorus, polymetry, lyric variety).

In the area of theme and plot, post-Aristophanic comedy—which, however paradoxical this may sound, already began during Aristophanes' latter days—to a considerable extent imitated the satyr play[6] without taking over the satyrs: that is, in casting about for new stories to dramatize, it often left the

---

his witty little dialogues from mythical stories as he found them in handbooks (e.g., the *Library* of Apollodorus).

[5]Aristophanes' *Frogs*, put on the stage in 405, may be called its last surviving masterpiece.

[6]There is the interesting case of Evanthius, a critic working in Late Antiquity, who in his treatise *De fabula* (to be found as no. XXV in Koster, *Prolegomena* 122-26) gives the name "Satyra" to the comedy period between Old and New (124.58)! In Nesselrath, *Mittlere Komödie* 43, I venture the suggestion that the reason for this rather peculiar case of naming may be found in the fact that a considerable number of Middle Comic plays dealt with mythical travesty just as the satyr plays of old did and that this may be echoed—though in a surely distorted way—by Evanthius (who may be called a "late-comer" within a long tradition of literary criticism) calling Middle Comedy "Satyra." In some satyr plays, in fact, new-born children played a not insignificant part, e.g. young Perseus in Aeschylus' *Diktyulkoi* (fr. 47a, 786-820 Radt); for Sophocles' *Ichneutai* see below, note 34.

contemporary and political themes of Old Comedy behind and looked to various myths and their treatment in epic and tragedy.[7] All this happened during a fundamental change in theme and emphasis of comic plays which apparently took several decades to develop fully; and in the course of these transitional decades, one certain field of mythical stories—those dealing with the birth and childhood of gods—came to be regarded by a number of poets as having at least as much dramatic potential as several others. It is at this point that θεῶν γοναί-plays[8] began to form a special, separate kind of group within the large flowering of mythological parody in the Attic Comedy of those times.

A rapid survey of some of the relevant themes to be found in θεῶν γοναί-plays will show that there was indeed considerable comic potential in this sort of plot. At least four plays dealt with the story of Aphrodite's birth,[9] and the sixth Homeric Hymn (the

---

[7]See, for example, the excerpt of Platonius, *On the Difference of (Periods of) Comedies* in Koster, *Prolegomena* 5.42-47: οἱ δὲ τῆς μέσης κωμῳδίας ποιηταὶ καὶ τὰς ὑποθέσεις ἤμειψαν...ὑποθέσεις μὲν γὰρ τῆς παλαιᾶς κωμῳδίας ἦσαν αὗται· τὸ στρατηγοῖς ἐπιτιμᾶν καὶ δικασταῖς οὐκ ὀρθῶς δικάζουσι καὶ χρήματα συλλέγουσιν ἐξ ἀδικίας τισὶ καὶ μοχθηρὸν ἐπανῃρημένοις βίον. ἡ δὲ μέση κωμῳδία ἀφῆκε τὰς τοιαύτας ὑποθέσεις, ἐπὶ δὲ τὸ σκώπτειν ἱστορίας ῥηθείσας ποιηταῖς ἦλθον.... "The poets of Middle Comedy changed the plots, too... In Old Comedy plots had been of the following kind: to blame generals and judges who did not judge correctly, and people who heaped up money by unjust means and had taken up a criminal way of life. Middle Comedy let go of these kinds of plots, and its poets turned to ridiculing stories told by poets.... "

[8]Some years ago Winkler, "Akko" 138, proposed a rather different meaning for the word γοναί in θεῶν γοναί-titles than was—and still is—generally assumed, namely "offspring." According to that meaning, Ἀθηνᾶς γοναί (e.g.) would mean something like (in current idiom) "Daughters of Eve," and this and other θεῶν γοναί would have been, according to Winkler, "not mythological burlesques dealing with the literal offspring of a god but humorous presentations of mortals who exemplified or perverted the works and nature of a god." This view, however, is hard to reconcile with some of the real evidence—fragmentary though it may be—which is still left of these plays. In Nesselrath, *Mittlere Komödie* 230, note 143, I have argued that fragments like Hermippus fr. 2 K.-A. and Araros fr. 13 K.-A. yield a satisfactory sense only if the word γοναί in the title of the plays to which these fragments once belonged means "birth."

[9]There once were Ἀφροδίτης γοναί by Philiscus (*PCG* VII p. 357: the title Ἑρμοῦ καὶ Ἀφροδίτης γοναί very probably has to be split up; see note 24

second one to Aphrodite in that collection) suggests a possible story-line for these comedies,[10] telling how Aphrodite, right after her birth from the sea, went up into heaven and was immediately the center of much attention and admiration, as she literally turned every god's head (every *male* god's, anyway: lines 15-18). In later comedy, a similar stir is sometimes caused by the arrival of a new and beautiful young hetaira in town,[11] and we may suspect that the comical Aphrodite's appearance was similarly depicted; even real-life hetairai sometimes cultivated aspirations to appear like Aphrodite and to approach her status.[12] To return to the Homeric Hymn: immediately after Aphrodite had presented herself on Olympus there was a desperate scramble by every male god around to win the hand of this wonderful newcomer in marriage (lines 17-18). The hymn does not tell us how this frantic vying for Aphrodite's favors ended, but from a well-established mythical "fact" we may imagine that on the comic stage a delightfully ironic dénouement could finally be built up: wouldn't it have made wonderful fun to show that actually the ugliest and least well-positioned of all the contenders, namely grime-and-soot-covered, limping Hephaestus, managed to fool everybody else and carry away the prize, the lovely and youthful Aphrodite?[13] Along some such lines as these, Ἀφροδίτης γοναί could have been developed on the comic stage; unfortunately, all this must largely remain a matter of conjecture, as of the four plays mentioned, only one more substantial fragment is left, to which I shall return later (pp. 20-22).

The second most popular birth-story on stage seems to have been that of Dionysus, which formed the subject of at least three

---

below); Polyzelus (*PCG* VII p. 553); Nicophon (fr. 1-5 K.-A.); and Antiphanes (fr. 57 K.-A.).

[10]See Wilamowitz, *Glaube der Hellenen* II 154 [152], note 2.

[11]Compare the reaction of Chaerea in Terence's *Eunuch* 292ff. (though the new girl Chaerea pines for turns out to be a free citizen in the end).

[12]Historical hetairai sometimes seem to have affected Aphrodite-like displays in public: e.g., the famous Phryne (Athenaeus 13.590ff.), who also posed as a model for the Cnidian Aphrodite made by Praxiteles (Athenaeus 13.591a); some others even were deified after death and became the center of cults and temples (Schneider, "Hetairai" 1356.13ff.).

[13]This last development is no part of the Homeric hymn, but the well-established mythical "fact" of Hephaestus being Aphrodite's husband would, of course, easily lead to such a conclusion.

plays.[14] One of its attractions certainly was that—unlike the Aphrodite theme—here a plot ripe with marital and extramarital complications could be developed. Dionysus was a product of gross adultery by the supreme god of the Greek pantheon, Zeus, and consequently a target of the bitter jealousy that led Zeus' wife Hera to start (every now and then) one of those lively (not to say vehement) intramarital spats, a glimpse of which can already be had in the amusing scene at the end of *Iliad* 1 (lines 536-570).[15] Unfortunately, the remains of these plays are so slight that we cannot form any real idea about their plot lines (apart from the assumption that Zeus' adultery and Hera's jealousy certainly had a part to play). One of Lucian's *Dialogues of the Gods* (12 [9]), however, may give us at least some idea how the story could be treated on the comic stage. In Lucian's little piece Poseidon, who wants to visit Zeus, is prevented from doing so by Zeus' faithful servant, who, after talking more or less embarassedly around the real matter, finally has to admit that Zeus is not altogether well because he has just given birth to little Dionysus. The scene as rendered makes most delightful reading, and an analogous scene on stage would probably have produced even more hilarity among its spectators.[16]

---

[14]Διονύσου γοναί were written by Polyzelus (fr. 6-7 K.-A.); Demetrius I (*PCG* V p. 8); and Anaxandrides (*PCG* II p. 243).

[15]When answering Thetis' request in *Iliad* 1.518-523, Zeus exhibits an obviously well-founded awareness of the troubles he is going to have with his wife. Indeed, from the moment Zeus sits down at the divine dinner table, Hera opens her barrage (lines 540-543; see also lines 551-559). Already in the first preserved fragment of the Homeric *Hymn to Dionysus* there is an explicit allusion to Zeus fearing the wrath of Hera when he gave birth to Dionysus: σὲ δ' ἔτικτε πατὴρ ἀνδρῶν τε θεῶν τε / πολλὸν ἀπ' ἀνθρώπων, κρύπτων λευκώλενον Ἥρην (lines 6ff.). See also the treatment of this story in Ovid's *Metamorphoses* III 259ff., especially lines 310-315.

[16]Even if Lucian has not taken his dialogue from a direct predecessor in comedy (see above, note 4), he clearly shows in what kind of setting a Διονύσου γοναί could have been successful: a sequence of such "domestic" scenes, showing the gods as quite ordinary (and fallible) beings, would have produced comically very effective contrasts with their "normal" divine status (for comedy's development of such contrasts see below, pp. 10, 16, 22-25).

Two plays were devoted to the birth of Pan,[17] and here the nineteenth Homeric Hymn and another of Lucian's *Dialogues of the Gods* (2 [22]) suggest possible story-lines (probably both in rustic settings): the hymn tells how Hermes falls in love with an Arcadian girl[18] and gets her pregnant. The nurse-to-be (or even the mother herself?[19]) leaps up in fright and dashes away upon first seeing the newborn child (which rather looked like Rosemary's baby with his horns, his goat's feet and his loud and alarming voice).[20] Hermes, nevertheless, takes him up as his son and proudly presents him to the gods on Olympus, who take much pleasure in seeing the child, most of all Dionysus (lines 30-47). The Lucianic dialogue suggests something more sophisticated, but no less comical: here Hermes—who apparently has forgotten the Arcadian tryst he was once involved in—is approached by Pan some time after his birth and has to learn to his embarrassment that this goat-like creature is in fact his son! Obviously, these two story-lines are rather different from each other;[21] and though, again, we cannot say with any degree of confidence that they appeared (or, in the case of the Homeric Hymn, reappeared) on the comic stage, they at least give an idea how on stage, too, two plays having the same title could proceed along fairly different lines.

Of each of the remaining birth-stories taken over by comedy, only one title has survived in each case (but there may have been more): In the staging of the birth of Zeus[22] secret

---

[17]They were produced by Philiscus (*PCG* VII p. 357) and Araros (fr. 13-15 K.-A.).

[18]In line 34, νύμφῃ ἐϋπλοκάμῳ Δρύοπος, νύμφῃ probably means just "girl"; see Càssola, *Inni Omerici* 576.

[19]In rendering τιθήνη in line 38, Allen-Halliday-Sikes, *Homeric Hymns* 408 opt for "mother"; but Càssola, *Inni Omerici* 577, objects that there is no sure early instance for this meaning of the word.

[20]Similar things are told about the newborn Priapus: see Herter, "Priapos" 1917.48-1918.4.

[21]Even the identity of the mother is different: in the hymn, she is a daughter of Dryops, remaining unnamed herself. In Lucian's case she is the well-known Penelope, daughter of Icarius and afterwards virtuous wife of Odysseus. Lucian chose this version, no doubt, because it added spice to the story.

[22]A Διὸς γοναί was produced by Philiscus (*PCG* VII p. 357). If the papyrus fragment *CGFP* 215 did not come from this play (see below, pp.

dealings and the cunning deception of a marital partner surely provide an exciting story-line. A mother in distress (Rhea) has to conceal a newborn baby (Zeus) from a tyrannical and in fact cannibalistic father (Cronus). An anonymous[23] papyrus fragment (*CGFP* 215) shows how this bare outline of a plot could indeed be filled with characters who—while being petty and downright base—surely were entertaining and comic, too.

As for the birth of Hermes,[24] the fourth Homeric Hymn is already so rich in presenting dramatic confrontations of a comic sort (the infant Hermes still in his swaddling clothes defending himself against the threats of an angry Apollo [lines 235ff.] and later confronting even Zeus himself on high Olympus in this "outfit" [lines 327ff.]), that one may well wonder whether in fact only one comic play took up this hilarious story; for the eleventh [seventh] of Lucian's *Dialogues of the Gods* shows yet another possible way to dramatize the theme of the divine young rascal outwitting his elders. In a conversation with Apollo, Hephaestus asks whether Apollo has already seen Maia's charming new-born child and declares himself to be positively delighted by this fine young creature. Apollo, however, is not really able to share in Hephaestus' delight, because he has already experienced the child's expert thievery!

For dramatic representation of Athena's birth[25] we have yet another of Lucian's dialogues (13 [8]), where Hephaestus, having just split Zeus' head with his sharpest ax to bring about this wondrous birth, immediately falls in love with the new-born maiden and starts pursuing her—to no avail, of course, as the

---

23-25), there once would have existed at least a second comic play dealing with the birth story of Zeus. There once was, in fact, a Ζηνὸς γοναί by the tragedian Timesitheus (*TrGF* I 214 Snell); but as only the title of this play is known, we cannot be sure whether it was a tragedy or a satyr play.

[23]See below, p. 24.

[24]A Ἑρμοῦ καὶ Ἀφροδίτης γοναί is recorded among the play titles ascribed to Philiscus (Suda φ 357 = test. 1 K.-A.; cp. *PCG* VII p. 357); but as the births of Hermes and Aphrodite according to Greek myth took place in settings and situations that were very different from each other, there is hardly a way one might possibly think of to connect them in a single play. Thus the Suda entry probably has to be split into a Ἑρμοῦ γοναί and an Ἀφροδίτης γοναί, as is already the opinion of Meineke, *Historia critica* 281ff.

[25]Hermippus, Ἀθηνᾶς γοναί (fr. 2-6 K.-A.).

myth tells us. Lucian's dialogue, to be sure, was a literary piece meant purely for recitation and not for real staging; therefore Lucian could lead the imagination of his listeners (and his readers) to the very point of Athena's birth itself and, indeed, make Hephaestus cry out in surprise, when the divine maiden dashes fully armed out of her father's head. In a dramatic play this incident naturally could not be directly shown on the stage (as the remains of Hermippus' ’Αθηνᾶς γοναί in fact demonstrate); the comic poet had to confine himself to staging the events before and after this birth, so that, in this case, we cannot expect too many similarities between Lucian's treatment and the lost one by Hermippus (see below, pp. 12-14).

As for Apollo and Artemis,[26] the story of their birth as told in surviving classical literature (in the *Hymn to Apollo* and in even greater detail in the Callimachean *Hymn to Delos*) would suggest that this instance of θεῶν γοναί was really rather more suited for the tragic than the comic stage, for it is hard to think how an element like Leto's long wandering and suffering could have formed part of a comedy; and on the birth of the Muses[27] we have—apart from Polyzelus' paltry fragments—nothing that might give us an idea of its possible dramatization. Still, our evidence puts it beyond reasonable doubt that there once existed comic adaptations of both these stories, and the harder it is to think of possible comic plots in these cases, all the greater must have been the amount of ingenuity that was required for the writing of these plays.[28] In the case of the Μουσῶν γοναί-play, a

---

[26]Philiscus, ’Αρτέμιδος καὶ ’Απόλλωνος ⟨γοναί⟩ (*PCG* VII p. 357).

[27]Polyzelus, Μουσῶν γοναί (fr. 8-11 K.-A.).

[28]In comparison, one may cite the Αἴολος of Antiphanes (fr. 19-20 K.-A.): How could this originally Euripidean play, with its scandal-ridden theme of incest (by which Aristophanes, for one, felt scandalized more than once) and its bloody dénouement, be made over into a comedy? In Nesselrath, *Mittlere Komödie* 205-9, I have suggested a possibility which assumes that Antiphanes in some ways—and certainly at the end—had to deviate radically from the Euripidean plot. In the cases of ’Αρτέμιδος καὶ ’Απόλλωνος γοναί and of Μουσῶν γοναί the poets had to display a similar degree of boldness. Looking at the drastic changes that the poet of *CGFP* 215 introduced in his depiction of the characters of Rhea and Cronus (see below, pp. 24ff.), one may feel encouraged that they really could be that bold.

bit of evidence has survived to give us, in fact, at least a clue (see below, pp. 15-17).

II

After this preliminary survey of the θεῶν γοναί-plays, according to their subject-matter, some more general observations about this kind of play by now seem possible, even though pitifully few fragments of them remain.[29] The common features which can be deduced in this way suggest that θεῶν γοναί-plays probably represented the most homogeneous group within the multi-faceted field of mythological comedy; for θεῶν γοναί-plays seem to have had in common a number of characteristics that set them apart from other plays in which a myth was parodied or travestied:

1) As the still-extant stories of divine births that are found in the Homeric Hymns show,[30] a god's birth story in many cases had humorous and even downright comic elements even before it came into the hands of a comedian, while for exactly the same reasons it was not very much suited for tragic treatment.[31] Comic writers who wanted to make θεῶν γοναί into comedies therefore could not do what they did rather often when they wanted to put a myth on the stage; that is, simply look back to a tragic predecessor who had already dramatized this myth, take over his plot and deform his speeches and his story-line so as to make a parody out of it; Euripides, especially, provided copious and suitable material for this kind of comic reworking.[32] As the

---

[29] We are fortunate, however, that with regard to comedies with mythical themes one can at least try to combine the fragmentary evidence of the plays themselves with treatments of the myth outside comedy. I tried this approach when I discussed other mythical plays of Middle Comedy in Nesselrath, *Mittlere Komödie* 204-41.

[30] I might add the evidence from Lucian's *Dialogues of the Gods*, because it is unlikely that—in these cases, anyway—he got his material out of comic plays (see above, note 4).

[31] The situation is different for clandestine *human* births, which could result in tragic predicaments for the mother. See the *Ion* of Euripides and the Amphitryon story, of course.

[32] How this process came about may still be observed in Aristophanes: in his heyday he parodied single scenes from Euripidean plays (in *Acharnians* and *Thesmophoriazusae*), while one of the last plays he

number of tragedies that dealt with divine births is likely to have been near zero,[33] θεῶν γοναί-writers had to look to other sources. A good source for stories about gods' births must have been didactic epic (like Hesiod's *Theogony*), gods' hymns (the first part of this paper has already shown how much material could be found there), and probably also folktales.[34] In dramatizing such sources, comic poets had—at least in some cases—to do more "original" work than when they simply could parody an already existing tragic plot.

2) The very nature of these stories implies that the presence and frequency of gods is much higher in this category of comic plays than in any other; in many cases, in fact, gods must have been the only participants. This may sound like a banality, but compared to other sorts of comedies it certainly is a distinguishing mark. According to Aristotle (*Poetics* 1448a17ff. and 1449a32-34), the essence of a comic play lies in the degrading of characters; to strip the gods involved in the story of their heavenly majesty and make them look low and base (so as to render them a laughing-stock) certainly was one of the main sources of comic contrast in θεῶν γοναί-plays. There were already models extant for this, not in tragedy, of course, but in earlier literature, namely epic: the dinner-scene at the end of *Iliad* 1 (already mentioned above, p. 5), beginning with the marital quarrel between Zeus and Hera and ending with a boisterous exuberance worthy of a public ale-house down on earth, or the titillating tale of Ares' and Aphrodite's adultery in the middle of *Odyssey* 8 shows how already Homer could make the Olympic gods look very human indeed. Old Comedy, too, knows how to make fun of gods: Aristophanes has a few scenes where some

---

wrote, *Aiolosikon*, seems to have been a continuous reworking of the single Euripidean play *Aiolos*.

[33]For the Ζηνὸς γοναί play by the tragedian Timesitheus see note 22 above.

[34]In some cases, a satyr play may have provided a model, too, e.g. Sophocles' *Ichneutai* (fr. 314 Radt) for retelling the story of the mischievous deeds of the baby Hermes. When taking over a story from a satyr play, however, comedy of course had to do completely without Silenus and his satyrs; so the comic poet would have had to find other carriers of the humor that was to be displayed and thus alter the plot-line considerably.

rather debased characters from Olympus make their appearance, e.g., the dumb pair Polemos/Kydoimos in *Peace* (lines 236-288), the divine ambassadors of very dubious dignity in *Birds* (lines 1565-1692), and (last but not least) Dionysus in *Frogs* (passim; especially lines 285-308 and 479-493). But all these instances, in epic as well as in comedy, do not consist of more than single scenes; the writers of θεῶν γοναί had the task of presenting silly (and all-too-human) gods during the whole length of their plays.

3) So far, we have noted features that seem to have their origin already in archaic Greek literature, while the greatest literary development of the "classical" fifth century, tragedy, seems to have played no role at all. Were then the comic poets who produced θεῶν γοναί-plays only looking back and digging up themes and comic modes of the distant past? This rather one-sided picture needs to be corrected. In one crucial aspect, at least, divine-birth plays anticipated something that was to become a dominant feature of the future New Comedy: poets of θεῶν γοναί-plays apparently were the first[35] to present on the comic stage the theme of children illegitimately conceived and clandestinely brought into the world. Many things that go with these scandalous happenings (and are ubiquitous in New Comedy) must already have been present and, indeed, in most cases provided a central feature ("trespassing" husbands, jealous wives, conspiring servants, etc.).

Taken together, the characteristics enumerated here seem to provide θεῶν γοναί-plays with something of a Janus-like quality: while searching for new themes, their poets looked back into the past and found stories already present in pre-classical

---

[35] One possible exception is the comic representation of the birth of Helen, which was already part of Cratinus' Νέμεσις (fr. 114-127 K.-A.), of Aristophanes' Δαίδαλος (fr. 191-204 K.-A.), and possibly of Eubulus' Λάκωνες ἢ Λήδα (fr. 60-63 K.-A.; a separate play titled Ἑλένης γοναί does not seem to have existed). There is also the depiction of a comical "Birth of Helen" on a South Italian "Phlyax vase" (Bari, Museo Nazionale 3899) produced about 370 BC. See the discussion in Taplin, *Comic Angels* 82ff. The birth of Helen, however, is not necessarily a case of "a child being clandestinely brought into the world." Neither the play of Cratinus nor that of Aristophanes (nor the play connected with the Phlyax vase) needs to have had the same atmosphere of domestic intrigue that seems likely for many of the later θεῶν γοναί-plays.

literature; but when adapting those stories to the stage, they "refitted" them in a way that would prove significant for the domestic comedies about illegitimate and concealed children in the latter part of the fourth century. Looking simultaneously backward and forward, plays about θεῶν γοναί seem to be quite fitting representatives of the transition period between Old and Middle Comedy to which they belong.

III

Having made a first survey of the (admittedly not abundant) remains of θεῶν γοναί-plays and having drawn some conclusions about probable common features of that kind of play, can we now even go a step further and attempt something like a history of its development? Scanty as the evidence is, one may indeed (with all due caution) try to tease out the probable chronological sequence of these plays.

The apparent πρῶτος εὑρετής and discoverer of the comic potential of θεῶν γοναί-plays, Hermippus, still belongs squarely to Old Comedy: he was active mainly in the 430's and 420's, though he may still have produced plays in the years after 420. There is scarcely a possibility to move him further down the timescale (not beyond 410, at any rate); so his Ἀθηνᾶς γοναί may even belong to the 430's. A mythological play of that kind, apparently unrelated to the political vicissitudes of the day, might seem to be rather untypical for Old Comedy; therefore already Meineke (*Historia critica* 279) thought that Ἀθηνᾶς γοναί might have been produced during the years when comic liberty had been restricted by the decree of Morychides and the poets were forced to look for "safer," i.e. apolitical themes. If that is true, Hermippus' play would have been in a position rather similar to that of the Ὀδυσσῆς of Cratinus, which in our tradition has explicitly been linked with political restrictions.[36] Cratinus retold the story about

---

[36]Compare the comments of Meineke, *Fragmenta* 93, and see Platonius, Περὶ διαφορᾶς κωμῳδιῶν (in Koster, *Prolegomena* 3.13-4.30): τῆς δημοκρατίας ὑποχωρούσης...καὶ κρατυνομένης τῆς ὀλιγαρχίας ἐνέπιπτε τοῖς ποιηταῖς φόβος...σκοποῦ γὰρ ὄντος τῇ ἀρχαίᾳ κωμῳδίᾳ τοῦ σκώπτειν δήμους καὶ δικαστὰς καὶ στρατηγούς, παρεὶς ὁ Ἀριστοφάνης τοῦ συνήθως ἀποσκῶψαι διὰ τὸν πολὺν φόβον Αἴολον τὸ δρᾶμα τὸ γραφὲν τοῖς τραγῳδοῖς ὡς κακῶς ἔχον διασύρει. τοιοῦτος οὖν ἐστιν ὁ τῆς μέσης κωμῳδίας τύπος,

Odysseus and the Cyclops more or less as he found it in the *Odyssey*, that is, without significantly "rationalizing" the fabulous and strange elements in it. Hermippus may have proceeded likewise: fr. 2 K.-A. probably belongs to a context where the astonishing birth of Athena out of Zeus' head was related in a kind of messenger speech:

ὁ Ζεύς "δίδωμι Παλλάς" ἠσί "τοὔνομα"

"I give her," says Zeus, "the name 'Pallas'"

Other parts of the story were portrayed more directly ("acted out"). In fr. 3 K.-A. someone (Hera?) accuses someone else (Zeus?) of extreme duplicity, i.e. of putting on the appearance of an innocent lamb, but hiding a serpent's mind within:

τὴν μὲν διάλεκτον καὶ τὸ πρόσωπον ἀμνίου
ἔχειν δοκεῖς, τὰ δ' ἔνδον οὐδὲν διαφέρεις
δράκοντος

you seem to have the speech and countenance of a lamb,
but inside you are not at all different from a snake!

These words would make a fine flourish within any vociferous marital conflict; it is more than likely that Hera, Zeus' wife, reacted quite indignantly when first being confronted with her husband's bringing forth Athena; so fr. 3 K.-A. may very well

---

οἷός ἐστιν ὁ Αἰολοσίκων Ἀριστοφάνους καὶ οἱ Ὀδυσσεῖς Κρατίνου... ("When democracy retreated...and oligarchy was strengthened, fear came over the poets...for the aim of Old Comedy had been to ridicule the people, judges, and generals, but Aristophanes now, beset by fear, gave up his customary ridiculing and joked about the bad quality of the play *Aiolos* that the tragedians had written. Such therefore is the character of Middle Comedy, instances of which are Aristophanes' *Aiolosikon* and Cratinus' *Odysses*..."). See also 5.49-5.52 τοιαῦτα δὲ δράματα (i.e., apolitical plays that make fun of other poets' productions) καὶ ἐν τῇ παλαιᾷ κωμῳδίᾳ ἔστιν εὑρεῖν, ἅπερ τελευταῖα ἐδιδάχθη λοιπὸν τῆς ὀλιγαρχίας κρατυνθείσης. οἱ γοῦν Ὀδυσσεῖς Κρατίνου οὐδενὸς ἐπιτίμησιν ἔχουσι, διασυρμὸν δὲ τῆς Ὀδυσσείας τοῦ Ὁμήρου... ("plays of that kind can also be found in Old Comedy, those that were brought on stage at its end, when oligarchy had already gained strength. Therefore the *Odysses* of Cratinus does not ridicule anybody, but makes fun of Homer's *Odyssey*..."). All in all, Platonius' comments, though pervaded by pleonastic verbosity, remain rather vague. See Nesselrath, *Mittlere Komödie* 31-34.

come out of Hera's mouth and belong to a vivid altercation between those divine (but so often estranged) marital partners played out in full on the stage.

In its own time, Hermippus' comedy about Athena's birth seems to have been a lone forerunner. It is only one or two decades later that the "season" of θεῶν γοναί-plays began in earnest, and it may strike one as a rather peculiar fact that it is two lesser-known poets who provide for more than half of the plays of this kind: Philiscus and Polyzelus.

Philiscus is on the record with the production of only seven[37] (or eight) plays in all, but four or—more probably—five (see notes 24 and 37) of them dealt with the birth of gods (of Hermes, of Aphrodite, of Artemis and Apollo, of Zeus, and of Pan). No fragments of these plays have been preserved, although eminent scholars have in the past attributed the papyrus fragment CGFP 215 to Philiscus' Διὸς γοναί (see below, pp. 23-25); this attribution, however, is fraught with uncertainties, and I shall consider another possible author for this remarkable piece later on. As there is so little really known about Philiscus, we can establish the time of his activity only by a roundabout argument, and with that only approximately: there is a story that Philiscus' portrait was painted by the famous Parrhasius (test.* 2 K.-A.);[38] if this is true, Philiscus should have been active towards the end of the fifth century. The rather small number of Philiscus' plays and the high percentage of θεῶν γοναί-plays among them suggest two things: that he was successful—if at all—only for a limited period and that his success may have been due mainly to comedies devoted to this theme. Perhaps one of those (presumably the first) was a great hit with the Athenian public, and after that Philiscus tried to

---

[37]We get a number of seven, if we leave the title Θεμιστοκλῆς out of the list that is provided by the Suda (φ 357 = Philiscus test. 1 K.-A.). It clearly cuts an odd figure among the rest, and already Meineke, *Historia critica* 424, thought that it might have been the title of a play by the homonymous tragic poet Philiscus (who is no. 89 in *TrGF* I). On the other hand, if we really have to split the recorded title Ἑρμοῦ καὶ Ἀφροδίτης γοναί into two (a Ἑρμοῦ γοναί and an Ἀφροδίτης γοναί; see above, note 24), we return to the number of eight.

[38]For other considerations about the dating of Philiscus see Nesselrath, *Mittlere Komödie* 229, note 140 (where the number of Philiscus' recorded plays is erroneously given as six).

repeat this success by trying out the same recipe with other divine-birth stories (in modern times, ephemeral artists have been known to proceed similarly). If this is a plausible scenario for Philiscus and the high number of θεῶν γοναί-plays on his record, it may well tell us something about the popularity that plays of this kind (or at least some of them) enjoyed when they first hit the stage.

A little bit more is known about Philiscus' contemporary Polyzelus, who all in all produced three plays about gods' births: Of his Ἀφροδίτης γοναί only the title has survived. Also the fragments of his Διονύσου γοναί yield very little of any substance, but we may be a bit better off in the case of his Μουσῶν γοναί: for them, at least fr. 9 K.-A. does provide some clues. I give the text (with some typographical simplifications) as it is in *PCG* VII p. 557. It is a prose reference, starting with a proverbial saying, and has therefore been preserved in a number of paroemiographical collections:[39]

ὥσπερ Χαλκιδικὴ τέτοκεν ἡμῖν ἡ γυνή· ταύτης [scil. τῆς παροιμίας] Πολύζηλος μέμνηται ἐν Μουσῶν γοναῖς, ἐπί τινος πολλὰς θυγατέρας ἀπογεννώσης, ἐπειδὴ Χαλκίδα τῆς Εὐβοίας πόλιν φασί ποτε ἀνθῆσαι δόρασί τε καὶ πλήθει τετρώρων ἁρμάτων. οἱ δέ φασιν οὐ τὴν πόλιν, ἀλλὰ τὴν ἡρωίδα Χαλκίδα εἰρῆσθαι· Κόμβην γάρ φασι τὴν ἐπικληθεῖσαν Χαλκίδα, ἐπειδὴ χαλκᾶ ὅπλα ἐποιήσατο πρώτη, συνοικήσασαν ἀνδρὶ ἑκατὸν[40] παίδων γενέσθαι μητέρα ...

"The woman has born us children like one from Chalcis." this (saying) is brought up by Polyzelus in *The birth of the Muses*, in connection with a woman who bears many daughters. They say that the Euboean town Chalcis once blossomed with spears and a wealth of four-horsed chariots. Others, however, say that not the town but the heroine (of the same name) is meant; for they say that Kombe—who was also called Chalcis because she was the first to create bronze (χαλκᾶ) weapons—lived together with a man and became the mother of a hundred children ...

---

[39] All of them have, as usual, been carefully documented in Kassel-Austin, *PCG ad loc.*

[40] Meineke conjectured ἑπτά (instead of ἑκατόν), comparing the Κόμβη ἑπτατόκος who is mentioned in Nonnus 13.148.

In this prose reference some words of the original text may, in fact, have been preserved (τέτοκεν ἡμῖν ἡ γυνή);[41] words that apparently come out of the mouth of someone who likens his wife—who, it seems, has just given birth—to a woman of Chalcis that had become proverbial for her abundance of children. Already Meineke (*Historia critica* 281, and *Fragmenta* 871) thought that this might be a clear reference to no one else but Mnemosyne, after she has (recently?) given birth to the Muses—a multiple birth if ever there was one.[42] This is not yet all that these four words can yield. Who else can be the speaker of τέτοκεν ἡμῖν but Zeus himself, the father of the Muses? If this attribution of the words is right, a further remarkable fact would result from it: if it is really the supreme god Zeus who utters the words ὥσπερ Χαλκιδικὴ τέτοκεν ἡμῖν ἡ γυνή, he would in fact be comparing a divine birth—that of his daughters, the Muses—to a mere human one (that is, by the woman Kombe/Chalcis). Now this amounts to something paradoxical, because this comparison produces a kind of "inverted" (and in its context even absurd) contrast: to grasp the remarkable occurrence that Mnemosyne has just given him nine[43] daughters at once, the highest god on Olympus can't think of anything else but the similar case of a mere mortal. It is probable that this curiously "perverted" contrast was intended by the poet. Was Polyzelus trying to make Zeus look like a down-to-earth father who felt rather overwhelmed when being confronted with nine new-born daughters, and who took refuge in a proverbial human example? If true, this whole mythical story as presented by Polyzelus would look rather "domesticated"—with Zeus reacting like a father who has to learn that his wife

---

[41]Already Kock (*ad loc.*) thought that in the first six words a whole iambic trimeter was hidden: ὥσπερ δὲ Χάλκις τέτοκεν ἡμῖν ἡ γυνή, and he certainly was led by the iambic rhythm of τέτοκεν ἡμῖν ἡ γυνή. "ipsa poetae verba servata esse istud μέμνηται praestare nequit" (Kassel-Austin, *PCG ad loc.*). They may be too cautious here, however.

[42]In *Theogony* 53-60 Hesiod narrates how Zeus slept with Mnemosyne on nine consecutive nights, and then, in due time, Mnemosyne produced her ninefold offspring.

[43]Kock (*ad loc.*), accepting Meineke's conjecture of ἑπτά (see above, note 40), thought that in Polyzelus' play only seven Muses were involved. This is not a necessary assumption, however, and would alter the picture very little, in any case.

produced much more offspring than he would have imagined in his wildest fears. There may, in fact, be a hint of lamentation in the words ὥσπερ Χαλκιδικὴ τέτοκεν ἡμῖν ἡ γυνή, and to understand this, one needs only to remember that in classical Athens getting a wealth of female children was normally regarded as more of a calamity than a boon, since providing a dowry for a daughter could eat up a considerable part of the family fortune. If all this is not too speculative, Zeus may in fact have been presented by Polyzelus in this play very much like an unfortunate Athenian father who all of a sudden has to cope with a whole bunch of expensive daughters! Perhaps this wealth of daughters was even introduced as a kind of punishment for Zeus' persistent chasing of women: the word γυναικοφιλής[44] in fr. 11 K.-A. may well point to this distinctive trait of the Father of Gods and Men. All this, of course, would imply a considerable "humanization" and "Atticization" of the myth about the Muses' birth, a development not yet perceptible in the fragments of Hermippus' Ἀθηνᾶς γοναί. This kind of change in the treatment of myth would, however, fit rather well into a more general pattern, for similar processes in the adaptation of myths to comical purposes—"high" myths being demoted for comic contrast—are discernible in a number of fragments of other mythological plays of this period.[45]

[44]Could it be rendered here with "womanizer"?

[45]In Nesselrath, *Mittlere Komödie* 204-35, I have tried to show that "domestication" and "Atticization" of myths are features to be found in more or less all mythical plays by Middle Comedy poets, as far as something still can be made out about them. The contrast with the treatment of the myth in Cratinus' Ὀδυσσῆς (*Mittlere Komödie* 236-40) suggests that Old Comedy's approach to such mythical themes was rather different: Old Comic poets like Cratinus got ridicule out of myths by taking their fabulous features "for real" and presenting them in a mockingly absurd way on the stage (e.g., the big pot that was to serve Polyphemus' anthropophagic inclinations in Cratinus' play probably was displayed very conspicuously on the stage as Cratinus' Polyphemus combines his original cannibalistic gourmandise with all the subtleties of a sophisticated cuisine [see fr. 150 K.-A.]). Middle Comic poets made myths a matter for laughing by ingeniously rationalizing and toning down fabulous features (e.g., the famous chasing dog Lailaps becomes a pampered pet animal in Eubulus' Πρόκρις, fr. 89 K.-A.). In Μουσῶν γοναί, Polyzelus seems to be well on the way to the comic domestication of

Like Philiscus, Polyzelus was active during the last years of the fifth century and probably some time beyond.⁴⁶ There remain another five contributors to this category of comic play for whom, however, the genre did not have the central role it had for Philiscus and Polyzelus. Each of them wrote only one θεῶν γοναί-play (though in one case I shall argue that we may be entitled to look at least for a second one), and this fact may already be a hint that the comic attractions of θεῶν γοναί were starting to decline.

The first two of those five, Nicophon and a little-known Demetrius, who are reckoned among the poets of Old Comedy by Diogenes Laertius (V 83 = Demetr. I test. 1 K.-A.), wrote comic plays during roughly the same time-span as Philiscus and Polyzelus. Nicophon, in fact, is the comic poet who figures next to Polyzelus on the Lenaean victors' list which has in part been preserved by an inscription (*IG* II² 2325.131 = Nicoph. test. 4 K.-A.), and his Ἄδωνις was a rival of Aristophanes' *Plutus II* in 388. This gives us at least a vague idea into what period we probably have to put Nicophon's sole play about a divine birth, an Ἀφροδίτης γοναί. The extant five fragments of this play (1-5 K.-A.)—though that is a higher-than-average frequency of citations for a play of this altogether obscure period—unfortunately yield nothing about its plot or characters. With Demetrius we are not much better off; in his case, even the existence of a θεῶν γοναί-play by his pen must remain something of a conjecture: a papyrus fragment (*CGFP* 77 = test. 2 K.-A.) has preserved the first part of a title which may in full have been Διονύσου γοναί; to look for fragments in this case is hopeless.

The next three poets may at last be called "real" Middle Comedy poets,⁴⁷ for their careers began only in the 380's. They

---

myth; another probable example of this among the θεῶν γοναί-plays is discussed below (pp. 23-25).

⁴⁶See Polyzelus test. 4 K.-A., which puts him in the company of other poets who were producing plays around the turn of the century, and the introductory comments on his play Δημοτυνδάρεως (*PCG* VII p. 553); see also Nesselrath, *Mittlere Komödie* 203.

⁴⁷In Nesselrath, *Mittlere Komödie* 333-38, I argue that there are a number of reasons to restrict the period that should properly be called "Middle Comedy" to the years 380-350 BC. The thirty years (approximately) before 380 seem to have witnessed how one by one the "typical" features of Old Comedy dropped out of the production of comic plays while in the

are thus a whole generation younger than Hermippus and still one or two decades younger than the other four who were discussed in the preceding paragraphs. These older four really belong rather to the transition period between Old and Middle Comedy.

The first of the three poets who started in the 380's is probably Aristophanes' son Araros.[48] He seems to have been rather heavily promoted by his father, who gave him the last two plays he wrote, *Kokalos* and *Aiolosikon*, for staging; with *Kokalos*, Araros managed to win the first prize in the year after the second *Plutus*, 387 (Araros test. 3 K.-A.). Left on his own, however, he turned out to be rather a failure: the record of his poetic career does not list more than six titles of his own, and whether any of them ever was a success is far from clear—quite to the contrary, Araros seems to have developed a rather embarassing reputation for ψυχρότης, which became the butt of a cruel joke by a much more successful rival comedian, Alexis (fr. 184 K.-A. = Araros test. 4 K.-A.). However, we cannot really be sure that Alexis' judgment was fair or applied to all the plays Araros produced. One of those six plays mentioned depicted Πανὸς γοναί (fr. 13-15 K.-A.); fr. 14 and 15 are almost hopeless as far as plot reconstruction is concerned,[49] but fr. 13 is more promising: it could have been part of a messenger's speech describing how quickly after his birth the young Pan grasped the μόναυλος:

⟨ ⏑ ⟩ ἁρπάσας μόναυλον εὐθὺς - πῶς δοκεῖς;
κούφως ἀνήλλετο ...

... and when he had grabbed the single flute, at once—
what do you think?—lightly up he leapt ...[50]

---

thirty years (again approximately) after 350 all the features (successively or maybe in some cases even simultaneously) made their entrance on the stage that finally added up to the "typical" appearance of New Comedy.

[48]See Araros test. 1 and 3 K.-A. with Nesselrath, *Mittlere Komödie* 192.
[49]Though fr. 14 ἄθικτος· ἡ παρθένος ("untouched: the young maiden") might give a hint, that such an ἄθικτος played a part in the story and that under attack by the newborn Pan's amorous advances she might not have remained ἄθικτος for very long—all this, however, is a rather long shot.
[50]On baby gods literally leaping out of their cradle see Kassel, *Infantes atque parvuli pueri* 17-20 (=*Kleine Schriften* 13-16).

Who is the narrator of this lively episode, and what did Pan do, after he had provided himself with a musical instrument? Was Araros' play successful with his audience, and what was its relationship with the homonymous play by Philiscus? Barring new material, we may never get an answer to these questions.

The next of the three, Anaxandrides, was a considerably more important and acclaimed poet than Araros, and his career on the Attic stage seems also to have been much longer-lasting, for he wrote plays from the 380's into the 340's.[51] He seems, however, only once to have tried his hand at a θεῶν γοναί-play, and of this, a Διονύσου γοναί, unfortunately, everything but the title is lost.

We are more fortunate with the last poet who has to be considered here, Antiphanes. There is evidence that Antiphanes started only slightly later than Anaxandrides and that he was active at least until about 330.[52] The total number of his plays is reputed to have been huge; our various sources (Antiphanes test. 1 and 2 K.-A.) put them between 260 and 365. The number of titles that have been preserved is much smaller, but still considerable (139), and one of these is Ἀφροδίτης γοναί. In this case, we have, for once, a title which has been transmitted together with a rather long fragment (fr. 57 K.-A.):

> τονδὶ λέγω, σὺ δ' οὐ συνιείς; κότταβος
> τὸ λυχνεῖόν ἐστι. πρόσεχε τὸν νοῦν· ᾠὰ μὲν
> ⟨ ᴗ – ᴗ – ᴗ ⟩ πέντε νικητήριον.
> (Β.) περὶ τοῦ; γελοῖον. κοτταβιεῖτε τίνα τρόπον;
> 5 (Α.) ἐγὼ διδάξω· καθ' ὅσον ἂν τὸν κότταβον
> ἀφεὶς ἐπὶ τὴν πλάστιγγα ποιήσῃ πεσεῖν -
> (Β.) πλάστιγγα; ποίαν; (Α.) τοῦτο τοὐπικείμενον
> ἄνω τὸ μικρόν - (Β.) τὸ πινακίσκιον λέγεις;
> (Α.) τοῦτ' ἔστι πλάστιγξ - οὗτος ὁ κρατῶν γίγνεται.

---

[51]See Anaxandrides test. 1-6 K.-A.; especially test. 5, an inscription (*IG* Urb. Rom. 218) that provides dates for plays by Anaxandrides between 375 and 349. His Πρωτεσίλαος probably belongs even before 385, and fr. 46 K.-A. (from Τηρεύς) points to the early 340's (all this evidence is discussed in Nesselrath, *Mittlere Komödie* 194-95).

[52]For the beginning of Antiphanes' career see test. 2 K.-A. (taken from the third anonymous "Prolegomena on Comedy" in Koster *Prolegomena*, which usually is a source of high value; see Nesselrath, *Mittlere Komödie* 45-51). For a possible end, see test. 1 K.-A.; but there is much controversy about how long his career lasted. See Nesselrath, *Mittlere Komödie* 193.

10 (Β.) πῶς δ' εἴσεταί τις τοῦτ'; (Α.) ἐὰν θίγῃ μόνον
    αὐτῆς, ἐπὶ τὸν μάνην πεσεῖται καὶ ψόφος
    ἔσται πάνυ πολύς. (Β.) πρὸς θεῶν, τῷ κοττάβῳ
    πρόσεστι καὶ Μάνης τις ὥσπερ οἰκέτης;...

    ᾧ δεῖ λαβὼν τὸ ποτήριον δεῖξον νόμῳ.
15 (Α.) αὐλητικῶς δεῖ καρκινοῦν τοὺς δακτύλους,
    οἶνόν τε μικρὸν ἐγχέαι καὶ μὴ πολύν·
    ἔπειτ' ἀφήσεις. (Β.) τίνα τρόπον; (Α.) δεῦρο βλέπε·
    τοιοῦτον. (Β.) ⟨ὦ⟩ Πόσειδον, ὡς ὑψοῦ σφόδρα.
    (Α.) οὕτω ποιήσεις. (Β.) ἀλλ' ἐγὼ μὲν σφενδόνῃ
20 οὐκ ἂν ἐφικοίμην αὐτόσ'. (Α.) ἀλλὰ μάνθανε.

... I mean this one, don't you understand? The lampstand is a kottabos. Now pay attention; I'll put up five eggs and five apples as prize.[53] - (B.) For what? That's funny. What is the way in which you will play kottabos? - [5] (A.) I'll teach you: Insofar as one sends off the kottabos and makes it fall onto the disk - (B.) The disk? What is that? - (A.) That's this little thing that lies up there on top - (B.) You mean the tiny tablet? - (A.) That's the disk—that person becomes the winner. - [10] (B.) But how is one going to know that? - (A.) If one only touches it, it will fall onto the manes, and there will be a very loud clatter. - (B.) Wow, the kottabos has a Manes, too, as a servant? ... Take the cup and show me, in which way one must do it. - [15] (A.) You must crook your fingers crab-like, just like a flute-player does, pour in a little wine—not much!—and then send it off. - (B.) How? - (A.) Look here: like that. - (B.) My goodness, how very high! - (A.) That's how you will have to do it. - (B.) But not even with a sling [20] could I for one come as high as that! - (A.) Well, learn it![54]

In these lines (which have been preserved by that polymath of table-lore, Athenaeus of Naucratis) we witness how one person (A.) endeavors to teach another (B.) the rules and skills of the kottabos game. The "student" (B.) seems to be rather bewildered by the new game and is made to look silly at times by reacting somewhat naively to the propositions the "teacher" makes. As in so many other cases of fragment quotation in a secondary source like Athenaeus, the speakers' names have not

[53]The translation uses (only e.g.) Blaydes' conjecture ⟨καὶ μῆλα θήσω⟩.
[54]The translation is based on that by Gulick, *Athenaeus* 71-73. It has been modified, though, in a number of places, not least because the text (and most of all the division of speakers) is somewhat different in *PCG*.

been preserved, but one may venture a suggestion which probably has a better-than-average chance of hitting the mark: if this scene can be connected with the title of the play—and there is no reason why it shouldn't—there is, then, the distinct possibility that the naively reacting learner may be none other than the newborn Aphrodite herself.[55] It has already been observed (above, p. 4) how in the sixth Homeric Hymn (the second *Hymn to Aphrodite*) all the male gods are stunned by Aphrodite's supreme and irresistible beauty when she first comes up to Olympus, and wish to marry her on the spot. Could the "teacher" in the Antiphanes fragment be one of those gods vying with each other for the goddess' favors? By "generously" offering to Aphrodite to instruct her in the kottabos game he might in fact try to get into closer "contact" with this charming creature; and if I read Aphrodite rightly in this scene as acting the part of an innocent, but readily excitable young girl, she may have exhibited an almost Lolita-like combination of youth, apparent innocence and sex-appeal in this play. Yet another thing is to be noted: the kottabos game, around which this scene is built, had its origins in Sicily, but became a very conspicuous element of Greek social life on the mainland too, and it is found rather often in the fragments of Athenian comedies of these times.[56] If this fragment really shows us Aphrodite being taught the kottabos game by one of her admirers on Olympus, the "domestication" and even "Atticization" of the scene is remarkable indeed, though comparable to other instances where Antiphanes and other Middle Comic poets transform a mythical setting into a domestic Athenian affair and thus comically "deflate" the original myth (see above, note 45).

At the end of our survey, there still remains what might be called the most significant piece of evidence for a θεῶν γοναί-play of those times, a papyrus fragment which, so far, has received only fleeting attention in the course of this paper: *CGFP* 215.

[55]In that case, the participle in line 6 would, of course, have to be feminine (ἀφεῖσ'; see Nesselrath, *Mittlere Komödie* 234, note 150).

[56]See Cratinus fr. 124; Eupolis fr. 95, fr. 399; Aristophanes fr. 231; Ameipsias fr. 2; Hermippus fr. 48; Plato Comicus fr. 46f., fr. 71; Cephisodorus fr. 5; Callias fr. 12; Nicochares fr. 13; Eubulus fr. 15 K.-A. All these citations (except Eupolis fr. 95) are presented together by Athenaeus in the course of his disquisition on the Kottabos game (15.665b-668f), of which our Antiphanes fragment is also a part.

(ΡΕΑ) 'τί οὖν ἐμοὶ τῶν σ[ῶν μέ]λει;' φαίη τις ἂν
ὑμῶν. ἐγὼ δ' ἐρῶ [τ]ὸ Σοφοκλέους ἔπος·
'πέπονθα δεινά.' πάντα μοι γέρων Κρ[όνος
τὰ παιδί' ἐκπίνει τε καὶ κατεσθίει,
5   ἐμοὶ δὲ τούτων προσδίδωσιν οὐδὲ ἕν,
ἀλλ' αὐτὸς ἔρδει χειρὶ καὶ Μεγαράδ' ἄγων
ὅ τι ἂν τέκω 'γὼ τοῦτο πωλῶν ἐσθίει.
δέδοικε γὰρ τὸν χρησμὸν ὥσπερ κυν[
ἔχρησε γὰρ Κρόνῳ ποθ' Ἀπόλλων δραχ[μήν,
10 κᾆτ' οὐκ ἀπέλαβε. ταῦτα δὴ θυμὸν πνέ[ων
ἑτέραν ἔχρησε[ν οὐκέτι] δρα[χ]μῶ[ν ἀ]ξ[ίαν,
οὐ σκευάρια, μὰ τὸν Δί', οὐδὲ χρήματα,
ἐκ τῆς βασιλείας δ' ἐκπεσεῖν ὑπὸ π[αιδίου.
τοῦ]τ' οὖν δεδοικὼς πάντα καταπί[νει τέκνα.

(RHEA) "Now what have I got to do with your problems?" one of you might say. I shall reply in the words of Sophocles: "Dreadful are my sufferings." Old Cronus is drinking and eating all my children up, [5] and he does not give me even one single part of them, but perpetrates this all by himself: He takes all my babies to Megara, sells them and gobbles down the proceeds. You see, he is afraid of that oracle like a hare of a hound,[57] and here's the reason: Once Apollo gave[58] Cronus a loan of a drachma—[10] and then he didn't get it back. That sent him into a white-hot rage, and so he gave him something else ... : [59] No pots and pans, oh no, and no other things to borrow—he gave him the oracle that he would be driven out of his kingdom by his own child! And as he is afraid of that, he gobbles up all his children ...[60]

This long monologue (of which at the break-off point of the fragment no end is yet in sight; it was possibly a prologue) is obviously spoken by Rhea, the distressed and suffering wife of cruel Cronus, who (so far at least) has deprived her of all her children by selling them on the Megarian slave market and keeping all the proceeds for himself—an almost depressingly rationalistic, but nevertheless ingenious reinterpretation of

---

[57]In line 8, the translation uses Immisch's supplement ὥσπερ κύν[α λαγώς.

[58]The ingenious play with the double meaning of ἔχρησε in lines 9 and 11 can be reproduced only weakly in a modern language ("gave ... gave").

[59]The supplements in this verse are problematic (and therefore left out of the translation: see Nesselrath, *Mittlere Komödie* 232, note 146).

[60]The translation is based on the one by Page, *Literary Papyri* 231-33.

Cronus' disgusting τεκνοφαγία. Everything in this fragment points to a situation in which Rhea either has just given birth to Zeus or is shortly going to do so. The play to which this speech once belonged should have been, therefore, a Διὸς γοναί, and that was the main reason why in 1930 Koerte and Gallavotti independently and almost simultaneously assigned this fragment to the one author who was known to have written a play about Διὸς γοναί, Philiscus.[61] Of this play, however, no other line—not even a single word—has been preserved, and so doubts about the ascription have been voiced very early and have lingered down to the present day.[62] There are indeed good reasons for uncertainty having mainly to do with the quality of writing exhibited by this fragment. The author of these lines must have had a good feeling for the comical effectiveness of ambiguous language, for his verses show a masterly interweaving of different levels of meaning. On one level they do indeed keep to mythical "facts" (when Rhea starts her lament, she seems to talk quite literally about the καταφαγεῖν of her poor children by Cronus, and later on Cronus really seems to dread the fateful prophecy he received about one of his children—which is why he resorted to the καταφαγεῖν of them in the first place). On another level, however, the statement of these "facts" is interspersed with comments by which they are emptied of their original content and thus deflated and ridiculed (e.g., the words in line 4, τὰ παιδί' ἐκπίνει τε καὶ κατεσθίει, come to mean ὅ τι ἂν τέκω 'γὼ τοῦτο πωλῶν ἐσθίει in line 7, i.e., "squandering the proceeds of the children's sale on food and drink"). On top of all that, Rhea's description of the whole deplorable situation produces outrageously absurd distortions of mythical "chronology" and genealogy (e.g., Cronus getting his prophecy from his grandson Apollo, whose father Zeus

---

[61]Austin, *CGFP* 200ff. followed Koerte's and Gallavotti's lead, and in Nesselrath, *Mittlere Komödie* 229ff., I also more or less acquiesced in this ascription, though already then with some doubts ("Zwingend ist die Zuweisung...an Philiskos...freilich nicht," 230).

[62]One of the editores principes, G. Vitelli, wanted to assign this fragment to the Κρόνος of Phrynichus, but chronological reasons concerning the Sophocles citation in lines 2-3 seem to militate against this (see Nesselrath, *Mittlere Komödie* 229ff.). In any case, the editors of *PCG* (VII p. 357) have decided to place *CGFP* 215 among the Adespota in Vol. VIII which will be published soon.

is either not yet born or only a baby himself), and it makes all the gods involved—including the speaker Rhea herself—look petty and mean. Cronus is reduced to the pathetic figure of a callous and avaricious drunkard; Rhea makes herself look not very much better by her own words (she is ranting and lamenting not because her beloved children are so cruelly treated, but because she gets none of the money that Cronus pockets for the sale of them); Apollo cuts the figure of an immature choleric (he flies into a rage because he didn't get back a petty sum) and one may presume that other divine personnel involved in this play were treated similarly. To sum up, this fragment deals with its story in such an inventive and irreverent way that one is reminded of the art of Aristophanes. All these observations, of course, do not totally preclude the attribution of these wonderful lines to Philiscus—even though he is, for us, nothing more than a very obscure writer active for (it seems) only a couple of years around 400, of whom next to nothing is otherwise known. Perhaps they were part of his one great hit, the one that induced him to go on and produce more θεῶν γοναί-plays (see above, p. 14). One may, however, still feel entitled to wonder why some other bits and pieces of at least this play have not anywhere been preserved. *CGFP* 215 can be read today, because its contents appealed to someone still in the first century AD and were written down then on the papyrus that was first published in 1930. Of Philiscus, there is not even a mention in our most important source for Middle Comic poets, Athenaeus. Shouldn't he have had more to offer if he was capable of such lines as are uttered by that wonderfully comic Rhea, distressed and mean at the same time?

Because of Middle Comedy's almost dishearteningly sparse remains and the glaring gaps in our knowledge about it which result from this situation, *CGFP* 215 may be the work of almost any poet who was active between 400 and 350 BC. It may belong, in fact, to a poet who is better known to us from other fragments. Therefore (just to show what is possible or conceivable) I would here like to suggest another ascription of these lines which—to me, anyway—does appear to be at the very least not implausible: it has already been stated (see above, p. 20) that in the case of Antiphanes there is a huge gap between the total sum of plays he is supposed to have written and the number of titles that have actually been preserved. Even if we accept only the lowest number that is in our traditions about the total sum (i.e., 260), this gap still amounts to more than 120 plays between this figure and the number of titles we know (139). Is it possible that among those 120-plus was a Διὸς γοναί? As for the wit and liveliness which are exhibited in such a masterly fashion by the author of CGFP 215, it can be shown that Antiphanes was fully capable of producing the same kind of ingenious humour in his plays.[63] On this basis, an attribution to Antiphanes makes at least as much sense as one to the little-known Philiscus.

Wherever we may finally place this intriguing papyrus fragment, it brilliantly demonstrates what could be made of the theme of a god's birth in comedy. At the same time, however, it may also represent a kind of terminus in the development of this sub-genre: one cannot possibly go much further in bringing gods down to the level of rather mean human beings. At a certain point, moreover, the possibilities of this kind of mythological play must have been more or less exhausted. The Athenian spectators surely must have grown tired of it, especially when some of these stories had already been presented to them three or four times. Thus it is probably no mere coincidence that poets like Anaxandrides and Antiphanes, who were very productive within a wide range of comic themes, produced only one (or possibly two, in the case of Antiphanes) of these plays each, and that was probably early in their careers, chronologically not much distant from the "specialists" in θεῶν γοναί-plays, Philiscus and Polyzelus. After the 380's, it seems, the theater-going public's interest had to be sustained by other fare. In general, mythological comedy was

---

[63]The fragments of Antiphanes' Αἴολος (fr. 19-20 K.-A.) still show how that play apparently began on a paratragic level which effectively parodied Euripidean art, but afterwards deformed the originally deeply moving plot into a hilarious burlesque in which the once tragic hero Macareus probably was portrayed as a wine-swilling glutton with the unflattering nickname ἀσκός (see Nesselrath, *Mittlere Komödie* 207-9)—a degradation similar to that undergone by Rhea and Cronus in CGFP 215. In fr. 17 K.-A. (᾽Αθάμας), the hero Athamas may have been put on stage like a penurious mercenary (See Nesselrath, *Mittlere Komödie* 327, note 122); in fr. 110 K.-A. (Καινεύς), we may still have a detail of the description of the—here comically deformed—battle between Lapiths and Centaurs which employed a highly figurative narrative style to describe the rather mundane happenings of a brawl after dinner and drinking (see Nesselrath, *Mittlere Komödie* 277-78).

being reduced progressively to only a small fraction of the comic plays that were produced during the following decades.[64] Before the births of gods completely vanished from the stage, however, they certainly helped to establish at least one theme which was, in fact, to become of considerable importance a few decades afterwards when comic plots had definitely returned from the high spheres of Olympus into the human—and sometimes all-too-human—world of the Athenian oikos: the theme of clandestine childbirth brought about by "illegitimate" sexual encounters became, with all its piquant corollaries, a stock motif for a sizable number of plays in the later fourth century, after it seems to have been pioneered, indeed, by the writers of θεῶν γοναί-plays.

These plays may after all have made up only a minor part of what was going on in the theater of Dionysus during comic competitions. As the preceding pages have tried to show, however, their development and history seems to be better traceable and discernible than most other genres of comic play of those times, and they may be considered as contributing something of their own to the slowly evolving features of later comic writing and thus making up a not insignificant part of the momentous transition that was finally to lead to New Comedy.[65]

---

[64]See Nesselrath, *Mittlere Komödie* 200-2.

[65]The Englishness of the original version of this paper was very much improved by Prof. Andrew Dyck, and the final version profited just as much from the kind help of Prof. Gregory Dobrov. To both I express my warmest thanks.

The Fabrication of Comic Illusion

Niall W. Slater

> But art has no goal. It evolves but it does not necessarily progress. Just as the history of politics isn't simply a progress towards parliamentary democracy, so the history of painting isn't simply a progress towards photographic realism.
>
> —Sir Anthony Blunt,
> in Alan Bennett's *A Question of Attribution*

Among the many changes from Old to New Comedy is one basic to the framing of the action on stage and therefore to our interpretation of the plays in their entirety: it is the creation of a consistently maintained dramatic illusion. Gregory Sifakis focused the discussion of this question with his bold claim that "illusion as a psychological phenomenon was entirely alien to Greek theatrical audiences...."[1] While many would regard that now as an overstatement, it was a useful overstatement nonetheless. It liberated us from the view that Aristophanes was groping his way toward nineteenth-century illusionistic comedy, rather like some people's view of an early Renaissance painter, painstakingly working toward vanishing point perspective; we now can see that Aristophanes might rather have his own aesthetic and structural principles in which a striving after illusion played no part.

Whether one then accepts Old Comedy as fundamentally non-illusory drama[2] or prefers still to see breaking of illusion in the parabases and other metatheatrical devices in Aristophanes,

---

[1]Sifakis, *Parabasis* 7. Green, "Seeing and Depicting" 15-50, esp. 40, has recently pointed out how differently the vase painters see tragedy and comedy. For a succinct bibliography on the question of illusion in comedy, see Green, "Seeing and Depicting" 26, note 37.

[2]I use the term of Styan, *Drama, Stage and Audience* (see esp. 180-223).

it is in any case clear that stage convention and practice have changed significantly by the time of Menander's plays. Direct address to the audience essentially disappears, except for the occasional use of ἄνδρες in a soliloquy,[3] as do references to stage machinery[4] and address to the flute-player (an exception being *Dyscolus* 880).[5] Above all, there are no claims about the quality of the play or abuse of the playwright's rivals, such as we know in Old Comedy.

This triumph of illusion is sometimes attributed simply to the influence of Euripides or more generally tragedy, sometimes to a loss of imagination and nerve following the Athenian defeat in the Peloponnesian War. It seems more valuable to examine, not the Zeitgeist, but the changing conditions of production in the Greek theatre. The evidence suggests that several interrelated developments within the period we now dub Middle Comedy, including the repetition of plays, the rise of stock character types, and the decline or at least transformation of the chorus, all contributed to the fabrication of a consistent stage illusion in comedy. Let us look briefly at these in turn.

[3]E.g., *Samia* 269. See Gomme and Sandbach, *Menander, ad loc.* for a list of further examples. Frost, *Exits and Entrances* 116-17 *ad Samia* 725 suggests that the μαρτύρων referred to are members of the audience, but the allusion is subtle and not absolutely required.

[4]Frost, *Exits and Entrances* 29-31 discusses the use of the *ekkyklema* at *Aspis* 299ff., originally suggested by Jacques, "Mouvement des acteurs" 51-52, and further discussed by S. Halliwell, (cited from *LCM* 8.2 [1983] 31-32 in Frost, *Exits and Entrances* 30, note 28); there is no explicit comment in the text, however. For the use of the *ekkyklema* in *Dyscolus* 690-758, see Gomme and Sandbach, *Menander* 239-41, *ad loc.* and Frost, *Exits and Entrances* 58, with full discussion. Cnemon's line at 758, εἰσκυ]κλεῖτ' εἴσω με seems sufficiently explicit, but there is no parody or play with the convention, as in Aristophanes. See also my review of Frost in "The Players Come Again."

[5]See Frost, *Exits and Entrances, ad loc.* and Handley, *Dyskolos* 283-86, *ad loc.* Of interest in this regard is the "Bari Dancers," an Apulian calyx crater dating around 365-350 BC and showing two aulos players with wings dancing around an altar; see the discussion in Taplin, "Auletai" and, more fully, Taplin, *Comic Angels* 70-78. Taplin, *Comic Angels* 105-10, is a very useful survey of possible metatheatrical play with the aulos-player. It is notable, however, that all of his examples come from Old Comedy, with the sole exception of the only surviving (and quite corrupt) fragment of Antiphanes' *Auletes*.

The simple fact that plays were now being restaged or toured beyond the original Athenian performance encouraged new kinds of comic writing. Certainly some plays in the fifth century had more than one production: we know of Aeschylus restaging a play in Sicily during his lifetime. Evidence for deme theatres in Attica in the late fifth century may not be conclusive proof for touring productions of comedies and tragedies staged earlier in Athens,[6] though we do know that tragedies were restaged in the theatre in the Peiraeus. The real explosion of demand for theatre comes in the fourth century. An anecdote about Anaxandrides, from Chamaileon on comedy, tells us that he was *unusual* because, instead of revising his failed plays and producing them again (for the secondary market?), he simply destroyed them (Athenaeus 9.373f-374b; cf. Eustathius 1834.15):

> πικρὸς δὲ ὢν τὸ ἦθος ἐποίει τι τοιοῦτο περὶ τὰς κωμῳδίας· ὅτε γὰρ μὴ νικῴη, λαμβάνων ἔδωκεν εἰς τὸν λιβανωτὸν κατατεμεῖν καὶ οὐ μετεσκεύαζεν ὥσπερ οἱ πολλοί. καὶ πολλὰ ἔχοντα κομψῶς τῶν δραμάτων ἠφάνιζε, δυσκολαίνων τοῖς θεαταῖς διὰ τὸ γῆρας.

> Being of a morose disposition, [Anaxandrides] used to do this with his comedies: whenever he failed to win, he took and gave them to the dealers in frankincense to chop up with it, and he never revised them, as most writers did. In this way he destroyed many plays which had been elaborately composed, because his old age made him peevish toward the spectators.[7]

Perhaps Anaxandrides was conservative in other ways too. Nesselrath notes the rarity of anapaestic tetrameters, a characteristic recitative metre of Old Comedy, in the remains of

---

[6]On the late fifth century deme theatre at Trachones see Green, "Seeing and Depicting" 18-19, and the articles by O. Alexandri cited there (from *Ergon* [1980] 24-25, *Praktika* [1980] 64-67, and *Ergon* [1981] 44-45). Taplin, *Comic Angels* 5, makes a good case for interpreting *Clouds* 523, πρώτους ἠξίωσ' ἀναγεῦσ' ὑμᾶς, to imply that Aristophanes had other venues in which he *could* have produced *Clouds*.

[7]Translation by C. B. Gulick from the Loeb edition of Athenaeus.

Middle Comedy: two of three examples are in Anaxandrides.[8] Our sample is not genuinely random, and the metre is employed by actors as well as chorus, but its use is nonetheless noteworthy.

A geographically expanded audience had less interest in specifically Athenian politics. Nesselrath notes this decline: some political comments remain, but they are "local color,"[9] like Attic geographical references. Perhaps these latter were of especial interest on the touring circuit of the deme celebrations of the rural Dionysia. Because such references are inorganic to plot, far from breaking the illusion, they help suture the audience into the play experience. References to demes and demotics seem to be about as frequent in Middle Comedy as in Old, but the names are not the subject of puns, as they were in Aristophanes.[10] Once again, Anaxandrides harks back more to the spirit of Aristophanes, when he makes a joke at the expense of the deme of Sunion, implying that they were careless about citizen registrations.[11]

An export market for comedy grew up as well. There is a growing consensus that the South Italian vases which we conventionally call phlyax vases, based on the notion that they represent native phlyax drama, in fact often depict performances of Greek, indeed specifically Athenian, scripted comedy. Oliver Taplin has given us one of the more striking pieces of evidence with his demonstration that a South Italian vase depicts a performance of Aristophanes' *Thesmophoriazusae*,[12] and more evidence, including the use of Attic (rather than Doric) Greek on vases to indicate what figures are saying, continues to be noted. Richard Green in particular has shown that the Apulian vases

---

[8]Nesselrath, *Mittlere Komödie* 335. We cannot demonstrate that any of these uses was choral or in an epirrhematic exchange with the chorus, but it is tempting to speculate.

[9]Nesselrath, *Mittlere Komödie* 335.

[10]Whitehead, *Demes* 338-45, esp. 339.

[11]Anaxandrides, *Anchises* fr. 4 K.-A. 3-4: πολλοὶ δὲ νῦν μέν εἰσιν οὐκ ἐλεύθεροι, / εἰς αὔριον δὲ Σουνιεῖς. Cf. Whitehead, *Demes* 340. There may have been a similar joke about the deme Potamos in Menander's Διδύμαι, since Harpocration says, s.v. Ποταμός·... ἐκωμῳδοῦντο δὲ ὡς ῥᾳδίως δεχόμενοι τοὺς παρεγγράπτους, ὡς ἄλλοι τε δηλοῦσι καὶ Μένανδρος ἐν Διδύμαις. Whitehead, *Demes* 292, note 7, suggests this joke may go back to Strattis in the fifth century, since he wrote a Ποτάμιοι.

[12]See Taplin, "Phallology, *Phlyakes*," "Classical Phallology," and *Comic Angels* 36-41.

showing comic scenes were manufactured primarily in Taranto, which provided a ready audience for Greek touring companies, but such vases were *not* being painted in the South Italian hinterland.[13] The conclusion is clear: what we have been calling phlyax drama is in fact Greek comedy, and primarily Middle Comedy, as produced by Greek touring companies, the forerunners of the Artists of Dionysus.[14]

The international market for plays helps explain the disappearance of direct, metatheatrical references to the comic competition. Stephen Halliwell has recently observed[15] that "gibes and counter-gibes of collaboration, plagiarism and the like, had by [the last third of the fifth century] become a stock comic *topos*—a recurrent motif in the twin techniques of self-promotion and denigration of others that played an explicit part in the rivalry of comic poets competing for public prizes." This motif simply disappears in the next century—though plagiarism does not. Middle Comedy playwrights stole freely from each other without recorded reproach, as Richard Hunter notes in his commentary on Eubulus fr. 67 K [= 67 K.-A.], where line 4 is essentially identical to Xenarchus fr. 4 K.-A. line 6.[16] The sea-change in the world of comedy is obvious: charges of plagiarism

---

[13]Green, "Phlyax Vases" 49-56, 55.

[14]While the *Thesmophoriazusae* vase is invaluable evidence for Attic drama in South Italy, the concern of Taplin, *Comic Angels* 44-45, over the paucity of other specific associations of surviving vases with known Aristophanes plays seems misplaced. Surely the majority, indeed the vast majority, of Greek performances in South Italy were of contemporary plays. One would assume that Aristophanes was no larger a proportion of the current repertoire in the fourth century than G. B. Shaw is today—a classic, not a staple, in other words.

[15]Halliwell, "Authorial Collaboration" 515-28; especially 519. Cf. Slater, "Play and Playwright References" 103-5. See note 25 below on Timocles.

[16]Hunter, *Eubulus, ad loc.* Hunter notes that such borrowing was "particularly frequent in the Middle Comedy fragments," and provides this list of examples: Philemon fr. 114 K.-A. [=123K]/Straton fr. 1 K.-A. [=219 Austin]; Eubulus fr. 122 K.-A. [=125K]/Alexis fr. 284 K.-A. [=282K]; Eubulus fr. 109 K.-A. lines 1-2 [=110K]/Ephippus fr. 15 K.-A. lines 3-4 [=15K]; Antiphanes fr. 89 K.-A. [=89K]/Epicrates fr. 5 K.-A. lines 4-9 [=5K]. See also his references to Stemplinger, *Das Plagiat*, and Kroll on the general subject of plagiarism.

would simply be unintelligible in a touring production, which may well not have been written for the Athenian market to begin with.

The career of Menander provides striking evidence for the writing of plays for a non-Athenian market.[17] Over one hundred titles of his plays are known, far more than he could have produced at Athenian festivals during his lifetime. The inference that some were written for non-Athenian performances is obvious. The further question arises as to what texts we have. In the absence of positive evidence, we should presume that we have the performance versions of the touring companies (we hear of no state archival copies of comedy, as we do for tragedy).[18]

This does not mean that certain more abstract metatheatrical elements were excluded from the comic stage immediately, but they become rarer and more generalized. One especially interesting fragment is from Timocles' *Women at the Dionysia*, fr. 6 K.-A., lines 8-19, where an unnamed speaker discusses how watching the myths of tragedy is a comfort or perhaps a therapy for the audience in their own personal griefs.

> τοὺς γὰρ τραγῳδοὺς πρῶτον, εἰ βούλει, σκόπει
> ὡς ὠφελοῦσι πάντας. ὁ μὲν ὢν γὰρ πένης
> 10 πτωχότερον αὑτοῦ καταμαθὼν τὸν Τήλεφον
> γενόμενον ἤδη τὴν πενίαν ῥᾷον φέρει.
> ὁ νοσῶν τι μανικὸν Ἀλκμέων' ἐσκέψατο.
> ὀφθαλμιᾷ τις· εἰσὶ Φινεῖδαι τυφλοί.

[17]Since coming to this conclusion on the basis of Menander's career alone, I find that Taplin, *Comic Angels* 94, note 14, argues for an increasing market outside Athens based on the larger outputs of fourth century playwrights (perhaps 130 reported titles each for Antiphanes and Alexis).

[18]We must at least consider the possibility that the original productions at the City Dionysia and Lenaia contained references to other comic plays and comic playwrights, but such references were excised from the touring productions which are the source of our texts. Such a system of double texts is rather inefficient, however, and if such ever existed, I would assume it quickly gave way to writing a single, "international" text. One might point here to the interesting contemporary case of Woody Allen's *God: A Play*, which is virtually unperformable outside New York City, because of its explicit metatheatrical references to things experienced by actors and audience in the subway on the way to the theatre, etc. The few productions that take place tend to re-write the text massively.

>   τέθνηκέ τῳ παῖς· ἡ Νιόβη κεκούφικε.
> 15 χωλός τις ἐστί· τὸν Φιλοκτήτην ὁρᾷ.
> 16 γέρων τις ἀτυχεῖ· κατέμαθεν τὸν Οἰνέα.
>   ἅπαντα γὰρ τὰ μείζον' ἢ πέπονθέ τις
>   ἀτυχήματ' ἄλλοις γεγονότ' ἐννοούμενος
>   τὰς αὐτὸς αὑτοῦ συμφορὰς ἧττον στένει

> Consider first, if you will, how the tragedians help everyone. For the man who's poor finds Telephus to be even poorer than himself and so bears his own poverty more easily. The sick man sees Alcmaeon raving mad. Someone has eye disease—well, the sons of Phineus are blind. Someone's child has died—Niobe is a comfort. The lame sees Philoctetes, an old man in misfortune learns about Oineus. So each one, having learned of all the greater misfortunes having befallen others, laments his own lot the less.

Tragedy as the opiate of the people, in other words.[19] Note that nothing in the passage implies that the audience must have seen a *particular* play, that is, a particular author's version of the myth; paradoxically, the tragic myths are viewed as having a comforting reality to them.

More puzzling are two fragments from Alexis' play, the Γυναικοκρατία or *Womenocracy*. The first, fr. 42 K.-A., has often been cited in discussions about whether women attended the theatre in Athens.[20]

> ἐνταῦθα περὶ τὴν ἐσχάτην δεῖ κερκίδα
> ὑμᾶς καθιζούσας θεωρεῖν ὡς ξένας

> You women must sit there in the farthest section[21]
> to watch, since you're strangers.

We know essentially nothing about this play beyond what the title and the two fragments tell us. Boettiger, who saw this fragment as the strongest evidence against his view that women did not attend the theatre, argued that, like the *Ecclesiazusae*, the

---

[19]On the virtually magical view of poetry's powers implied here, see Pohlenz, "Anfänge" 142-78, 168-69. Pohlenz sees in particular here the influence of Gorgias' theory of ἀπάτη.

[20]See most recently Henderson, "Women" 133-47, 140-41.

[21]Literally, "wedge,"—the outermost wedge of seats (i.e., with the worst sightlines) is meant. See Henderson, "Women" 140-41.

Gynaikokratia portrayed a topsy-turvy world of women invading what was in fact a male public space.[22] Later Kann also took the view that the *Gynaikokratia* was about women attempting to control a public sphere.[23] Who speaks? To whom? And what are they watching? We simply do not know the answers to the first two questions, but I would agree with Jeffrey Henderson, who says, citing the subject of the next fragment, that "we are entitled to assume that the festival in question was theatrical."[24] That fragment, 43 K-A., deals with an actor.

> ὁ δέ Κίλιξ ὅδ' Ἱπποκλῆς,
> ὁ ζωμοτάριχος ὑποκριτής
>
> This Hippocles of Cilicia,
> the pickled-fish actor

This is of course the only use of ζωμοτάριχος in this sense, so we are left wondering whether the epithet reflects one of Hippocles' eating habits, or is rather an aesthetic judgement upon his acting style. If the latter, it is doubtless unflattering. In either case, such personal comment is extremely rare in the period of Middle Comedy, and we can only conclude that Alexis was somewhat retrograde in this respect[25] (though we cannot date the *Gynaikokratia* in his long career).[26]

[22]Boettiger, *Kleine Schriften* 300-2. The social views which inform Boettiger's scholarship on this point become rather clear with his reference to "dieses neumodische right of Women (um mit der neuesten großen Verfechterin dieser Ordnung, der Miß Wolstonkraft, zu reden)...."

[23]Kann, *De iteratis* 78: "Ut in contione feminae in Ecclesiazusis, ita in theatro in Γυναικοκρατίᾳ imperium sibi parare volunt."

[24]Henderson, "Women" 141.

[25]Cf. also Alexis fr. 77 and 113 K.-A., both of which mention a Timocles who *may* be the comic poet. In fr. 77, Timocles is given as the source for a witticism about Chairephilos's sons: this may have been in a play, or it may have been in conversation. If this is the poet, and one of his plays is being quoted, this is most unusual, since even in Old Comedy, one poet rarely quoted another with approbation, due to the competitive mode of play production. In fr. 113, a Timocles is cited as a typical drunkard; Edmonds speculates that this may be the comic poet being criticized as Cratinus was in the fifth century, but again we cannot be sure (and he occurs in a list with two definitely mythical characters, Oinopion and Maron). Alexis fr. 184 K.-A. speaks of water being "ψυχρότερον Ἀραρότος," apparently a reference to Aristophanes' son, who had no

The evolution of stock characters and stock scenes represents a more complex level of borrowing from competitors and simultaneously moves comedy sharply toward illusion. Once again, the archaeological record is particularly helpful: terracotta figurines begin to appear, of which a famous example is the New York Group. As Richard Green has convincingly argued, however, they do *not* represent the cast of a single play; there are simply too many copies, over too long a period of time. As he points out, "No single play or set of plays could have been that popular or had so much re-play."[27] Instead they represent a growing standardization of masks and stock character types, which could be used and re-used in varying plays. Antiphanes (who seems to have averaged 5 or 6 plays a year and was clearly writing for more than the Athenian festival market) is therefore somewhat disingenuous in the famous complaint in his *Poetry* (fr. 189 K.-A.), where it is asserted that writing comedy is harder than tragedy because all the names, characters, and events must be invented anew each time.

---

particularly distinguished career as a comic poet. The use of the term ψυχρός here is intriguing, in that it echoes Aristophanes' own description of Theognis, the minor tragic poet, in *Thesmophoriazusae* 170: ὁ δ' αὖ Θέογνις ψυχρὸς ὢν ψυχρῶς ποεῖ (cf. also *Acharnians* 11 and 140). We should remember how long the career of Alexis was. Old Comedy elements, such as this kind of personal commentary, may have lingered long in his style.

[26]Edmonds, *Fragments,* ad fr. 41 [= fr. 42 K.-A.] speculates that the play might date after the rebuilding of the Theatre of Dionysus in 329 BC, but the division of the theatre into *kerkides* predates that rebuilding, so there is really no evidence for the date. Amphis also wrote a Γυναικοκρατία, of which only one fragment, 8 K.-A., survives, whose subject matter is not theatrical. On the other hand, Amphis's Ἔριθοι may well be the first evidence for the use of the metaphor of life as theatre. In a contrast between country and city living, Amphis says (fr. 17 K.-A. line 4; see p. 69 below): ἄστυ δὲ θέατρον {ἐστιν} ἀτυχίας γέμον. It is hard to judge from a four-line fragment, of course, but the use of the metaphor does not seem particularly metatheatrical here: rather, the theatre has become the preeminent place of display for the workings of τύχη, so that reference to the theatre is simply a matter of moralizing reflection.

[27]Green, "Seeing and Depicting" 32. See also his discussion of the group in Webster, *Monuments*[3] 45-47.

μακάριόν ἐστιν ἡ τραγῳδία
ποίημα κατὰ πάντ', εἴ γε πρῶτον οἱ λόγοι
ὑπὸ τῶν θεατῶν εἰσιν ἐγνωρισμένοι,
πρὶν καί τιν' εἰπεῖν· ὥσθ' ὑπομνῆσαι μόνον
5   δεῖ τὸν ποιητήν. Οἰδίπουν γὰρ † φῶ
τὰ δ' ἄλλα πάντ' ἴσασιν· ὁ πατὴρ Λάιος,
μήτηρ Ἰοκάστη, θυγατέρες, παῖδες τίνες,
τί πείσεθ' οὗτος, τί πεποίηκεν. ἂν πάλιν
εἴπῃ τις Ἀλκμέωνα, καὶ τὰ παιδία
10 πάντ' εὐθὺς εἴρηχ', ὅτι μανεὶς ἀπέκτονε
τὴν μητέρ', ἀγανακτῶν δ' Ἄδραστος εὐθέως
ἥξει πάλιν τ' ἄπεισι − ⏑ − ⏑ −
(ἔπει)θ' ὅταν μηθὲν δύνωντ' εἰπεῖν ἔτι,
κομιδῇ δ' ἀπειρήκωσιν ἐν τοῖς δράμασιν,
15 αἴρουσιν ὥσπερ δάκτυλον τὴν μηχανήν,
καὶ τοῖς θεωμένοισιν ἀποχρώντως ἔχει.
ἡμῖν δὲ ταῦτ' οὐκ ἔστιν, ἀλλὰ πάντα δεῖ
εὑρεῖν, ὀνόματα καινά, − ⏑ − ⏑ −
⏑ − ⏑ − κἄπειτα τὰ † διῳκημένα
20 πρότερον, τὰ νῦν παρόντα, τὴν καταστροφήν,
τὴν εἰσβολήν. ἂν ἕν τι τούτων παραλίπῃ
Χρέμης τις ἢ Φείδων τις, ἐκσυρίττεται·
Πηλεῖ δὲ πάντ' ἔξεστι καὶ Τεύκρῳ ποιεῖν

Tragedy's a cushy art altogether,
since first of all the spectators
know the plots already, before anyone speaks—
all the poet has to do is remind them.
All I need to do is say "Oedipus"
and they know the rest—his father Laius,
his mother Jocasta, his daughters, sons,
what will happen to him, what he's done. Or again
if someone says "Alcmaeon," in the same breath
he's included all the children, how he
went off his rocker and killed his mother, and how
Adrastus will enter and leave again...
And when the poets can't come up with anything
and have said absolutely everything in their plays
they lift the crane just like a finger
and the spectators get their money's worth.
That's not the way with us comic poets—
we have to invent everything: new names,
set-up, action, second act curtain,

opening.[28] If a Chremes or a Pheidon leaves out any of this, he's hissed off the stage, but Peleus and Teucer can do what they please.

Characters and plots were by no means unique. The rise and fall of the boastful cook in Middle Comedy demonstrates the dynamics of the market for comedy: type scenes (arrival, marketing, report on menus) evolve, which can be added to any play the cook appears in, but a decline for this particular figure sets in after mid-century,[29] and parasites, slaves, and young lovers fill the vacuum.

Finally, the decline of the chorus (apparent already in late Aristophanes) goes hand in hand with the fabrication of a comic illusion. Now the decline of the chorus does not mean necessarily the disappearance of the chorus: there were choral performances in late Aristophanes and in Menander,[30] and Kenneth Rothwell (pp. 99-118, below) provides evidence that the Athenians continued to pay handsomely to support tragic and comic choruses. The question is what relation this choral activity had to the plays being written. Richard Hunter has carefully examined the evidence for the chorus during the transition from Old to

---

[28]What I have translated "opening" might or might not be the prologue. The narrative of a conventional prologue would fall under "set-up," but the use of the word εἰσβολήν for "opening" seems deliberately vague: a play needed a strong opening which might be a dialogue scene, followed by a delayed prologue. "Second act curtain" is literally the catastrophe, the turning point of the action, which often comes in the fourth act of a New Comedy.

[29]Nesselrath, *Mittlere Komödie* 339, suggests a reading public is responsible. The type never disappeared, as Sikon in *Dyscolus* and various cooks in Roman comedy demonstrate, but their roles were much less prominent.

[30]On the chorus in late Aristophanes, see Handley, *Dyskolos* 55-61. For Menander, see Handley, *Dyskolos* 171-74 on lines 230-232 (cf. Frost, *Exits and Entrances* 27) and Gomme and Sandbach, *Menander, ad Epitrepontes* 169. Sifakis, "Aristotle, *E.N.*, IV, 2" 410-32 argues that in Middle Comedy it was common for the chorus to perform the parodos in character and uncharacterized interludes thereafter, with an emphasis on dancing which was "lively and even, in the opinion of some critics, obscene" (432). If this was the case for the performances Aristotle saw, however, it need not have been so outside Athens.

New Comedy,³¹ but several of the passages he discusses appear to be references *to* the chorus, rather than verses actually sung *by* the chorus: his best candidates for the latter are Alexis fr. 239 K.-A. [=237K], Anaxilas fr. 13 K.-A. [=13K], and Eubulus fr. 102-103 K.-A. [=104-105K]. In other words, there is very little evidence to contradict the picture that plays were being written to *allow* for the insertion of choral lyrics when a chorus was available to sing them, but there is also very little to indicate the presence of choruses more specific than Menander's typical drunken revellers, that is, choruses which had characters and verses written for them by the play's author.³²

This accords well with the picture we have been building up of both a domestic and an international audience for comedy. Plays written for the festivals in Athens could still expect production with a full chorus, and a playwright might choose to write lyrics for such a performance.³³ Most plays, however, were

---

³¹Hunter, "The Comic Chorus" 23-38.

³²Maidment, "The Later Comic Chorus" 1-24, does point out one problem for this uniform view. He notes that Aeschines, in a prosecution of Timarchus in 345 BC, refers to a joke made at Timarchus's expense by a comic actor performing at the Rural Dionysia (*In Tim.* 157): πρῴην ἐν τοῖς κατ' ἀγροὺς Διονυσίοις κωμῳδῶν ὄντων ἐν Κολλυτῷ καὶ Παρμένοντος τοῦ κωμικοῦ ὑποκριτοῦ εἰπόντος τι πρὸς τὸν χορὸν ἀνάπαιστον ἐν ᾧ ἦν εἶναί τινας πόρνους μεγάλους Τιμαρχώδεις.... The actor Parmenon (393 O'Connor) is known and had one Lenaean victory: *IG* II/III² 2325; see Mette, *Urkunden* 179, and Ghiron-Bistagne, *Recherches* 350. Note that the actor specifically spoke in anapaests, the typical metre of the parabasis. This seems astonishingly late for such direct address to the audience and for such a personal attack. We do not know the playwright or the play. I can only suggest that a parabatic tradition may have survived longer at the Rural Dionysia than at the city festivals, but even this is a rather unsatisfactory explanation, for Kollytus was one of five "genuinely urban demes"; see Whitehead, *Demes* 26. We also know of a fourth century performance of Sophocles' *Oinomaus* there: Demosthenes, *De Corona* 180. Perhaps a certain conservatism was a function of the deme festival differentiating itself from the great city festivals. The passage does not, as suggested by Maidment, "The Later Comic Chorus" 13 (and note 3), necessarily imply that "the chorus in contemporary comedy was present throughout the dialogue [and] also took a definite part in the dialogue."

³³We might note that the absence of any such lyrics from Menander is not conclusive proof that he never wrote such lyrics. Again, the most

written with an eye on the international market, where production conditions were much more varied. At Delphi in the third century BC, we have inscriptional evidence for a single comic chorus of seven which was shared by three troupes of comic actors. Sifakis assumes that these choristers were professional.[34] That does not mean, however, that these choristers regularly toured with any one of the competing troupes. More likely they were based at Delphi. More commonly the Hellenistic inscriptions mention only chorus trainers,[35] which suggests that touring troupes for major festivals might recruit and train a local chorus. One wonders how much rehearsal time was available and therefore how high a standard such choruses could attain. Even if the playwrights wished to hold onto this oldest element of comedy, amateur choristers were extraneous to the theatre of professionalized and highly specialized comic actors in the great guilds of the Artists of Dionysus. Lesser companies simply did without choruses, and the productions were no less intelligible.[36]

---

likely assumption is that we possess the touring versions of his plays, which would lack such details; cf. note 18 above.

[34]Sifakis, *Hellenistic Drama* 72, cf. 116.

[35]Sifakis, *Hellenistic Drama* 116-20.

[36]The scanty evidence from South Italy is fertile ground for speculation on the questions of whether comic performances there normally had choruses. Taplin, *Comic Angels* 55-60 and 75-78, believes that choruses were part of South Italian performances (though perhaps smaller in number than in Athens), but we should perhaps be a bit more cautious. His belief in choruses allows him to provide an interesting explanation of the so-called "Choregoi Vase," which he himself admits (76) is the best evidence he can provide (nor are the Delphi inscriptions persuasive for choruses in South Italy—see pp. 48-49). An analysis of the "Choregoi Vase" is beyond the scope of this note, but I would suggest that Taplin too easily dismisses the difficulty that the two labelled choregoi are shown on the stage, not on the orchestra level. Might they then be actors playing characters with a function but not necessarily personal names, much like the Logoi in *Clouds*? Though much later, Plautus may provide evidence for what he and his contemporaries could see performed in Taranto and elsewhere. Hunter, "The Comic Chorus" 37-38, prefers to see Greek choruses behind the *piscatores* of the *Rudens* and the *advocati* of the *Poenulus*. Whether that is so or not, however, nothing persuaded Plautus to attempt any use of a traditional chorus in the orchestra in his plays. I suspect that there were some performances with chorus in the

Interconnected with this decline of the chorus was the fundamental change in theatre architecture brought about by the raised stage. Though the stage was never completely cut off from the orchestra level,[37] this change reduced any possible interchange between chorus and actors to the moments of the latter's entrances and exits. If not quite so powerful as the nineteenth-century picture frame proscenium, the raised stage of the Hellenistic theatre ratified the divide of the dramatic world in two, and the actors inhabited a world of consistent verisimilitude.[38]

Before closing, we should cast one glance at the possible influence of tragedy on this process, in particular at an extremely interesting fragment that has only recently come to light. It has most recently been edited by Anton Bierl,[39] who argues that it comes from a comedy, not a satyr play, as Kannicht maintains.[40]

```
                          ε]ἰς οἶδμ' ἀπολίσθο[ι
                          ]τορ    ις [
                          ]νασε   ιαις
    4                     ]σεμελης[ ]  [ ]ς ὕμνον
                          ]  βλα[ ]  [  ]θεος Ἀρκάς
                          ]σκεπτομεν[   ]' σοσσυνην·
        ] υλε   δης       ] ει παρέδωκεν
    8   ∪∪−∪∪−  −∪]πεφευγὼς ἤθυρον ἐγιὼ νέος ἀντρας^ων
```

---

cities of Magna Graecia, but they are likely to have been the exception rather than the rule.

[37]Sifakis, *Hellenistic Drama* 130-35.
[38]Cf. Slater, "Transformations of Space" 1-10.
[39]Bierl, "Dionysos" 353-91.
[40]Kannicht-Snell *TrGF* II 217 comments on the metre and gives a list of words which seem too "tragic" for a comedy. The text has also been edited in Gauly, *Musa Tragica* 251-53; See also p. 302 where the editors adopt the suggestion of W. Luppe (cited from *ZPE* 72 [1988] 36) that the verses come from a "parabasenhafte[r] Epilog" to a satyr play (250). The degree of illusion-breaking tolerable in satyr play is open to debate. Interesting, in this regard is the discussion in Green, "On Seeing and Depicting" 47-49, of the satyrs' metatheatrical discussion of masks that they carry in Aeschylus's *Isthmiastae*. One can only say that the degree of metatheatricality in P. Köln 242A exceeds anything else in our limited evidence heretofore.

	⏑⏑–⏑⏑–	⏑⏑]ουργος ἁπλοῦς, πάσης κακίας ἀμˌίˌαντος
	⏑⏑–⏑⏑–	⏑⏑–]˳οσισου καρπὸν μˌὲν ἑλὼν τὸν ˌὅρˌειον
	⏑⏑–⏑⏑–	⏑⏑]αιτο πάλαι θηρῶνˌ ἐφόδοις ἀκόˌμισˌτον
12	⏑⏑–⏑⏑–	⏑⏑] παιδεύσας ὥριον ἥβˌην ἐφύλαξα
	⏑⏑–⏑⏑–	καρπὸ]ν ὀπώρας ἦρα βαˌθείας ἐπὶ ληνˌούςˌ
	⏑⏑–⏑⏑–	⏑⏑]ν εἰς θνητοὺς ἀνέˌφηνα ποτὸν Διονˌύˌσου
	⏑⏑–⏑⏑–	–]σος ὁ μύστης οὔποˌτε λήγων ἐπὶ Βάκχωι
16	⏑⏑–⏑⏑–	⏑⏑–]δε θεοῦ πρώτηˌ πλοκάμοις ἀνέδησεν
	⏑⏑–⏑⏑–	⏑⏑]ων λήθη χάρισινˌ κείναις ἀνέλαμψεν
	⏑⏑–⏑⏑–	⏑⏑]αι θίασος. τοιάδεˌ κομπεῖν ἐδιδάχθην
	⏑⏑–⏑⏑–	⏑⏑–⏑] μέγας φησὶνˌ ἀοιδὸς Σαλαμῖνος
20	⏑⏑–⏑⏑–	⏑⏑]ης ταμίας, νῦν δ' εˌἰ̣ς ἀπάτας κεκύλισμαι
	⏑⏑–⏑⏑	]ας παῦρος ὑπουργˌῶν ταῖς ψευδομέ᾽ να[ις]' .... [
	⏑⏑–⏑⏑–	–]αραπέμψει τὸν ἀˌπ' ὀθνείας ἐπεγείρων
	⏑⏑–⏑⏑–	–]γνωτε, θεαί · τραγˌικῶν ὁ παρὼν πόνος ὕμνων
24	⏑⏑–⏑⏑–	–]˳ος ὁρίζει μὴ τˌὰ̣ δικαίως καλὰ μόχθωι
	⏑⏑–⏑⏑–	–]φθέντα μόλις θˌῆτε παρέργου τρίτα φόρτου
		ˌαδεν ὀρθῆι Διόνυσος
		βˌραβεύσας γ' ἐν ἀγῶνι

1	...[he] slipped off into the billowy wave...[41]
4	...of Semele...hymn...
	...Arcadian god...
	...observing...
	...handed over....
8	...having fled, as a child I played [in] the caves...
	...a simple worker..., undefiled by any evil...
	...picking the mountain fruit...
	...long ago uncultivated, to [?] the approaches of beasts...
12	...I guarded the young fruit I trained...
	...[the fruit] of autumn I carried to deep winepresses...
	...to mortals I revealed the drink of Dionysus...
	...the initiate never ceasing...to Bacchus...
16	...and the first [female follower?] of the god bound with curls...

[41] My translation is of course deeply indebted to that in Bierl, "Dionysos" 355-56, and his commentary. A number of terms would not in other contexts be unambiguously theatrical, but here it is very tempting to take ἐδιδάχθην as "I rehearsed, learned my part," ψευδομέ᾽να[ις]' as "fictions, plots," and τρίτα as "third prize."

>   ...forgetfulness shone forth in those joys...
>   ...thiasos. I was taught to boast of such things...
>   ...the great bard of Salamis says...
> 20   ...the steward, and now I've been rolled into deceptions...
>   ...doing little service to the fictions...
>   ...rousing him from that far-off bourne, [he] will send...
>   ...goddesses. The present labor of tragic hymns...
> 24   ...defines so that justly beautiful things not...with toil...
>   ...scarcely consider third [prize?] a sideline burden...
>   ...Dionysus rightly...
>   ...judging in the competition...

In an important article which lays out the metatheatrical dimensions of this text, Bierl suggests that we may have a spokesman for comedy complaining that, under the influence of Euripides, comedy has fallen into a use of illusion, which is appropriate rather to tragedy.[42] Because all of the lines lack at least one metron at the beginning, some very basic elements of the interpretation are obscure. There may be one, two, or three speakers. The verses may come from a parabasis or an agon. I do accept that the "bard of Salamis" (ἀοιδὸς Σαλαμῖνος) in line 19 is Euripides and that εἰς ἀπάτας κεκύλισμαι in line 20 does refer to theatrical illusion.[43] What is unclear is whether the speaker of line 20 is necessarily acting as a spokesman for, or judge of, the genre of comedy. Certainly the direct reference in line 23 to tragic hymns is at home only in a comedy, not a satyr play. The idea that the speaker is specifically describing the influence of tragic ἀπάτη on the writing of comedy may be more a result of the conventional belief in Euripidean influence on comedy than a direct inference from this tantalizingly fragmentary text. The

---

[42]Bierl, "Dionysos" 385 (commenting on line 20): "In our text the comic poet, or the speaker representing comedy, notes in the first person that he has been rolled or has rolled himself into illusion, i.e., the tragic form of Euripides. He may be saying that with the new comic style there is scarcely any distinction between tragedy and comedy. In the following lines he wants to express his opposition to this kind of comic composition."

[43]See Bierl, "Dionysos" 365-68 (with notes), for an excellent discussion of ἀπάτη as theatrical illusion; cf. Slater, "Space, Character and ἀπάτη." One point Bierl does not address seems of particular interest to me: why does the speaker refer to ἀπάτας, rather than simply ἀπάτην? Could ἀπάτας mean "plays with illusionistic plots," or could it mean that there are different kinds of dramatic illusions?

fragment is also hard to date, but Bierl's suggestion of a turn-of-the-century date, not far from the death of Euripides, seems in keeping with the subject matter. Bierl's interpretation of τρίτα in line 25 as "third prize" does suggest some further support for this date. On the conventional view that the number of competing comedies at the City Dionysia was reduced to three during the war years and only later restored to five, the reference to third prize (as apparently the worst position one could attain) suggests a date at the end of the fifth century rather than in the next.[44]

Such a date too fits the concern over the fates of both tragedy and comedy that is evident in *Frogs*. I believe it is not just the wisdom of hindsight which sees in that play's debates concern both for the political fate of Athens and for the dramatic genres she had so preeminently nourished. Great artistic achievements commanded the attention of an ever-widening public, so large that it was soon beyond any centralized control. The archon basileus could determine what was seen in Athens but not elsewhere.

Illusion triumphed in the fourth century comic theatre not because tragedy was so compelling a model for dramaturgy but because a diverse and internationalized audience created an enormous demand for a standardized and portable product. Illusion may not even have been a conscious goal of the playwrights in this process, and some, including perhaps Anaxandrides and the author of P. Köln 242A, may have resisted the demands of distribution and market forces. Illusion was not inevitable. As much as anything else, it may have been the incidental result of the "framing" of comic action which took place both physically on the raised stage and metaphorically through the abstraction of the comedy from its specifically Athenian festal setting.

---

[44]For my argument in favor of the reduction during the war years (against the proposal of Luppe that five plays continued to compete throughout the war), see Slater, "The Hypotheses to Aristophanes' *Peace*" (with bibliography).

The Poet's Voice in the Evolution of Dramatic Dialogism

Gregory W. Dobrov

> лингвистика этого двуголосого слова не знает
> linguistics knows nothing of this multivocal word
> —M. Bakhtin

The significance of self-presentation and the relation of the author's voice to other elements in a dialogue or narrative are notoriously elusive issues of literary analysis. Why might an author encourage us to identify him/her explicitly or implicitly with the voice of a speaking subject? Must we acknowledge the voice of the Creator from outside His creation or do we construct this "author" as a secondary fiction? More subtle than an intrusion of the authorial "I" are moments when a character becomes, as it were, a puppet in the hands of a clever ventriloquist, i.e., when we sense the author's presence/voice in the speech of a fictional figure as this speech departs from, or surpasses, its speaker in intelligence, sophistication, tone or scope (e.g. of time, awareness, cultural context, etc.).[1] How do we negotiate encounters of "author" and "figure" such as the point in Aristophanes' *Peace* (43-48), for example, where a slave is made to hypothesize the interpretation of his own performance by two members of the audience, or when a disgruntled rustic improvises tragic parody? Stimulated in large measure by the work of

---

[1]In *Orestes*, for example, Euripides finds subtle expression for his own learning, his "learned voice," by imparting to his dramatic figures knowledge far beyond their means (so Zeitlin, *Closet of Masks* 53). McLeish, *Theatre of Aristophanes* 86, goes further to imagine a reflexive "poneria of style: that is the feeling that the occasion is a game whose rules depend on the mood of the moment, and which the players are watching with as much delight as the spectators."

cultural philosopher Mikhail Bakhtin, recent approaches to such questions have revealed new dimensions of genre, text and performance that challenge our understanding of even basic phenomena such as "voice" and "dialogue." The spectrum of authorial voices between Homer and Heliodorus is arguably brightest at the band marking the political satire of Old Comedy. In this paper I explore the phenomenology of the comic poet's voice and how it follows the convergence of language, character, theme, and plot from early Aristophanes through Middle Comedy towards the focal point of "the probable" (τὸ εἰκός, *Poetics* 1451b9) in New Comedy. Aristotle's insight has been called a "brilliant penetration into the latent possibilities of the most advanced practice of his time."[2] Indeed, the establishment of an implicit dramatic theory of "the probable" informs the evolution of a new and constrained dialogism[3] in the comic stagecraft of the fourth century.

From the very first, when Hesiod names himself in the prologue of the *Theogony* and narrates personal details in *Works and Days* we face the problem of relating poet, figure, (character, persona) and work: "Who is Hesiod?" asks a recent commentator; "Somebody must have written his poetry, so why deny the claims of the text itself?"[4] This reflexive moment in literary history, it is argued, reveals "a finely articulated and carefully developed posturing of the poetry itself, an individual voice and a character that were first invented by preliterate bards, then manipulated and brought to the form they take in the preserved corpus by the needs of an important cultural institution." *Works and Days* and *Theogony* mark an advance in fiction-making by "personalizing the speaking voice and inventing a narrator with an identity and a personality.... If there is a single achievement of the poetry that

---

[2]Webster, *Later Greek Comedy*[1] 114-15.
[3]For an able study of Bakhtinian dialogism see Holquist, *Dialogism*. See also Wall and Thompson, "Cleaning up Bakhtin" (esp. the bibliography on pp. 68-70) and Goldhill, *Poet's Voice*. A somewhat more limited interest in voice is exhibited by Hubbard, *Mask of Comedy*, and Fisher "Multiple Personalities."
[4]Lombardo and Lamberton, *Hesiod* 6-7.

reaches us under Hesiod's name that stands out over all the others, it is that: the invention of the poet."[5]

The impact of this invention on the literature of the next three centuries was profound and has recently received much attention with a productive concentration on the nature of the authorial "I" in archaic lyric.[6] Lesbian poetry is enjoying a vogue outside Classics, a development attested, for example, by a steady stream of publications on the reception of Sappho in French and English literature.[7] Within Classical Studies itself the debate between the "solo hypothesis" and traditional views of the epinikion genre has had the stimulating effect of problematizing much that was taken for granted down to the function of topical references and fundamentals of performance. The surviving works of composers from Alcman to Pindar are scripts belonging to a complex exchange between poet and audience that in many ways anticipates the festival performances of the fifth century.[8] The dialogism of tragedy,[9] deployed in the theatrical space and

---

[5]Lombardo and Lamberton, *Hesiod* 16. For a good discussion of the poet's persona in the Archaic period see Nagy, "Early Greek Views," especially 47-69.

[6]For a collection of essays on the first-person fiction in archaic poetry see Slings, *The Poet's "I."* Important entries in the Pindaric debate are: Lefkowitz, "Who Sang Pindar's Victory Odes?" and *First Person Fictions*; Davies, "Monody, Choral Lyric"; Burnett, "Performing Pindar's Odes"; Carey, "Performance of the Victory Ode" and "Victory Ode in Performance"; Heath and Lefkowitz, "Epinician Performance"; Heath, "Receiving the κῶμος"; Bremmer, "Pindar's Paradoxical ἐγώ"; Ley, "Monody, Choral Song"; and Morgan, "Pindar the Professional."

[7]Highlights of modern Sapphic studies include the following: DeJean, *Fictions of Sappho* (cf. the article of the same name) and "Sappho, c'est moi"; Duclos, "Higginson's Sappho"; Greenberg, "Erotion, Anactoria"; Gregory, "Rose Cut In Rock"; Gubar, "Sapphistires"; Harvey, "Ventriloquizing Sappho"; Holstun, "Lesbian Elegy in Donne, Marvell, and Milton"; Leighton, *Victorian Women Poets*; Mueller, "Lesbian Erotics"; O'Higgins, "Sappho's Splintered Tongue"; Powell, "Afterwords"; and Zonana, "Swinburne's Sappho."

[8]E.g., Gentili, *Poetry and its Public*, and Kurke, *Traffic in Praise*.

[9]"Dialogism" (see note 3 above and pp. 90-93) denotes the quality of involving more than one voice in a text or script engaged in reflexive interaction. The ways in which two or more voices operate in a given narrative are explored by Bakhtin in a number of works, especially

played in real time, represents a new level of complexity in which the poet's voice would appear to have a greater formal range of expression. It is in the comedy of Aristophanes, however, that the fictional poet makes his boldest appearance, an entrance in which a long tradition of self-representation reaches a climax.[10]

The unstable partial identity between protagonist and playwright in comedies such as *Acharnians* and *Wasps*, for example, as well as direct self-presentation in the parabases are hallmarks of Old Comedy. In the fifth-century scripts that survive we have evidence of a remarkable moment, a supernova, as it were, of creative energy in which the amalgamated material of a long tradition explodes in a dazzling flash leaving behind the dimmer shapes of the fourth century. Aristophanes' brilliance owes much to the direct and indirect presence of his poetic persona throughout: the protagonists, plots, and parabases of his highy topical satires necessarily involve the fictional playwright on many levels. Moments at which Aristophanes appears to ventriloquate through a figure such as Dicaeopolis (e.g., *Acharnians* 377-382, 501-503) or the cloud-chorus (*Clouds* 510-626) are but the tip of an iceberg whose extent has not been fully appreciated. The glaring affronts to our sense of verisimilitude are symptomatic of a style in which no distinct boundary protects the *dramatis personae* from invasion by (the fictionalized) "Aristophanes." The dialogism of Old Comedy is thus not yet rigidly structured by the identity of character and voice. Remarkable here is the facility with which a given speaking subject may be distorted and overshadowed by the "poet" beyond the limits of consistent character. Individual stage-figures, moreover, are often made to speak several styles and to mix several "languages."

An important and palpable feature of the subsequent (Middle and New Comic) styles, then, is the apparent depersonalization of dramatic discourse with respect to the "poet" himself as the author withdraws from his work leaving the characters in a play-world that insists on its autonomy through

---

Dostoyevsky's Poetics. On the varieties of dialogism and their reception in contemporary criticism see the final section of this paper.

[10] On the centrality of self-reference and allusion in Greek literature see Hubbard, *Mask of Comedy* 33-40.

the dramatic illusion. The realism of New Comedy subordinates voice to character much more strictly. In what follows, I concentrate on these transformations by aligning similar elements from scripts spanning the full century between *Acharnians* and *Dyscolus*. I argue from the fragmentary evidence of Middle Comedy that an important stylistic shift took place in this period which abandoned much of what was fundamental to Aristophanes and set the stage for Menander. The current surge of interest in dialogism stimulated by Bakhtin adds a new dimension to the study of dramatic discourse and literary reflexivity that will be helpful in tracing the role of the poet's voice in the evolution of Greek comedy.

Plutarch's Problem

An interesting, if somewhat enigmatic, beginning for an inquiry into the relationship between language and character is suggested in the epitome of Plutarch's *Synkrisis of Aristophanes and Menander*.[11] Plutarch begins with observations on the style of the former:

> ἔνεστι μὲν οὖν ἐν τῇ κατασκευῇ τῶν ὀνομάτων αὐτῷ τὸ τραγικὸν τὸ κωμικὸν τὸ σοβαρὸν τὸ πεζόν, ἀσάφεια, κοινότης, ὄγκος καὶ δίαρμα, σπερμολογία καὶ φλυαρία ναυτιώδης. καὶ τοσαύτας διαφορὰς ἔχουσα καὶ ἀνομοιότητας ἡ λέξις οὐδὲ τὸ πρέπον ἑκάστῃ καὶ οἰκεῖον ἀποδίδωσιν· οἷον λέγω βασιλεῖ τὸν ὄγκον ῥήτορι τὴν δηνότητα γυναικὶ τὸ ἁπλοῦν ἰδιώτῃ τὸ πεζὸν ἀγοραίῳ τὸ φορτικόν· ἀλλ' ὥσπερ ἀπὸ κλήρου ἀπονέμει τοῖς προσώποις τὰ προστυχόντα τῶν ὀνομάτων, καὶ οὐκ ἂν διαγνοίης εἴθ' υἱός ἐστιν εἴτε πατὴρ εἴτ' ἄγροικος εἴτε θεὸς εἴτε γραῦς εἴθ' ἥρως ὁ διαλεγόμενος.

Aristophanes' language, then, shows much incongruence and dissimilarity: a tragic element and a comic; the pretentious and the prosaic; the obscure and the commonplace; grandeur and elevation; vulgar garrulity and nauseating nonsense. Despite this, his style fails even to

---

[11]*Moralia* 853a-854d. Here I follow the example of a rare and stimulating study of Menandrean style and stagecraft, Sandbach, "Menander's Manipulation." The translations are based on those in Russell and Winterbottom, *Ancient Literary Criticism* 531-32.

assign appropriate and suitable language to individual characters—grandeur to a king, cleverness to an orator, lack of sophistication to a woman, prosaic words to an ordinary man, vulgarity to a street-lounger. Instead, it puts any words in the mouth of any character, as though out of a hat. You can't tell if it's a son talking or a father, a farmer or a god, an old woman or a hero.

The salient criticisms here are directed against an unrealistic mixture of linguistic resources and the apparent lack of effort to adapt language to character. Particularly interesting is the mention of "much incongruence and dissimilarity," τοσαύτας διαφοράς καὶ ἀνομοιότητας. The context shows that the problem lies with the diction as assigned to individual figures. Plutarch appears to suggest that, within the limits set by a single character, Aristophanes' script violates certain standards of appropriateness and suitability (τὸ πρέπον ἑκάστῃ καὶ οἰκεῖον) in a way that precludes linguistic characterization. An Aristophanic character, on this reading, is given an unrealistic mixture of registers, styles, and even voices (e.g., a peasant mixing Euripides and obscenity). By contrast, Menander "shows what mastery of language really is":

ἡ δὲ Μενάνδρου φράσις οὕτω συνέξεσται καὶ συμπέπνευκε κεκραμένη πρὸς ἑαυτήν, ὥστε διὰ πολλῶν ἀγομένη παθῶν καὶ ἠθῶν καὶ προσώποις ἐφαρμόττουσα παντοδαποῖς μία τε φαίνεσθαι καὶ τὴν ὁμοιότητα τηρεῖν ἐν τοῖς κοινοῖς καὶ συνήθεσι καὶ ὑπὸ τὴν χρείαν ὀνόμασιν· ἐὰν δέ τινος ἄρα τερατείας εἰς τὸ πρᾶγμα καὶ ψόφου δεήσῃ, καθάπερ αὐλοῦ πάντρητον ἀνασπάσας ταχὺ πάλιν καὶ πιθανῶς ἐπέβαλε καὶ κατέστησε τὴν φωνὴν εἰς τὸ οἰκεῖον. πολλῶν δὲ γεγονότων εὐδοκίμων τεχνιτῶν, οὔθ' ὑπόδημα δημιουργὸς οὔτε προσωπεῖον σκευοποιὸς οὔτε τις ἱμάτιον ἅμα ταὐτὸν ἀνδρὶ καὶ γυναικὶ καὶ μειρακίῳ καὶ γέροντι καὶ οἰκότριβι πρέπον ἐποίησεν· ἀλλὰ Μένανδρος οὕτως ἔμιξε τὴν λέξιν, ὥστε πάσῃ καὶ φύσει καὶ διαθέσει καὶ ἡλικίᾳ σύμμετρον εἶναι, ...

Menander's language, on the other hand, is so polished and its constituents so harmoniously united that, despite the varied emotions and characters involved and the fact that it has to suit all kinds of personages, it gives a single impression and maintains its uniformity by means of common, everyday words that are in normal use. Should the action however demand something fanciful or impressive, he opens all the stops of his instrument, as it were, and then quickly and convincingly closes them again and restores the tone to its usual quality. Of all the famous craftsmen there have been, no cobbler has made a shoe, no costumier a mask, no tailor a cloak, that would fit at the same time a man, a woman, a boy, an old man, and a household slave. Yet Menander has so contrived his language as to make it appropriate to every nature, disposition, and period of life.

Menander is praised, above all, for the verisimilitude of his language which has been purged of incongruity. The emphasis here is on uniformity and consistency ([ἡ φράσις] μία τε φαίνεσθαι καὶ τὴν ὁμοιότητα τηρεῖν) that lend themselves well to the realistic drawing of character. Plutarch has long puzzled his readers with the apparent implication that Menander developed a *single type of language* for all characters. "I must confess," notes F. H. Sandbach in this connection, "that I find it easier to support the view that Menander distinguished his speakers by their language than to find clear evidence for a single style."[12] This is surely correct, and we should rather place the emphasis in the analysis above on the phrase [ἡ δὲ Μενάνδρου φράσις] συνέξεσται καὶ συμπέπνευκε κεκραμένη πρὸς ἑαυτήν "(Menander's language is) polished and its constituents harmoniously united." I suggest a reading of this passage on a level of abstraction sufficient to allow the stated unity to be one of method: Menander's approach, unlike that of Aristophanes, is to adapt language (the contents and style of which may differ) to each character *in the same way*, i.e. by giving each character a consistent and homogeneous language free of unrealistic intrusions, admixtures, and incongruities. A stumbling block in the interpretation of Plutarch's *Synkrisis* has been the heavy-handed concluding metaphor which suggests a single, concrete language for all characters. Taken simply, of course, this suggestion finds little support either in the text of Menander or in Plutarch's own analysis. The claim for a unity of language is best understood in contrast to Aristophanes, whose vocabulary and usage appear wildly unpredictable and unrealistic. The general stock of words and idioms in Menander may be said to be relatively uniform, while still allowing for considerable variation

---

[12]Sandbach, "Menander's Manipulation" 114.

in syntax and style.¹³ In its criticism of Aristophanes, the *Synkrisis* identifies different modes deemed appropriate to different characters: "grandeur to a king, cleverness to an orator, lack of sophistication to a woman, etc." *Between* characters Menander's style may differ somewhat, but within the limits of a single character's speech Menander shows no trace of Old Comic complexity and discontinuity. Since it is precisely in this complexity and discontinuity that I locate my generalized notion of "the poet's voice" in Aristophanic comedy, the contrast drawn by Plutarch may be seen to imply the process of depersonalization (with respect to the poet and his voice) through which the stage figures of New Comedy acquire a more clearly defined and realistic verbal mask as the "personality" of the Creator fades from His work.

Modern discussions of comic language have repeated Plutarch's observations with some refinement, to be sure. "Aristophanes abstains from giving each of his characters a distinctive language," notes K. J. Dover. The dramatist's stage personae "develop essentially through what they say without any help from the way in which they say it." Old Comic character in this analysis represents "a compromise between convention and naturalism."¹⁴ The implication here of a link between theatrical convention and language receives support from New Comedy in which the marriage of naturalism and (dramatic) illusion suggests the influence of tragedy. Indeed, Plutarch makes clear that the characters of Aristophanes don't sound much like those of Menander. The latter, as we learned from the *Synkrisis*, gives his characters language that is more coherent, predictable, and lifelike than what one critic has called the "shifting network of fictionalized representations, the glossolalia of Aristophanic

---

¹³On vocabulary, see Sandbach, "Menander's Manipulation" 115-20 (also 130-36) and Del Corno, "aspetti del linguaggio" 13-48.

¹⁴Dover, "Language and Character" 248. In *Frogs* 196 (concerning line 51), however, Dover clearly supports the notion of some sort of linguistic characterization. The line in question, taken as "a sour aside," is effective in that it "best fits the progressive characterization of [Xanthias'] role." This role is discussed more fully on pages 45-46 of the same work. In other words, what stage-figures say (and how they say it) may, in fact, contribute to their characterization.

characterization."[15] The polymetry and variety of delivery (spoken, recitative, song) in Aristophanes further complicate the fabric of his plays in a way that distinguishes it from that of later comedy. Old Comedy, in other words, has a great deal of external variety in addition to the variety that so annoyed Plutarch within the limits of a given character.

A prominent aspect of the evolution of the comic genre is the evolution of theatrical discourse as it defines the dramatic figure ("character") in the environment of given stage conventions and a given level of dramatic illusion. Where does the "poet" end and a "character" begin? This is a problem that has received special attention since the appearance of an influential paper by J. Gould: that of separating "the figures of drama... —as bounded individuals—from the (figural) language of the narrative."[16] Since dramatic language and characterization undergo significant changes between Cratinus and Menander it is worth asking how the relationship between "character" and "language of the narrative," i.e., between "figure" and "discourse" (as controlled and often appropriated by the author) evolves with the genre.[17] In this connection, I identify and foreground three aspects of the Old Comic dialogism— "polyphony," "discourse irony," and "improvisation"—which, in their stark transformation, exemplify the significant changes evident across the board in the fourth century "middle" and "new" comic styles. I shall elaborate Plutarch's complaint by suggesting that, in a play such as *Acharnians*, Aristophanes' style is deliberately *polyphonic*, i.e., it incorporates many voices and styles with little homogenization in the service of realism and with little concern for defining character by means of voice, style,

---

[15]Goldhill, *Poet's Voice* 195.

[16]Goldhill, "Character and Action" 108. Goldhill and others in this collection take Gould, "Dramatic Character" as their point of departure.

[17]Goldhill, "Character and Action" 112, notes that Roland Barthes (*S/Z* 178) "questions the validity of this opposition of character and discourse. Discourse and character, he writes, can be seen in 'good narrative writing' as mutually and inextricably implicative: 'from a critical point of view...it is as wrong to suppress character as it is to take him off the page in order to turn him into a psychological character (endowed with possible motives): *the character and discourse are each other's accomplices*' [original emphasis]."

or linguistic register. Closely related to this polyphony is *discourse irony*, i.e., the ironic mismatch at many points in a play between a given character (i.e. who he/she is *supposed* to be: farmer, slave, etc.) and things this character says, does and knows. Dicaeopolis and Trygaeus most certainly exceed their "natural" competence as common-sense rustics when they base their speech and behavior on tragic models in a sophisticated and critical way. Discourse irony in Aristophanes is often a symptom of what I have termed "ventriloquism," i.e. the direct or oblique invasion of a character by the voice of the poet. This irony becomes especially apparent at moments where Aristophanes propels and develops his plot through the deceptively casual actions of a character whose role is played as a series of *improvisations*. Relatively free of the stock character-types and rigid social situations that inform the design of later comedy, Aristophanes allows his ideas to evolve as if by accident from the spontaneous movements of his stage-figures. As with irony of speech and knowledge, the serendipitous progress of figures such as Peisetaerus and Euripides' Kinsman is a literary ruse, i.e., the careful presentation of the poet's design as the unrehearsed improvisations of a buffoon or trickster.

In the work of Aristophanes the author's mind and presence are simultaneously asserted and masked in a way that calls to mind the ventriloquist's art: we enjoy the enigmatic tension between the character and its vehicle (e.g., a puppet), between a fictive dialogue and the reality of a complex solo-performance. Discontinuities of voice and character are, in fact, the stock-in-trade of ventriloquists who habitually invade and disrupt their fictional character for comic effect. In the conclusion to this paper I extend Plutarch's *Synkrisis* in light of recent work on "voice" from the perspective of Bakhtinian dialogism to suggest that between Aristophanes and Menander we observe the mutation of a dialogical genre from one in which the playwright is free to "ventriloquate" through his stage-figures to one in which the characters are linguistically secured as autonomous and stable literary constructs, i.e. one in which voice and language are rigidly structured by character. Old Comedy with its unrealistic and "ventriloqual" use of polyphony, discourse irony, and improvisation, yields to New Comedy with its narrowly circumscribed inventory of speakers and linguistic registers approaching what in recent Bakhtinian criticism has been termed "primary dialogism," "that interplay of voices and concepts which is found in realist fiction and daily life."[18] I shall also consider the literary-historical significance of this transition within the social context of Old Comic political satire.

The vehicle for my project shall be an exploration of the harangue, an evolving comic topos that endures throughout the entire history of the genre. This is usually a set speech to the audience (or as an aside) in which a central character, upon his first entrance (as in *Acharnians* and *Dyscolus*) complains about his fellow man, either as an entire class or as represented by one or another element of humanity or human behavior: women, imposters, greed, drunkenness, etc. The harangue, moreover is an intrinsically worthy representative of its genre since it offers many opportunities, as a topos, for exaggeration, anticlimax, surprise, and witty commentary on human nature. From its origins as an unstructured complaint in the hands of Aristophanes, the harangue develops features that mark it as a topos where stylization of form and content go hand-in-hand.

One Hundred Years of Haranguing

Criticism and outrage are the life-blood of comedy. The five lines attributed to the "pre-historic" poet Susarion (Susar. test. 8 K.-A.) set the stage from the very outset by linking the harangue form with the theme of ψόγοι γυναικῶν (see below, pp. 66-68): "Women are an evil! Nevertheless it is impossible, neighbors, to live in one's house without (this) evil. For both to marry and not to marry is evil." We find another harangue at the much more real and important starting point of Aristophanes' career. His earliest surviving work, *Acharnians* of 425 BC, opens with a long

---

[18]Miller, "Dialogism of Lyric" 183-84, drawing on Morson and Emerson, *Rethinking Bakhtin* 52-53. Primary dialogism "designates that set of relations which governs the exchange of complete 'utterances' between individuals, social groups, and/or their fictional representatives: the utterance being, as Bakhtin defines it, the basic unit of speech delimited not by the sentence, the proposition or the paragraph, but by the completion of one speech act by one speaker and the beginning of a second by another."

and lively tirade spoken by the protagonist. In the attempt to clarify the principles of Aristophanic characterization and humor, critics have made a variety of suggestions. Thus Dover would constrain the potential of comic language by a rather harsh rule in accordance with which Aristophanes *never* invites us "to turn our attention to two different levels of humour operating simultaneously."[19] More recently Michael Silk has proposed that language and character in Aristophanes be understood in terms of a general notion of "imagist representation."[20] The apparent limitations of such formulae should not overshadow their value for further inquiry into a challenging subject. In my own attempt to articulate the relationship between the various linguistic "coordinates" discernible in Aristophanes' work, i.e., the script, poet's voice and persona, the dramatic figures, and the spectators themselves, I begin by setting side by side two representative samples from the endpoints of the extant tradition: the harangues of Dicaeolpolis (*Acharnians* 1-42) and of Menander's Cnemon (*Dyscolus* 153-168).

The opening of *Acharnians* is a particularly appropriate beginning as it isolates the stage figure's voice in the expression of a complaint that is of central relevance to the play as a whole. As a discursive (i.e. trimeter) topos attested in all stages of Greek Comedy, moreover, the harangue will serve to focus the discussion and to make comparisons across comic strata more intelligible. Dicaeopolis' monologue, of which I give only a sample, illustrates well the challenge presented by the language of the Aristophanic protagonist:

1   Ὅσα δὴ δέδηγμαι τὴν ἐμαυτοῦ καρδίαν,
     ἥσθην δὲ βαιά, πάνυ δὲ βαιά, τέτταρα·
     ἃ δ' ὠδυνήθην, ψαμμακοσιογάργαρα.
4   φέρ' ἴδω, τί δ' ἥσθην ἄξιον χαιρηδόνος;
        . . . .

[19]Dover, "Language and Character" 241.

[20]Silk, "The People of Aristophanes" 159: "Aristophanes' characters, ... have their realist elements, or moments, or sequences, disrupted by imagist elements, or moments, or sequences. And though realist elements, or moments, or sequences, remain, the presence of the disruptive serves to differentiate the representation as a whole from realism proper."

POET'S VOICE 59

```
26                      εἰρήνη δ᾽ ὅπως
          ἔσται προτιμῶσ᾽ οὐδέν· ὦ πόλις πόλις.
          ἐγὼ δ᾽ ἀεὶ πρώτιστος εἰς ἐκκλησίαν
          νοστῶν κάθημαι· κᾆτ᾽ ἐπειδὰν ὦ μόνος,
30        στένω κέχηνα σκορδινῶμαι πέρδομαι,
          ἀπορῶ γράφω παρατίλλομαι λογίζομαι,
          ἀποβλέπων ἐς τὸν ἀγρὸν εἰρήνης ἐρῶν,
          στυγῶν μὲν ἄστυ τὸν δ᾽ ἐμὸν δῆμον ποθῶν,
          ὃς οὐδεπώποτ᾽ εἶπεν, ἄνθρακας πρίω,
35        οὐκ ὄξος οὐκ ἔλαιον, οὐδ᾽ ᾔδει 'πρίω,'
          ἀλλ᾽ αὐτὸς ἔφερε πάντα χὠ πρίων ἀπῆν.
```

I've been stung in the very heart one too many times.
And I've enjoyed little, very little,... four things, to be exact.
Yup, but my pains have been in the sand pile-zillions!
As for fun... Let's see, what've I enjoyed, a real happytude?
. . . . .
[The Prytaneis] give no thought to peace
or how it might be arranged. Ah, city, city!
I'm always the first one to come here and to take my seat
in the assembly. Then, since I'm all alone
I whine, I yawn, I stretch, I fart,
I wonder, I doodle, I pluck myself, I ponder the situation
and look to the countryside yearning for peace.
I hate the urban center here and long for my village home
There I never hear "charcoal for sale,"
"vinegar for sale," "oil for sale." My village doesn't
even know the phrase "for sale." It produces everything
itself and such as*sale*ants are nowhere to be found.

This monologue incorporates most of the linguistic strata characteristic of Aristophanes' trimeter style. I illustrate a modified version of Dover's categories in light of Geoffrey Arnott's recent work on comic openings (with apologies for not printing the full Greek text):[21]

1) Contemporary Usage (from colloquial to formal registers): Lines 19-22, for example, are straightforward, containing neither specialized nor comic terms: ὁπότ᾽ οὔσης κυρίας ἐκκλησίας / ἑωθινῆς ἔρημος ἡ πνὺξ αὑτηί, / οἱ δ᾽ ἐν ἀγορᾷ

---

[21]Dover, "The Style of Aristophanes" 224, suggests the categories "normal language," "the spoken language," "technical language," "the language of serious poetry," and "peculiarly comic language." In this connection, I must also acknowledge my debt to the perceptive analysis of *Acharnians* 1-18 in Arnott, "Comic Openings" 19-22.

λαλοῦσι κἄνω καὶ κάτω / τὸ σχοινίον φεύγουσι τὸ μεμιλτωμένον, "come the morning of a sovereign Assembly day, this here Pnyx is empty while they're in the agora chatting and running around dodging the red-rope." Of a colloquial color are the phrases such as φέρ' ἴδω, τί δ' ἥσθην, "Let's see, what've I enjoyed?" (line 4), ἀπέθανον καὶ διεστράφην, "I (nearly) broke my neck and died" (line 15), εἶτα δ' ὠστιοῦνται πῶς δοκεῖς, "then they'll come pushing and shoving like you wouldn't believe!" (line 24), and τοῦτ' ἐκεῖν' οὑγὼ 'λεγον, "this is just what I was talking about"(line 41).[22]

2) **Technical terminology**: τραγῳδικόν, "tragic" (line 9, as a term of [sophistic?] literary criticism, cf. *Knights* 1378-1380 for parody of the sophistic use of -ικός), ἔσεισέ μου ... τὴν καρδίαν, "rattled my heart" (line 12, perhaps a medical term). Aristophanes certainly knows how to exploit specialized expressions and new morphology (e.g., the many new nouns in -σις and -τις)[23] and likes to play with jargon such as the bombastic string of superlatives at *Clouds* 260 and *Birds* 429-430 that, no doubt, refelect sophistic argot.

3) **Poetic language**, i.e., the language of epic, lyric, or tragedy (with the likelihood of parody) maintains a prominent presence throughout the work of Aristophanes. Here we have a few limited examples: ἄξιον γὰρ Ἑλλάδι "worthy of Hellas" (line 8, Euripides' *Telephus*, fr. 720 N²); ὦ πόλις πόλις "ah, city, city!" (line 27, Sophocles' *Oedipus* 629). In light of the subsequent involvement with Euripides' *Telephus*, however, the glancing allusion at line 8 is a harbinger of an extended involvement on the part of *Acharnians* with a tragic text.

4) **Comic usage and invention**: Aristophanes' arsenal includes obscenities such as πέρδομαι, "fart" (line 30), and παρατίλλομαι,"pluck myself" (line 31, with obscene potential as in *Lysistrata* 89 and line 151); rhetorical tricks (cf. the asyndeton in these lines and at line 38); and lexical innovations such as the words ψαμμακοσιογάργαρα. "sand pile-zillions" (line 3), and χαιρηδόνος, "happy-tude" (line 4).

---

[22]For an interesting discussion of this idiom in its various forms from Aristophanes to Terence see Bain, *Actors and Audience* 207. For further bibliography on a number of similar phrases belonging to everyday speech see Bain, "Misunderstood Scene" 92 (esp. note 21).

[23]On this particular linguistic phenomenon see Browning, "Greek Abstract Nouns" 60-74, and Rawlings, *Prophasis* 39-40.

POET'S VOICE   61

To this list we could add a number of special types of language such as the use of dialect, quotation and parody of non-literary texts (decrees, oracles), and the occasional use of nonsense and onomatopoeia. An Aristophanic favorite, moreover, is the pun of which we have a typically untranslatable example in line 35. The verb πρίω (imperative of πρίασθαι) "buy x," "x for sale," is repeated three times as a vendor's cry. The form which follows in line 35, ὁ πρίων, is a pun on the notion of something irritating (the noun for "saw" or participle "one who saws") imparting to the vendor and his trade the quality of being rasping, annoying. It is important to note that the leading characters in Aristophanes' plays often exhibit a linguistic virtuosity similar in complexity (if not in precise technique) to this performance by Dicaeopolis. This passage appears quite free of the formulae which later mark *Bauformen* and topoi such as the prologue and harangue, respectively.

The soliloquy of Cnemon, Menander's misanthrope, provides an interesting contrast of form and content. Whereas Dicaeopolis' complex harangue is gradual and oblique in approaching its subject, i.e., lamenting the emptiness of the Pnyx in a mood of deep concern for the polis, Cnemon passes from a sardonic commonplace to make the simple and direct point that people won't leave him alone. He expresses his disaffection with humanity by means of a mythological exemplum with little, if any, stylistic affectation (*Dyscolus* 153-168 [Sandbach]):

153 εἶτ' οὐ μακάριος ἦν ὁ Περσεὺς κατὰ δύο
     τρόπους ἐκεῖνος, ὅτι πετηνὸς ἐγένετο
     κοὐδενὶ συνήντα τῶν βαδιζόντων χαμαί,
     εἶθ' ὅτι τοιοῦτο κτῆμ' ἐκέτηθ' ᾧ λίθους
     ἅπαντας ἐπόει τοὺς ἐνοχλοῦντας; ὅπερ ἐμοὶ
     νυνὶ γένοιτ'· οὐδὲν γὰρ ἀφθονώτερον
     λιθίνων γένοιτ' ⟨ἂν⟩ ἀνδριάντων πανταχοῦ.
160 νῦν δ' οὐ βιωτόν ἐστι, μὰ τὸν Ἀσκληπιόν.
     λαλοῦσ' ἐπεμβαίνοντες εἰς τὸ χωρίον
     ἤδη· παρ' αὐτὴν τὴν ὁδὸν γάρ, νὴ Δία,
     εἴωθα διατρίβειν· ὃς οὐδ' ἐργάζομαι
     τοῦτο τὸ μέρος ⟨τοῦ⟩ χωρίου, πέφευγα δὲ
     διὰ τοὺς παριόντας. ἀλλ' ἐπὶ τοὺς λόφους ἄνω
     ἤδη διώκουσ'. ὦ πολυπληθείας ὄχλου.
     οἴμοι, πάλιν τις οὑτοσὶ πρὸς ταῖς θύραις
     ἕστηκεν ἡμῶν.

> Didn't old Perseus have all the luck, I mean
> a double dose? First of all, he had wings and
> could avoid everybody milling about below;
> Second, he had this thing which he used
> to turn anybody who got in his way to stone.
> If only I now had it! Nothing would be
> a more common sight: stone
> statues everywhere! I can't stand it
> anymore, I swear! These days they
> just barge into my yard and babble away.
> I've gotten used to hanging out right on the
> big highway. I mean, I can't even farm
> this plot of land anymore; I can't go near it
> if I want to avoid passers-by. Now they chase me up
> into the hills. What a throng, what a crowd!
> Damn it, here's some guy at my door again!

Concerning the technique, it is clear that of the strata identified in the Aristophanic passage only one is in evidence here, namely, that of contemporary usage with traces of the colloquial.[24] What catches the eye as a possible counter-example is the reference to Perseus (εἶτ' οὐ μακάριος ἦν ὁ Περσεύς, etc.). Lines 153-159, however, stand in stark contrast to paratragic usage, which reflects a specific literary model (from a single word to an entire scene). Consider, for example, the words of Trygaeus' slave to his master at *Peace* 135-136 "οὐκοῦν ἐχρῆν σε Πηγάσου ζεῦξαι πτερόν, / ὅπως ἐφαίνου τοῖς θεοῖς τραγικώτερος," "you should have yoked the wing of Pegasus, so as to appear more tragic to the gods." The slave is made to underscore the comic script's usurpation of Euripides' *Bellerophon* in a way that simultaneously incorporates tragic language ("yoke the wing of Pegasus") and outlines the parodic purpose of the scene, i.e., to improvise from the tragic situation a new comic scenario. The metatheatrical dimension of this prologue permeates all levels of

---

[24]Menander is not, of course, incapable of using elevated or tragic language as Plutarch implies: "Should the action however demand something fanciful or impressive, he opens all the stops of his instrument, as it were, and then quickly and convincingly closes them again and restores the tone to its usual quality" (see pp. 52-53, above). The recognition scene in the *Perikeiromene* (lines 779-827 [Sandbach]) is an elaborate example of stichomythia that in vocabulary and meter follows the rules of tragedy. See Sandbach, "Menander's Manipulation" 125-28.

the performance and is especially palpable in the changes in language and meter. Trygaeus, for example, mounts his comic Pegasus (a dung beetle) and, by line 154, is lifted by means of the crane into the air. In the nineteen-line anapaestic sequence (lines 154-172) which follows, the protagonist mingles paratragic exhortation to his "steed" with expressions of terror at the prospect of falling to earth. Although the threats to Trygaeus' safety are extravagantly comic (e.g., the aroma of fresh feces in the Piraeus) they are confined to the fiction of the flight to Olympus. As the meter changes, however, he blurts out in plain colloquial Attic (lines 173-176):

> οἴμ᾽ ὡς δέδοικα, κοὐκέτι σκώπτων λέγω.
> ὦ μηχανοποιὲ πρόσεχε τὸν νοῦν ὡς ἐμέ·
> ἤδη στρέφει τι πνεῦμα περὶ τὸν ὀμφαλόν,
> κεἰ μὴ φυλάξει, χορτάσω τὸν κάνθαρον.

> Man, am I scared! Hey, engineer, jokes aside now,
> listen to me! I've got gas spiraling
> inside my gut and, if you don't watch it,
> I'll end up feeding the dung beetle.

Here, quite obviously, Trygaeus expands the range of his speech to include the production situation. The shift from anapaests to trimeters marks a transition from inside the comic fiction to the surrounding circumstances in which an actor, dangling from a rudimentary crane, expresses his misgivings about the stunt. The threat in line 176 (χορτάσω κ.τ.λ.) harmonizes quite well with the preceding scatological humor and there is little reason to dwell on the "rupture" of dramatic illusion here. Nevertheless, the metafictional nature of the comic flight is clearly marked in language, mood, meter, and action: 1) the humor of lines 154-172 is self-consciously suspended as the actor (Apollodorus, if we are to trust Hypothesis 3 [Platnauer])[25] lays joking aside in his new show of fear; 2) lines 154-172 colored by poetic turns of phrase such as δρομαίαν πτέρυγ᾽ ἐκτείνων / ὀρθὸς χώρει Διὸς εἰς αὐλάς, "extending your fleet wing(s) advance straight to the halls of

---

[25] For an interesting discussion of the text conveying this detail see Slater, "The Hypotheses to Aristophanes' *Peace*" 53-56, who argues from this hypothesis for the possibility of an comic actor's contest at the City Dionysia as early as 421.

Zeus" (lines 160-161), yield to uniformly colloquial speech (lines 173-179); 3) recitative anapaests are followed by iambic trimeter; 4) Trygaeus-Apollodorus no doubt emphasizes his words to the μηχανοποιός by means of some upward gesture. There is an effective irony here as the lofty diction and position of the hero are briefly interrupted by the banal details of production.

The mythological reference in the *Dyscolus*, by contrast, serves to make a general point and to introduce Cnemon's complaint in the harangue. Perseus, in fact, is invoked as a prototype of the successful misanthrope possessing powerful means to avoid human contact. The literary purpose of the harangue is very different from that of Dicaeopolis. In a detailed study of this and other mythological exempla in Middle and New Comedy, Udo Reinhardt suggests that such a digression would combine incongruity with *aprosdoketon* (surprise) which he characterizes as "eine Art 'Befremdungseffekt'."[26] The surface of Menander's text appears to be free of intertextual disruptions of the sort outlined above and the play, as a whole, does not engage myth through a well-known tragic model. This use of myth which, in modified form, occurs with some frequency in Plautus' prologues would appear to have its origin in Middle Comic burlesque, concerning which Nesselrath has written recently that "the promotion of mythical elements to a level of grotesque absurdity (as, say, in Cratinus) was no longer essential to the humor of mythological comedy in the Middle period. Quite the reverse, [the humor] lay in dismantling such elements and in the thoroughgoing rationalization of mythical events. Myth had thus become almost a vessel of sorts which, by this time, was taking in fourth-century contemporary material of every kind in great quantities: dining fashions, popular customs and pastimes, 'modern' urban characters as well as politics." The result of this change for character was that the erstwhile mythical figures were "reduced ever more to mere names, facades for ever more

---

[26]Reinhardt, *Mythologische Beispiele* 63: "So wirkt das Mythologische, vom Sprecher, von der Situation und auch vom γένος her unerwartet, als ἀπροσδόκητον: es erzielt eine Art 'Befremdungseffekt,' der gerade hier ganz wesentlich ist, mag ihn der Zuschauer auch nur kurze Zeit empfinden. In Verbindung mit der typischen Einleitungsformel erregt das Mythologische Aufmerksamkeit, löst von dem Alltäglichen zuvor, hebt heraus."

distinct types and characters of Athenian society. The form of mythical travesty had finally done its duty as the scaffolding of comic drama and was no longer necessary as the basis for comic plots."²⁷ To refine this picture, however, we should note that the specific (ab)use of a mythological exemplum does figure in New Comedy as an indirect means of characterization.²⁸

On a small scale, Menander's use of myth in *Dyscolus* illustrates these points well and, no doubt, represents a technique which had become a New Comic formula of sorts. Two contemporary parallels, Menander fr. 718 (Sandbach) and Aristophon fr. 11 K.-A., provide further illustration:²⁹

εἶτ' οὐ δικαίως προσπεπατταλευμένον   (Men. fr. 718)
γράφουσι τὸν Προμηθέα πρὸς ταῖς πέτραις
καὶ γίνετ' αὐτῷ λαμπάς, ἄλλο δ' οὐδὲ ἓν
ἀγαθόν; ὃ μισεῖν οἶμ' ἅπαντας τοὺς θεούς,
γυναῖκας ἔπλασεν, ὦ πολυτίμητοι θεοί,
ἔθνος μιαρόν. γαμεῖ τις ἀνθρώπων, γαμεῖ;
λάθριοι τὸ λοιπὸν γὰρ ἐπιθυμίαι κακαί,
γαμηλίῳ λέχει τε μοιχὸς ἐντρυφῶν
καὶ φαρμακεῖαι καὶ νόσων χαλεπώτατος
φθόνος, μεθ' οὗ ζῇ πάντα τὸν βίον γυνή.

²⁷Nesselrath, *Mittlere Komödie* 240, where he notes also that "Die mythischen Stücke der Mese waren weder Parabeln auf die Fehler der Zeitgeschichte noch völlig unpolitische Travestierungen der alten Sagen in ihrer ursprünglichen märchenhaften Form, sondern offenbar ein Mittelding zwischen diesen beiden Spielarten: Die Komiker der Mese-Zeit arbeiteten entweder den mythischen Stoff selbst oder eine schon vorhandene Fassung (meist eine Tragödie) von ihm in eine komische Geschichte um, ohne einen darüber hinausgehenden politischen oder pädagogischen Zweck zu verfolgen; ihr ganzes komisches Potential enthüllte eine solche Komödie erst dem, der auch ihre Vorlage oder das betreffende mythische Sujet (oder beides) gut kannte. Auf diese Weise wurden die Mythenstücke der Mittleren Komödie wohl noch viel mehr zum gehobenen literarischen Spiel, als es die Archaia vor allem in ihrer Schlußzeit unter den Händen des Aristophanes bereits geworden war."

²⁸Reinhardt, *Mythologische Beispiele* 65: "Die Konstante eines sonderbaren Charakters ist die entscheidende Triebkraft, einen Mythos ohne objektive Entsprechungen zur Situation aufzugreifen, bewertend einzuengen, in ganz spezifischer Weise auszudeuten. Mit dieser ingeniösen Verwendung erfüllt das Mythologische seine indirekt chararakterisierende Funktion."

²⁹See Handley, *Dyskolos*, on line 158.

> Isn't it fair that they paint Prometheus nailed to
> a rock with nothing to cheer him but a lamp?
> What I think the gods hate him for is that he created
> women. Ye gods, what a disgusting race!
> Married, you say? Is someone getting *married*?
> Well, from that point on he'll have to contend with wicked,
> secret lusts, adulterers enjoying themselves in his
> own bed, sorcery, and the dire malice of diseases
> with which a woman lives her whole life long.

Menander's catalogue of horrors consists of troubles indirectly inflicted on husbands by the otherwise beneficent Prometheus. The speaker here is, no doubt, driven to this misogynist outburst by a conflict with his wife whom he suspects (unfairly, of course) of adultery, sorcery, or other behavior which he imputes to married women. Although this passage conforms to the conventions of the harangue and mythical exemplum, there is a subtle difference in that the emphasis shifts from myth proper to the realm of art.[30] In *Dyscolus*, Perseus is envied directly for his supernatural tools (wings and lethal weapon) while the μυθολογούμενον of fr. 718 is engaged at a self-conscious remove by a spectator who comments on the iconography of Prometheus δεσμώτης. This reflexive twist has the effect of enhancing the topicality of the reference since it is a specific practice of contemporary painters that inspires the conflation of Hesiod with the tradition of Prometheus the Creator. This and other ψόγοι γυναικῶν,[31] *mutatis mutandis*, revive for the comic stage the

---

[30]This harangue is remarkable for the fact that its subject is the *representation* of the myth rather than the myth itself. See Reinhardt, *Mythologische Beispiele* 75. As several commentators note, the fragment may also contain a reference to the λαμπαδηφορία or λαμπαδηδρομία which was part of the Attic Promethia. See Deubner, *Attische Feste* 211, and Fraenkel, *Agamemnon* 324. Note the possibility of supplementing the first lines of the famous fragment of Antiphanes' *Poiesis* with εἶτ' οὐ (fr. 189 K.-A. printed and discussed by Slater above, pp. 37-38). We would then have another formal parallel in which the humorous emphasis is on the representation of myth and its significance for tragedy and comedy.

[31] Reinhardt, *Mythologische Beispiele* 74-87 (A cluster of these passages is found in Athenaeus 13.559b-c). It is remarkable that a close parallel, published from an Egyptian ostrakon by J.G. Milne in 1908 and 1923, makes explicit the tragic connection: πλάττων ὁ Προμηθεὺς τἄλλα θηρίων γένη / οὐδὲν γυναικῶν ἔπλασεν ἐξωλέστερον. / νὴ τὸν Δία τὸν

famous tirade in which Hippolytus blames Zeus for producing women.³² Although the typecasting tendencies of fourth-century comedy explain the frequency of harangues against *types* of people (with occasional studies in general opprobrium), the patriarchal mold of the genre insures that target of blame will often be a woman or type of woman (midwives, nurses, etc.) Thus we find a corollary to the misogyny of Menander's fr. 718 in the outburst against Eros in Aristophon's *Pythagoristes*:³³

εἶτ' οὐ δικαίως ἔστ' ἀπεψηφισμένος   (fr. 11 K.-A.)
ὑπὸ τῶν θεῶν τῶν δώδεκ' εἰκότως ⟨τ'⟩ Ἔρως;
ἐτάραττε κἀκείνους γὰρ ἐμβάλλων στάσεις,
ὅτ' ἦν μετ' αὐτῶν. ὡς δὲ λίαν ἦν θρασὺς
καὶ σοβαρός, ἀποκόψαντες αὐτοῦ τὰ πτερά,
ἵνα μὴ πέτηται πρὸς τὸν οὐρανὸν πάλιν,
δεῦρ' αὐτὸν ἐφυγάδευσαν ὡς ἡμᾶς κάτω,
τὰς δὲ πτέρυγας ἃς εἶχε τῇ Νίκῃ φορεῖν
ἔδοσαν, περιφανὲς σκῦλον ἀπὸ τῶν πολεμίων

Wasn't Eros disenfranchised fair and square by
the twelve gods? After all, he caused trouble and strife
while in their midst. He was so arrogant and overbearing
they cut off his wings to prevent him from
flying back to heaven and sent him into exile down here
to be with us. They gave his wings to Victory
to wear as conspicuous spoils stripped off the enemy.

μέγιστον, εὖ γ' Εὐριπίδης / εἴρηκεν εἶναι τὴν γυναικείαν φύσιν / πάντων μέγιστον τῶν ἐν ἀνθρώποις κακῶν κ.τ.λ. Reinhardt, *Mythologische Beispiele* 79 (with note 3), cites Euripides fr. 1341 Mette as a parallel. For the language see *Medea* 471, and Euripides fr. 7 and 537 Mette.

³²Euripides *Hippolytus* 616-624. Prometheus is, in some accounts, the creator of man (cf. Hesiod, fr. 268; Apollodoros 1.7.1, Pausanias 10.4.4., Hyginus, fab. 142). In the best-known treatments of his legend such as the *Prometheus Bound* he endows mankind with gifts ranging from fire to basic human sensibility, reason, and culture. Hesiod's *Theogony* and *Works and Days*, of course, make Prometheus responsible for the gods' creation of woman/Pandora. The speaker here superimposes the misogynist aetiology on the beneficent figure of Prometheus the Creator.

³³The parallels (e.g. fr. 198) surveyed by Reinhardt, *Mythologische Beispiele* 88-90, are not harangues at all but expressions of awe in line with a well-established tragic topos. For the "philosophical" background of this theme see Webster, *Studies in Menander* 214-15, who suggests that both the poet and Theophrastus were influenced by Middle comedy.

In these examples, as in *Dyscolus*, unitary complaints—one misogynist, the other anterotic—are introduced by a reference to a mythical figure which serves as foil to what follows. As we are coming to expect, the reference has less to do with another text than with the mythical subject itself, in this case the banishment of Eros and his transition from the familiar Ἔρως ὑπόπτερος to a mysterious wingless figure for which it is hard to find parallels in literature or art until the later development of the *cupido punitus* (*cruciatus*) theme. As with Menander's Prometheus the exemplum here brings the artistic representations of Eros and Nike to bear on the comic theme of Eros the troublemaker. It appears that Aristophon has elaborated his highly unusual myth of Eros by imagining the transfer of wings between two common sculpture-types (Eros and Nike) as a narrative supplement to complaints of the sort we find in a fragment of Alexis' *Apokoptomenos* and Eubulus' *Kampylion*: "who was it that first drew Eros or fashioned him in wax as having wings? That guy appears to have known little except how to draw swallows and was certainly ignorant of that god's behavior!"[34] Reinhardt suggests that this fragment may poke fun at the skeptical reanalysis of myth in the ἐρωτικοὶ λόγοι of the sort we find in Plato's *Symposium* and *Phaedrus*.

It is certainly no coincidence that the language, form, and use of myth in these harangues point to Middle Comedy. We are, in fact, dealing with a well-attested topos that appears to have taken shape in the Middle period and to have assumed strict formulary features including a limited length (fifteen or so lines, judging from our two complete examples). As most of the fragments of Middle Comedy are found in Athenaeus, we know little, if anything, about the context from which they were drawn. Characteristic of the harangue in Middle and New Comedy, however, is that it helps outline stock-character and situation while maintaining a certain independence from the specifics of the plot, a feature which tends to offset the inadequacy of our evidence. Although it is not possible to assign precise dates to these fragments, we can be confident that they gravitate to the

---

[34] Fr. 20 and 41 Kock, respectively, as cited by Kassel and Austin *ad* Aristophon fr. 11. See Reinhardt, *Mythologische Beispiele* 91-96, for this and other parallels cited from Meinecke and Kock.

central period of Middle Comedy defined recently by Nesselrath.³⁵ Two harangues from the work of Amphis, *Athamas* (fr. 1 K.-A.) and *Erithoi* (fr. 17 K.-A.), though incomplete, exhibit many characteristic features of the form. Here, contrasts are set up between wife and hetaira³⁶ and city and country:

εἶτ' οὐ γυναικός ἐστιν εὐνοικώτερον   (fr. 1 K.-A.)
γαμετῆς ἑταίρα; πολύ γε καὶ μάλ' εἰκότως.
ἡ μὲν νόμῳ γὰρ καταφρονοῦσ' ἔνδον μένει,
ἡ δ' οἶδεν ὅτι ἢ τοῖς τρόποις ὠνητέος
ἄνθρωπός ἐστιν ἢ πρὸς ἄλλον ἀπιτέον

Isn't a mistress nicer to you than your own
wife? Rightly so, and by a long shot!
You are, by law, stuck with your wife though
she despises you while a mistress knows that
her man must be bought by good behavior:
It's either behave or find someone else!

εἶτ' οὐχὶ χρυσοῦν ἐστι πρᾶγμ' ἐρημία;   (fr. 17 K.-A.)
ὁ πατήρ γε τοῦ ζῆν ἐστιν ἀνθρώποις ἀγρός,
πενίαν τε συγκρύπτειν ἐπίσταται μόνος,
ἄστυ δὲ θέατρον {ἐστιν} ἀτυχίας σαφοῦς γέμον

Isn't solitude golden?
The countryside is Father of Sustenance for
us; only the country knows how to conceal poverty.
The city, on the other hand, is a theater, a full house
before whom your misfortune is on display.

---

³⁵Middle Comedy has, of course, been variously defined (see Nesselrath, *Mittlere Komödie* 1-28). Nesselrath's considered and reasonable dating of the period involves a "nucleus" from 380-350 BC, the heyday of poets such as Anaxandrides, Eubulus, Epikrates, Ephippus, and early Antiphanes. This nucleus is preceded and followed by long transitional periods in which features of the other styles are seen side by side with those of Middle Comedy. The transitional periods are defined as 411-380 for Old to Middle, and 350-320 for Middle to New Comedy.

³⁶To place this and other ψόγοι γυναικῶν in a broader context, see Henry, *Menander's Courtesans*. In light of comedy's reliance on the accessibility of mythological exempla, the complaint in Antiphanes' *Poiesis* about the tragedy's use of myth (see note 30 above) appears especially disingenuous.

Of Antiphanes we have a curious harangue against those involved in a variety of lowly occupations. In this passage from the *Misoponeros* (fr. 157 K.-A.) we find Scythians as the incongruous foil introducing the catalogue of disreputable professions:

εἶτ' οὐ σοφοὶ δῆτ' εἰσὶν οἱ Σκύθαι σφόδρα,   (fr. 157 K.-A.)
οἳ γενομένοισιν εὐθέως τοῖς παιδίοις
διδόασιν ἵππων καὶ βοῶν πίνειν γάλα;
μὰ Δί' οὐχὶ τίτθας εἰσάγουσι βασκάνους
καὶ παιδαγωγοὺς αὖθις, ὧν μείζω ⟨ ∪ –
⏓ – ∪ – ⏓ μετά⟩ γε μαίας νὴ Δία·
αὗται δ' ὑπερβάλλουσι, μετά γε νὴ Δία
τοὺς μητραγυρτοῦντάς γε· πολὺ γὰρ αὖ γένος
μιαρώτατον τοῦτ' ἔστιν, εἰ μὴ νὴ Δία
τοὺς ἰχθυοπώλας τις † βούλεται λέγειν
⟨ ⏓ – ∪ ⟩ μετά γε τοὺς τραπεζίτας· ἔθνος
τούτου γὰρ οὐδέν ἐστιν ἐξωλέστερον

Aren't the Scythians, then, really clever?
I mean, they give their infants mare's or
cow's milk to drink, immediately at birth.
By god, they don't mess with nasty nurses
or pedagogues, of which there's no greater...
except midwives, by god. They take the
cake! Well, along with those begging-priests,
of course. This is by far the vilest bunch;
unless you want to talk about fishmongers...
and money-changers. There's no sort
more wretched than them!

Salient features of these last three fragments are the points of contrast for which the poets use realia (hetaira, solitude, Scythians) instead of myth. It is important to note, then, that the contrast or foil in the Middle Comic formula does not necessarily involve a μυθολογούμενον, i.e., the legendary exemplum has not become an invariable topos in the comic harangue. What is clear, however, is that the parataxis introduced by the formula εἶτα... οὐκ attaches a passage rather loosely to its wider context in which it (as contrast or foil) need not have any specific relevance beyond the point of the complaint. On the other hand, all the exempla we have seen so far share the quality of being accessible, i.e., they enjoy immediate recognition as items of general currency. The mythological figures are always well-known

(Prometheus, Perseus, or Amalthea) while the Scythians have become somewhat of a ethnographic cliché as milk-drinking barbarians who are ignorant of viniculture.[37]

Non-mythological harangue-fragments range in length from a few lines to a full tirade equivalent to that of Menander's Cnemon. In the former category are the two-liners from Xenarchus' *Hypnos* on women (fr. 14 K.-A.)[38] and Alexis' *Daktylios* (fr. 44 K.-A.) which, no doubt, is prefatory to an enumeration of the evils associated with intoxication: εἶτ' οὐχ ἁπάντων ἐστὶ τὸ μεθύειν κακὸν / μέγιστον ἀνθρώποισι καὶ βλαβερώτατον; "Isn't drunkenness the greatest of evils for mankind and the most destructive at that?" (One thinks of the typical premise involving a "young woman in trouble" as in *Epitrepontes* and *Samia*).[39] A thematic parallel is found in a short fragment of Antiphanes' *Bacchae* (fr. 58 K.-A.) in which the speaker implies that he envies Scythian men their good fortune of having sober spouses. In both Antiphanes passages (fr. 58 and 157 K.-A.) the poet exploits the ethnographic cliché of "milk-drinking Scythians" in misogynist harangues berating a variety of types: wives, midwives, nurses.

The specificity of these passages contrasts interestingly with the broad indictment of human nature in a longer harangue-fragment from Alexis' *Mandragorizomene* (fr. 145 K.-A.), my final example.[40] This passage inverts a familiar pattern as the criticism passes abruptly from general features of human behavior to the specifics of culinary practice. At the focus are the contradictions inherent in human nature:

---

[37]See Herodotus 4.2; Reinhardt, *Mythologische Beispiele* 97-98; and Long, *Barbarians in Greek Comedy*.

[38]Again ψόγος γυναικῶν: εἶτ' εἰσιν οἱ τέττιγες οὐκ εὐδαίμονες, / ὧν ταῖς γυναιξὶν οὐδ' ὁτιοῦν φωνῆς ἔνι;

[39]A familiar point of departure for New Comedy involves a young woman who gets pregnant during nocturnal revelry of one sort or another. This situation, naturally, is at first the cause of great tension which is ultimately resolved in the happy ending. Cf. the first extant lines (1-57) of Menander's *Samia* (Moschion's soliloquy).

[40]The examples given here do not, of course, exhaust the resources available to writers of Greek comedy for expressing a complaint. I have been rather strict, however, in keeping to a variety of stage-complaints marked by distinct, formal features.

> εἶτ' οὐ περίεργόν ἐστιν ἄνθρωπος φυτὸν (fr. 145 K.-A.)
> ὑπεναντιωτάτοις τε πλείστοις χρώμενον;
> ἐρῶμεν ἀλλοτρίων, παρορῶμεν συγγενεῖς.
> ἔχοντες οὐδὲν εὐποροῦμεν τοῖς πέλας,
> 5 ἐράνους φέροντες οὐ φέρομεν ἀλλ' ἢ κακῶς.
> τἀκ τῆς τροφῆς δὲ τῆς καθ' ἡμέραν πάλιν
> γλιχόμεθα μὲν τὴν μᾶζαν ἵνα λευκὴ παρῇ,
> ζωμὸν δὲ ταύτῃ μέλανα μηχανώμεθα
> τὸ καλόν τε χρῶμα δευσοποιῷ χρῴζομεν.
> 10 καὶ χιόνα μὲν πίνειν παρασκευάζομεν,
> τὸ δ' ὄψον ἂν μὴ θερμὸν ᾖ, διασύρομεν.
> καὶ τὸν μὲν ὀξὺν οἶνον ἐκπυτίζομεν,
> ἐπὶ ταῖς ἀβυρτάκαισι δ' ἐκβακχεύομεν.
> οὐκοῦν, τὸ πολλοῖς τῶν σοφῶν εἰρημένον,
> 15 τὸ μὴ γενέσθαι μὲν κράτιστόν ἐστ' ἀεί,
> ἐπὰν γένηται δ', ὡς τάχιστ' ἔχειν τέλος

> Aren't people silly creatures? Isn't their behavior
> full of contradictions? We love
> strangers and neglect our family.
> When we're well off we give nothing to
> our neighbors. When it's our turn to
> entertain we give a stingy feast, but for our
> daily meals we insist that our bread be white.
> We make the broth for it black, however,
> and ruin the bread's pretty color with the dip.
> Though we prepare to cool our drink with snow
> we're disgusted by food that's not hot.
> We spit out wine that's tart but wax
> Bacchic over sauerkraut. Hence the word
> from many men of wisdom: The best
> thing by far is never to have been born.
> Once you're born, to end it as soon as possible.

These passages reveal that, in the Middle Comic period, the harangue had developed distinct formulary features. The topos is invariably introduced by the conjunction εἶτα which, at its most vivid, connotes consequence, "esp. in questions or exclamations to express surprise, indignation, contempt, sarcasm, and the like, *and then... ? and so... ?*"[41] Thus at *Frogs* 21-23 Dionysus exclaims indignantly: εἶτ' οὐχ ὕβρις ταῦτ' ἐστὶ καὶ πολλὴ τρυφή, ὅ τ' ἐγὼ

---

[41] LSJ εἶτα II. Dover, *Frogs* 193 (on line 21) notes that this εἶτα is "commonly indignant and plaintive, as Nu. 1214, where the Creditor's first words are εἶτ' ἄνδρα τῶν αὑτοῦ τι χρὴ προϊέναι;"

μὲν... αὐτὸς βαδίζω καὶ πονῶ, τοῦτον δ' ὀχῶ; "Now isn't this the picture of insolence and great luxury? I mean, here I am ... with all the fatigue of walking while I let this fellow ride!" The pattern that develops in the harangue-monologue involves an introductory question in which εἶτ' οὐ(κ) ... ἐστιν presents the foil or issue (Perseus, Prometheus, Scythians, etc.) by placing grammatical and rhetorical emphasis on the predicate whereby a striking modifier (μακάριος, δικαίως προσπεπατταλευμένον / ἀπεψηφισμένος, εὐνοικώτερον, χρυσοῦν, etc.) is framed by the particles and the copula. There follows, in fragments of sufficient length, a more or less brief "application" which reveals the point of comparison, contrast, or causation, often with a relative pronoun lead-in (once ὅτι) or a pointed sequence inflected by means of appropriate particles (μέν ~ δέ, γάρ). This application is typically signaled by a verb in the third or fifth line, near, or in, initial position: (ἐγένετο) κοὐδενὶ συνήντα, γυναῖκας ἔπλασεν, ἐτάρρατε, διδόασιν, καταφρονοῦσ' ἔνδον μένει, ἐρῶμεν, etc. Thus the Scythians in the fragment of Antiphanes' *Misoponeros* (fr. 157 K.-A.), like Cnemon's Perseus, are brought in as an exemplum of how to avoid the evil at hand, in this case nurses who head the disreputable list. Amphis' *Athamas* (fr. 1 K.-A.) initiates criticism of "the wife" by way of the ἑταίρα as a foil. In his *Erithoi* (fr. 17 K.-A.), the same poet has a character like Cnemon illustrate the joys of solitude by setting up a stark contrast between country ("father of life") and city ("theater of misery"). The antithetical pattern is quite sustained in the full example of Alexis' *Mandragorizomene* (fr. 145 K.-A.). The folly of human nature is illustrated by means of a long series of behavioral paradoxes: we love strangers and neglect kin; when prosperous, we don't share with our neighbors; we're stingy in contributing to public meals but dine in luxury at home, etc. The extent of this last fragment, which appears to represent the complete harangue (sixteen lines), set alongside the harangue of Menander's Cnemon (fourteen lines), suggests a rough measure of standard length as well.

It is tempting to regard the New Comic harangue as a descendant of the fifth-century entrance-speeches like the opener of *Acharnians* discussed above. The stylization which sets in during the Middle period involves casting a character's "first words" in a strict mold of the καί-style (καί parataxis) around an easily accessible rhetorical foil.⁴² The wide variety of introductory strategies found in Aristophanes has been narrowed to the paratactic formula exemplified by the fragments of Middle Comedy. There is a world of difference between Lysistrata's initial ἀλλά, for example, and the fixed Middle Comic εἶτα. The former is revealed to be a genuine beginning *in mediis rebus* that contrasts a sentence we have not heard (e.g. "Look, not a soul to be found!") with the one that follows: ἀλλ' εἴ τις εἰς βακχεῖον αὐτὰς ἐκάλεσεν, "but if someone had invited them to a place of Bacchic worship...."⁴³ The formulaic εἶτα, on the other hand, has become a rather bland introductory conjunction. In a narrowing of its varied and long-lived role in the καί-style, this εἶτα, like καί, announces a new clause whose connection to what precedes (and what follows) may be quite weak. In her monograph on the καί-style, Sophie Trenkner argues that the distribution of καί, κᾆτα, κἄπειτα and εἶτα already in Aristophanes suggests "l'impression de l'identité des conjonctions."⁴⁴ The use of the καί-style for characterization of vulgar types and unadorned colloquial speech is relevant here as well, since the fourth-century harangues appear to be "pitched low," i.e., they often involve simple language and familiar exempla to characterize unsophisticated figures such as misanthropes and rustics.

Cnemon's complaint in *Dyscolus* suggests, moreover, that an important (perhaps central) function of the harangue-topos continued to be the introduction of a character or situation by means of an entrance-speech.⁴⁵ The misanthrope enters with a soliloquy quoted above (pp. 61-62) that defines him as a stock character, i.e., his concerns, his relation to others, and his potential role in the plot. The harangue is brought to a smooth conclusion by the entrance of Sostratus, who nicely embodies the point of Cnemon's complaint, i.e., that he has lost peace of mind on account of intruders and passers-by. As Sander Goldberg has

---

⁴²See Trenkner, *Le style kai*.

⁴³Henderson, *Lysistrata* 66: "Initial adversative ἀλλά appears frequently in oracles (cf. 770); it is used by Xenophon in dialogues (*Smp., Resp., Lak.*) and speeches (Denn. 20-1) and by Menander to open scenes (e.g. *Aspis* 97-98, *Georg.* 22-23). The tone is conversational, ..."

⁴⁴Trenkner, *Le style kai* 13; see also p. 78.

⁴⁵See Frost, *Exits and Entrances*, 43-44 on Cnemon's entrance and harange, *Dyscolus* 153-168.

pointed out, the harangue here will strike the external spectator (audience) and internal spectator (Sostratus) quite differently: For the audience, "the contrasts between irascible old man and mythological hero and between grandiose wish [to be Perseus himself] and trivial complaint are both unexpected and comic." Sostratus, on the other hand is terrified. "Overwhelmed by the ferocious appearance, extravagant language, and heavy sarcasm of the old man, he speaks only a feeble excuse, and that a false one, for his presence."[46] Cnemon's first words are essential in identifying him as a misanthrope and introducing his position in the plot in a way that, on a small scale, resembles the technique of the expository prologue. Though different in design from Aristophanic speeches, Menander's monologue and, no doubt, the Middle Comic harangues presented above have inherited something of their function from fifth-century stagecraft.

In distinction from Dicaeopolis' harangue-soliloquy, however, the fourth-century harangues maintain a higher level of generality. The Aristophanic protagonist identifies the time, place, and purpose of his activities with plenty of comical and topical commentary into the bargain. He makes very clear his political position and is critical of his compatriots' apathy. This prelude to Dicaeopolis' quest for a separate peace includes play with the festival context of the performance (lines 9-18). The reference to Cleon's "disgorging five talents" (line 6) as a possible reference to the poet's *Babylonians* fuses politics and comedy in a typically Aristophanic fashion.[47] The criticism of the performances by Theognis and Chaeris follows naturally and, in its turn, segues smoothly into social criticism of lines 19-42. Much of Dicaeopolis' humor is metaperformative: addressing the audience as a fellow-citizen in the Pnyx, he says his troubles are beyond reckoning. We begin in the realm of the festival and performance, however, from which Dicaeopolis narrates his joys and sorrows as a *spectator* with little reference to the political process. Since the protagonist's immediate purpose is not literary but political, the theater (as metaphor for polis) eventually yields

---

[46]Goldberg, *Menander's Comedy* 77.
[47]Hubbard, *Mask of Comedy* 35, 41-42, and Arnott, "Comic Openings" 21 (on *Acharnians* 6 as referring to *Babylonians*).

to the Pnyx, allowing us to catch the guiding thread of the plot.⁴⁸ Dicaeopolis' troubles are legion indeed, and he will end up withdrawing from the ἄστυ, or urban center, in order to do something about it. The later harangues of Menander and Alexis, by contrast, are devoid of explicit topicality and are largely confined to general observations and antitheses. Their focus is much less on the details of plot per se than on the broad features of the character type (misanthrope, disgruntled patriarch, young man in love, etc.)

It is hard to find much in the language of any one of these Middle Comic fragments that is distinctive. Thus in the *Misoponeros* (Antiphanes fr. 157 K.-A.) the variation of pejorative adjectives, βασκάνους (4), μιαρώτατον (9), ἐξωλέστερον (12), makes use of fairly common terms which are amply attested in earlier and later comedy. The central antithesis of *Erithoi* (Amphis fr. 17 K.-A.) sets up a contrast between the country as "the father of sustenance" and the city as a "theater, a full house before whom your misery is on display." The phrases ὁ πατὴρ τοῦ ζῆν and θέατρον ἀτυχίας σαφοῦς γέμον are interesting as hapax legomena, to be sure, and do stand out in the otherwise bland linguistic environment of the Middle Comic harangue.⁴⁹ Compared with the boldness of Aristophanes, however, these metaphors are very pale indeed. What is particularly interesting here is the apparent reluctance on the part of our poets to experiment with language in a way that would generate humor from the very process of play with morphology, syntax, or vocabulary. Similarly, the fragment of

---

⁴⁸ Slater, "Space, Character, and ἀπάτη" 401, notes the successive transformations of the theatrical space: "With Dicaeopolis' departure, the prologue is over. Aristophanes has used the flexibility of his theatrical space to the fullest—the playing space has changed from the undefined theatre to the Pnyx, back to an undefined space and now, with the first entrance into the skene, into Dicaeopolis' country home. He has also used this flexibility to establish some important and persisting equivalencies, or perhaps we should say areas of exchange, between the theatrical space and political space."

⁴⁹"All the world's a stage" metaphors are legion in Renaissance drama, the best-known, perhaps, being the soliloquy of Jaques in *As You Like It* (Act 2). Antiphanes fr. 17 K.-A. is a rare example in Greek drama of this topos-to-be. For a view of this topos as part of a new "metatheatrical" genre see Abel, *Metatheatre* 83.

Alexis' *Mandragorizomene* (fr. 145 K.-A.) is quite literally prosaic with the possible exception of the phrase ἐπὶ ταῖς ἀβυρτάκαισι δ' ἐκβακχεύομεν, "wax Bacchic over sauerkraut." Word-play, moreover, is subdued and seems confined to jingles and gentle antithetical irony. Thus in in the same fragment παρορῶμεν ~ εὐποροῦμεν (lines 3-4), ἐράνους φέροντες οὐ φέρομεν ἀλλ' ἢ κακῶς (line 5). The choice of ἐκβακχεύομεν in line 13 points to the preceding verse which describes the rejection of sour wine. There are no bold puns, no comic manipulation of morphology of the sort found in the Aristophanic χαιρηδόνος, ψαμμακοσιογάργαρα, or ὁ πρίων.[50] It would be easy, considering only these fragments, to underestimate the linguistic resources of the Middle Comic poets. It has been shown, for example, that in other contexts the new dithyramb figured as a distinct linguistic stratum in the work of the latter.[51] There is, however, an important contrast between the Old Comic use of, and reaction to, dithyramb and the Middle Comic use of the same. Whereas Old Comedy exhibits a "belligerent denial, in the first instance, of dithyrambic music and its representatives,"[52] Middle Comedy incorporates the language of the new dithyramb with little or no implicit comment on the genre itself. Thus while Old Comedy reacts, by way of parody, mockery, criticism, etc., to the poetic model as to an external object,[53] Middle Comedy assimilates the discourse of the model

---

[50]See Arnott, "Comic Openings" 17-21, for further discussion of these and other points in Dicaeopolis' speech. Arnott suggests that χαιρηδών may be dithyrambic parody rather than "pure" coinage. Making an interesting comparison of humor in *Dyscolus* and *Frogs* on p. 25 he notes: "But that is all [we find in Menander]: two instances in a hundred lines, to set against at least twelve verbal and visual jokes in the first thirty-two lines of the *Frogs*."

[51]In Middle Comedy dithyrambic language makes its appearance in a variety of fragments (Nesselrath, *Mittlere Komödie* 254, counts 43 fragments exhibiting traces of dithyrambic style). The salient features of the style include ubiquitous descriptive participles, cryptic periphrases for familiar objects, complex morphology (esp. adjectives), asyndetic relative clauses and appositives, and bold metaphors.

[52]Nesselrath, *Mittlere Komödie* 241-66.

[53] E.g. the explicit lampoons of dithyrhamb in Aristophanes such as the Cinesias scene in *Birds* (lines 1372-1409) and the dramatically more sophisticated fragment of Pherecrates' *Chiron* (fr. 155 K.-A. for which see the essay by Dobrov and Urios Aparisi below) on the "prostitution" of

thoroughly, subordinating potential comment or parody to other dramatic purposes.

These harangues share as much in the scope of their subject matter as they do in language and form. Throughout we find general criticism of contemporary mores and types: pedagogues, drunkenness, wives, city life, and the contradictions of human nature. The tone of the commentary has become more impersonal, timeless, and placeless—an impression which is no doubt exaggerated by the texts' fragmentary nature. With the exception of the generalizing "we" of the *Mandragorizomene*, the speakers of these passages use only the third person. There is, moreover, no hint of topical humor. It appears that the comic formula was a generalizing digression (often, no doubt, an aside) that required immediate contextualization by the action in order to be intelligible, as we have learned from the example of *Dyscolus* 153-168. In his own comparison of Aristophanes and Menander, Geoffrey Arnott notes the striking attenuation of verbal and visual humor in the latter, "consistent with his differently oriented theory of comedy."[54] Menander, he explains, places "emphasis on *plausibly structured, carefully integrated plotting and on the consistent presentation of character*, both of which seem at first sight to derive rather from the tragedies of Euripides than from the comedies of Aristophanes" (emphasis mine). The evidence of Middle Comedy suggests that this theoretical reorientation was underway long before the beginning of Menander's career.

The Poet's Voice in the Evolution of Comic Discourse

A dramatic moment in which a stage-figure is presented by means of a critical soliloquy should have great potential for characterization and character-development. It is curious that the harangue evolved into a generalizing topos, one which, by the middle of the fourth century, would appear to have supplanted

---

music. The action of the latter, according to pseudo-Plutarch (*De Musica* 1141d), involved Music, in the guise of a dishevelled woman, complaining to Justice about a host of musicians (especially Cinesias and Timotheos) and their terrible new techniques.

[54]Arnott, "Comic Openings" 26.

the flexibility seen in the work of Aristophanes. We note that as the diction, plots, characters, and action of Middle Comedy tend towards greater naturalism, we begin to lose sight of the many specifics which made the fifth-century political satires so compelling, especially the kaleidoscopic language and intense involvement with the particulars of contemporary reality. For all its lack of theatrical realism, Aristophanic comedy drew the spectators into a transaction of sorts which was frequently written into the script: the audience is addressed, exhorted and, in some cases, "heard" by the actors. This exchange involved much prominent and specific use of contemporary realia as well as that elusive figure, the poet himself whose "ventriloqual" presence (see above, pp. 47 and 56) was directly or indirectly palpable throughout a performance. The frequent instances of direct address in Aristophanes, in fact, served to incorporate the audience into the dramatic fiction. In the prologues of the early plays it is common for characters to digress briefly and engage the spectators as do Bdelycleon's slaves at *Wasps* 74-87. The one designated "Xanthias," for example, begins by saying φέρε νυν κατείπω τοῖς θεαταῖς τὸν λόγον, "Well now, let me tell the spectators the plot" (line 54). After a few conspicuously parabasis-like comments (lines 56-66) he gestures upward and informs the audience that Bdelycleon is asleep, literally, "on the roof" and that they, the slaves, have been charged with making sure that the litigious old man, Philocleon, does not escape from the house-arrest imposed on him by his son. The ensuing dialogue begins with the exchange (lines 71-77):

Ξα. νόσον γὰρ ὁ πατὴρ ἀλλόκοτον αὐτοῦ νοσεῖ,
     ἣν οὐδ' ἂν εἷς γνοίη ποτ' οὐδ' ἂν ξυμβάλοι
     εἰ μὴ πύθοιθ' ἡμῶν· ἐπεὶ τοπάζετε.
     'Αμυνίας μὲν ὁ Προνάπους φήσ' οὑτοσὶ
     εἶναι φιλόκυβον αὐτόν· ἀλλ' οὐδὲν λέγει.
Σω. μὰ Δί', ἀλλ' ἀφ' αὑτοῦ τὴν νόσον τεκμαίρεται.
Ξα. οὔκ, ἀλλὰ φιλο μέν ἐστιν ἀρχὴ τοῦ κακοῦ.

Xa. Our master's father is afflicted by a strange disease which no one could ever recognize or diagnose without our help. Go ahead, try to guess what it is! Amynias there, son of Pronapes, suggests "gambler-itis." Nope, wrong as can be.
So. I swear, he's judging from his own behavior!

> Xa. Well that's not it, though an "-itis" is indeed at the root of the problem.

There follow several more jokes at the expense of individual spectators as the slaves pretend to take and reject suggestions from the audience. At line 85 Xanthias finally gives up and resumes his prologue narrative in which he reveals that Philocleon is, in fact, sick with "jury fever." The script has thus briefly expanded the slaves' private conversation into a confrontational exchange between citizen-spectators outside the narrowly circumscribed initial fiction.

A common device used to conclude such metatheatrical digressions is to bring on a character who has not been involved in it. At *Wasps* 136, accordingly, Bdelycleon awakens and calls for his slaves at which point his wily father emerges from the smoke-hole for a comic jack-in-the-box routine. In a similar scene (*Peace* 43-48), to give another example, one of Trygaeus' slaves looks out into the audience and relates a conversation which he imagines to be taking place in the audience: an Ionian visitor explains to a young man seated next to him that the dung beetle is a riddling representation (αἰνίσσεται) of Cleon inasmuch as he "eats shit shamelessly." In this case the script hypothesizes its own interpretation revealing an awareness of an audience-response that survives the ephemeral performance.[55] In New Comedy, by contrast, the scope of audience address and scripted acknowledgment of the spectators has narrowed almost to the vanishing point, as David Bain has shown. There is little in Menander beyond glancing second-person plurals and the common "ἄνδρες" which reduce the spectators' identity to a

---

[55]In a somewhat different spirit, the opening of *Frogs* presents a comic Dionysus who is self-conscious about the quality of his humor and who, like Dicaeopolis of *Acharnians*, speaks overtly as an actor (cf. lines 1-2), spectator (lines 16-18) and reader (lines 52-54). The most sustained and powerful shift between the world of the play and the extradramatic world is, of course, the parabasis which has recently been studied in this connection by Hubbard, *Mask of Comedy*. In the hands of Aristophanes the parabasis was a regular component of the comic form in which the audience was addressed and, in some manner or other, included in the dramatic issues. The development of an ever stronger dramatic illusion contributes to filtering out many of these distinctive features.

singularity.⁵⁶ From the wide variety of appeals to, and invocations of, the spectaors as θεαταί and πολῖται by Aristophanes, we are left with a simple nod to a passive, apolitical, and generic group of "men."

Profound changes in language and style appear to have begun in the first half of the fourth century.⁵⁷ Insofar as we are able to judge from the fragmentary evidence, the differences between Aristophanes of the 420's and Antiphanes are vast by comparison to the differences between the latter and Menander. The Anonymus on Comedy (Koster, *Prolegomena* III, 9.44-10.45)⁵⁸ asserts that "the poets of Middle Comedy did not use the poetic style. They employed the familiar language so that their merits are rhetorical, poetic qualities being rare in their [work]. They all expend study on their plots."⁵⁹ This opposition between the ποιητικὸν πλάσμα of Old Comedy with its ὑποθέσεις οὐκ ἀληθεῖς, invention and linguistic innovation on the one hand, and the συνηθὴς λαλιά, λογικαὶ ἀρεταί, linguistic naturalism and priority of plot on the other hand, illustrates an implicit connection between the constituent elements of comedy as it evolves.⁶⁰ What can be said about the poet's voice and characterization in this evolution?

---

⁵⁶Bain, *Actors and Audience* 185-91. Scope is one thing, frequency another. "It is unwise," Bain concludes (pp. 205-6), "to be dogmatic about the amount of audience address in New Comedy."

⁵⁷On the language of New Comedy see Sandbach, "Menander's Manipulation"; Del Corno, "aspetti di linguagio"; Feneron, "Some Elements"; Gamberale, "L'inizio proverbiale"; Flury, "Liebessprache"; and, most recently, Wiles, *Masks of Menander* (esp. Chapter 8, "Language and Voice," pp. 209-27).

⁵⁸In the company of much worthless material this is indeed "the most valuable testimonium of ancient literary history concerning the three periods of [Greek] comedy" (Nesselrath, *Mittlere Komödie* 51).

⁵⁹τῆς δὲ μέσης κωμῳδίας οἱ ποιηταὶ πλάσματος μὲν οὐχ ἥψαντο ποιητικοῦ, διὰ δὲ τῆς συνήθους ἰόντες λαλιᾶς λογικὰς ἔχουσι τὰς ἀρετάς, ὥστε σπάνιον ποιητικὸν εἶναι χαρακτῆρα παρ' αὐτοῖς. κατασχολοῦνται δὲ πάντες περὶ τὰς ὑποθέσεις.

⁶⁰This emphasis of the Anonymus on Middle Comedy's "poetic poverty," "familiar language," rhetoric and plot may be compared interestingly to Platonius' more political analysis in which Old Comedy is associated with politics, "real" citizens, personal mockery and abuse, the chorus, and parabasis while Middle Comedy is concerned with

A striking aspect of an Aristophanic figure such as Dicaeopolis, as we have seen, is the way he is used to organize an impressive array of verbal and thematic elements in a performance that, strictly speaking, is unrealistic and discontinuous. Such a character is a locus for multiple linguistic registers and even multiple voices. There are, as a result, discontinuities of character to contend with. A notorious problem in *Acharnians*, for example, is the extent to which Aristophanes' authorial "I" invades the character of Dicaeopolis at lines 377-382 (and in his speech at lines 500-506). Having criticized the litigiousness of old men Dicaeopolis says:

αὐτὸς τ' ἐμαυτὸν ὑπὸ Κλέωνος ἅπαθον
ἐπίσταμαι διὰ τὴν πέρυσι κωμῳδίαν.
εἰσελκύσας γάρ μ' ἐς τὸ βουλευτήριον
διέβαλλε καὶ ψευδῆ κατεγλώττιζέ μου
κἀκυκλοβόρει κἄπλυνεν, ὥστ' ὀλίγου πάνυ
ἀπωλόμην μολυνοπραγμονούμενος.

I know well what I've had to take from
Cleon for last year's comedy—do I ever!
How he dragged me into the council-chamber,
and slandered and tounged me with his lies,
roaring like a torrent and showering me with spit.
I nearly died, overwhelmed by slime.

The personal response to Cleon is resumed in Dicaeopolis' Great Speech in which comedy is advanced as a suitable medium for telling the truth, however unpleasant (lines 502-505):

οὐ γάρ με νῦν γε διαβαλεῖ Κλέων ὅτι
ξένων παρόντων τὴν πόλιν κακῶς λέγω.
αὐτοὶ γάρ ἐσμεν οὑπὶ Ληναίῳ τ' ἀγών,
κοὔπω ξένοι πάρεισιν·

And Cleon can't slander me for
trashing the polis before outsiders.
This here's the Lenaea, and we're all alone;
No visitors have come yet.

---

mythology, mythical personages, oblique reference, abolition of chorus and parabasis. See Perusino, *Platonio* 17.

Is Dicaeopolis at these points to be regarded as the author, another poet such as Eupolis (Bowie), a generalized "comic hero" (so Dover), a momentary parabasis-like interlude (Whitman), a more sophisticated fiction of the "disguised poet" (Hubbard, Goldhill), deliberate Dionysiac obfuscation (Fisher), or nothing worth belaboring (Forrest)?[61]

The complex relationship between dramatic character(s) and the poet's voice in Aristophanes is further complicated if we acknowledge the difficulty of separating the parts of individual stage-figures from the discourse of the play, from the "total image of human existence that the play presents," in the words of J. Gould. "The play as a whole that is," he notes, "is the 'meaning' that is to be humanly intelligible, the play as a whole being an image, a metaphor of the way things are, within human experience—not a literal enactment of 'the way people behave'."[62] The "inner landscape" of a character such as Peisetaerus or Trygaeus draws freely on the full linguistic and thematic resources of the entire play, which, in turn, is a fiction coextensive with the world of the spectators (in contrast to the temporally and, often, spatially remote tragic *mythos*) and, as such, particularly rich in simultaneous possibilities. Aristophanic comedy exhibits many remarkable features that do not appear to have survived the famous playwright. In this final section I should like to outline several distinguishing "parameters" of this discourse relevant to the interaction of "poet" and character within the framework of "the play as a whole."

Polyphony: The scripts of Aristophanic political satires are woven of a mingled yarn whose individual strands are distinct and particular: colloquial speech, parody, topical allusions, comic formations, legalese, etc. The presence of the poet as the controlling mind is quite palpable in such writing, not necessarily as an intrusive "I" but often in the *unhomogenized internal variety of linguistic resources* organized in the form of a given

---

[61]On *Acharnians* 377-382 and 500-506 see Goldhill, *The Poet's Voice* 191-95; Fisher, "Multiple Personalities"; and Hubbard, *The Mask of Comedy* 43-47. For a variety of opinion on this issue see also A. Bowie, "Parabasis" 30, and E. Bowie, "Dicaeopolis" 183-85 (with Parker's reply in "Eupolis or Dicaeopolis?"); Dover, "Notes on *Acharnians*" 15; Whitman, *Comic Hero* 22; Forrest, "Aristophanes' *Acharnians*" 8-10.

[62]Gould, "Dramatic Character" 62.

character. The diversity of these resources and the rapid transitions from one level to another are an undisguised display of the poet's creativity at the expense of realistic character. As a poetic microcosm of the entire play[63] the dramatic figure is, of course, is not a "bounded individual" easily separable from his (con)text. At the same time, the language of Peisetaerus, for example, would appear to differ from that of, say, Dicaeopolis in its composition. Insofar as the former draws on the sophistic vocabulary and mannerisms (*Birds* 462-610), he differs from Dicaeopolis who sustains the persona of a rustic critical of his urban compatriots. Neither is "realistic," to judge by an absolute standard, but each exhibits unique, characteristic features: Dicaeopolis specializes in Euripidean parody, among other things, while Peisetaerus "speaks" Aesop and Pindar. The language of both participates in what I term Aristophanic "polyphony" but each character is given a unique mixture of the various strata identified above.

Improvisation: Throughout its transformation in the hands of its most famous fifth-century practitioner comedy never forgot its "improvisational beginnings," γενομένη δ' οὖν ἀπ' ἀρχῆς αὐτοσχεδιαστικῆς–καὶ αὐτὴ [τραγῳδία] καὶ ἡ κωμῳδία," in the phrase of *Poetics* (1449a9). The unselfconscious facility with which simple personae such as Trygaeus and Philocleon are made to manipulate both language and the very scenario of which they are a part results in a character development of sorts. Thus Dover notes of Xanthias, Dionysus' sidekick in *Frogs*, that he undergoes a "progressive characterization" through a series of manipulative utterances and actions.[64] The plot and fundamental "comic idea" are often directly dependent on the inspirations and decisions of the lead character who appears to invent as he goes along, propelling the "fantastic plots" (ὑποθέσεις οὐκ ἀληθεῖς), in the phrase of the Anonymus. The evolving comic scenario, in turn, appears to shape the character or, at least, to reveal new, unexpected potential. The interaction of internal invention (speech, self-expression) and external invention (improvised

---

[63]Gould, "Dramatic Character" 62-63.
[64]Dover, *Frogs* 196, on the attribution of line 51.

action) are vital for the Aristophanic plot.⁶⁵ The words and deeds of Peisetaerus, for example, trace a path of conversion from a self-professed *apragmon* to an ambitious city-planner and, finally, tyrant-god.⁶⁶ The creative, improvisational aspect of Aristophanes' lead roles are, in an important sense, metaphors of poetic creativity and an extension of the poet's voice, generally speaking. The identification between poet and protagonist ranges from explicit (Dicaeopolis) to subtle (Bdelycleon). "By projecting his own experience onto his main character" notes Hubbard of this phenomenon, "Aristophanes clarifies both the potential and the limitations of his comic art."⁶⁷

Discourse Irony: Unlike a tragic figure whom we might be tempted to regard as the "tip of an iceberg" concealing a subconscious, a family, and a past, the Aristophanic character is entirely on display to the point where the spectators are aware of more about him and the meaning of his words than is the character himself. Thus when a figure such as Tereus uses tragic language (*Birds* 92), or when Euripides' Kinsman is drawn into the "comic" tragedian's intrigue in *Thesmophoriazusae*, the spectator is given a broader perspective on the action than the dramatic figure, strictly speaking, is supposed to have. At many points in a comedy a player (or chorus) communicates to the audience the jokes and ideas of the poet "unwittingly" or in spite of himself. When Philocleon's slave includes in his exposition of the dramatic situation an endorsement of Aristophanic comedy and its methods (*Wasps* 54-67) we do not struggle with this

---

⁶⁵Notions of improvisation are prominent in Greenblatt, *Renaissance Self-Fashioning*, and Johnstone, *Improvisation and the Theatre*. "While other characters usually remain trapped in the stock roles to which their plot functions assign them," writes Slater, *Plautus in Performance* 16, "the clever slaves have the self-transformational power of the versipellis (skin-changer).... More importantly, though, the improvisational lead player knows how to use the humours and foibles of the other stock character to bend them to his schemes." In this respect (less the emphasis on "stock characters") Aristophanes has much in common with Plautus. For the cross-cultural relativity of "improvisation" in musical traditions see Merriam, *Anthropology of Music* 179.

⁶⁶This understanding of Peisetaerus' role is clarified by the line-attributions proposd by Marzullo and incorporated by Sommerstein in his text of *Birds*. See Sommerstein, *Birds* 201.

⁶⁷Hubbard, *The Mask of Comedy* 137.

discontinuity between "slave" and "dramatic critic" but rather allow the figure temporarily to assume a new fictional dimension (an aspect of "poet").[68] The complexity of Dicaeopolis' harangue is similarly presented for the reader/spectator to enjoy in its fullness while the dramatic figure is intent on his central problem. Cleon's "disgorging five talents" in line 6 discussed above, as a self-citation (alluding to Aristophanes' *Babylonians*), conspires with the chorus' promise at lines 300-301 to cut Cleon to shreds for the knights (i.e., *Knights*). Here the characters of the comedy are bearers of a sophisticated literary message which, strictly speaking, should be beyond the nominal roles of the protagonists. This pleasing irony—i.e., where the scope of a character's discourse is perceived by the spectators to exceed the his apparent intentions and understanding—is an Aristophanic hallmark. "No other characters in a Greek drama are so bookish, so learned," notes Froma Zeitlin of what I term "discourse irony,"—and she could well have been speaking of figures such as Dicaeopolis and Trygaeus—"*although they themselves are marvelously unaware of their erudition*" (emphasis mine).[69] A striking aspect of this irony is the ventriloqual moment where "poet" usurps the voice and/or role of a stage figure. The most sustained example of this is the parabasis in which the chorus appears, a certain points, to suppress its own identity to speak for the playwright.

The polyphony, improvisation, and discourse irony of linguistic characterization in Aristophanes are representative of a genre that is "in its very essence grounded in an atmosphere of developed agonistic competition and intense literary allusion, wherein the poets sought and created for themselves visible public identities."[70] Old Comedy is, in this respect, part of a long poetic tradition of allusion and self-consciousness.[71] A

---

[68]For an interesting perspective of a similar discontinuity in *Acharnians* see Fisher, "Multiple Personalities" 44: "I would conclude that the purpose of giving Dicaeopolis these multiple, shifting, roles, *personae*, and placing him in so many different settings, is deliberately obfuscatory: they help to suggest the complexity, the Dionysiac ambiguities, of the comic voice embodied in this hero, and the sustained ambivalence of his 'peace' and of his relation to the city."

[69]*Closet of Masks* 53, on Euirpides' *Orestes* (see note 1 above).

[70]Hubbard, *Mask of Comedy* 33.

[71]So Hubbard, *Mask of Comedy* 16-40, argues at some length.

fundamental aspect of the evolution of comic language and character, then, is the process whereby the poet as quasi-fictional persona/presence withdraws from the world and language of his play, thereby shifting in the self-reflexive orientation of the genre. The attenuation of the sociopolitical and satirical motivations driving the creation of (the playwrights') "visible public identities" effected a sea change in comic discourse: as the poet disengages from his public, the polyphony, improvisation, and discourse irony of the comic performance mutate into a realistic dialogism in which language and voice are subordinated much more strictly to character in a fiction insulated by a powerful dramatic illusion.

We must not overlook the significance of the fact that the poet's voice is heard most clearly in the engagé plays of the late fifth-century. As important agonistic events of the polis, these were in fact "assemblies" in which a prominent citizen (the playwright) persuaded his fellow-citizens by means of an appeal mingling amusement and politics.[72] The protagonists in these productions (and quite a few choruses) interact, in varying degrees, with the fictional persona of the "poet" in a way that underscores the political satire as a non-illusory performance played for the poet by the actors to the spectators. "Old Comedy is ubiquitously self-referential," notes Taplin in his comparison of genres, "Aristophanes is probably the most metatheatrical playwright before Pirandello. The world of the audience is never safe from invasion...by the world of the play."[73] Taplin opposes the world of the play to the world of the audience in an attempt to sharpen the contrast between fifth-century tragedy and comedy[74] in terms of "different modes of interplay between stage and auditorium." I suggest, however, that we transcend the simple distinction between "inside" and "outside" the play, "the world of the play," and "the world of the audience" (in Taplin's terms) since a performance such as *Wasps* embraces the spectators by

---

[72] For a discussion of this "comic appeal" and its place in the polis see Henderson, "Comic Competition" 307-13.

[73] Taplin, "Synkrisis" 164. See also his *Comic Angels* 67-78.

[74] Against the trend to see "cross-talk" beetween genres in, e.g., Zeitlin, "Closet of Masks," "Travesties," and Seidensticker, *Palintonos Harmonia*. See now Taplin, *Comic Angels* 63 (with note 21).

fictionalizing them (*demos* by synecdoche),[75] its own context (polis), the poet, and the dramatic process itself. Comedy, notes Henderson ("Comic Competition" 297), "create[d] a comic version of the city itself, where the partisan comic troupe reproduced the *demos* in festive caricature and the competitors for its favor in the guise of traditional figures of mockery." The fictionality of Old Comedy was obviously more elastic than that of its sister-genres (and later comedy) in that it could trace the complexity of the festival situation more completely and pervasively. Parody and the parameters of Aristophanic discourse outlined above are symptomatic of the complex three-dimensional dramatic world that at once admits to having author, context, players, and spectators—a fictional mode operative at every point in the performance. This presentation, re-presentation, by the playwright (himself of the polis) of the polis to itself points up the fact that what we call "metatheater" was an inherent feature of Old Comedy.

As the Greek dramatic genres matured in the latter quarter of the fifth century, their range of expression extended and deepened to become increasingly self-reflexive, i.e., they came to exhibit a heightened self-consciousness in script and performance and a self-awareness as influential media with a visible role in the Athenian polis. Work on Euripides and Aristophanes now commonly employs the term "metatheater" in a way that identifies reflexivity as an inalienable dimension of their stagecraft. "The city established...a spectacle open to all citizens, directed, acted, and judged by the qualified representatives of the various tribes," writes Jean-Paul Vernant of tragedy. "*In this way it turned itself into a theater; its subject, in a sense, was itself and it acted itself out before its public*" (emphasis mine).[76] Another critic has written similarly of Old Comedy that it "*represents the city to the city.*"[77] Social and dramatic self-consciousness went especially hand-in-hand at the City Dionysia as we see from the other festival events such as the Proagon, Eisagoge, Pompe and above all the civic ceremonies inaugurating the dramatic

---

[75]In Aristophanic passages such as *Acharnians* 496-508, *Wasps* 74-87, *Peace* 50-55, and *Birds* 753-797.
[76]Vernant and Vidal-Naquet," Myth and Tragedy" 33.
[77]Goldhill, *Poet's Voice* 185.

competitions: public recognition of benefactors of the state, display of the allies' tribute to Athens, front-row seats and gifts for orphaned sons of the war dead, and the selection of judges.[78] Indeed, it would be hard to exaggerate the extent to which the polis became a theater of literary and political fictions played by the *demos* to the *demos*. This process of self-representation, however, is motivated by the need to call established values, institutions, and practices into question and it is the self-critical force of Greek metatheatrics that show it to be an especially progressive, not to say subversive, phenomenon.

To return to *Archanians*: Dicaeopolis, who coincides at several points with the fictionalized poet, makes his complaint quite differently from the characters of Antiphanes and Alexis. His harangue is long, gradual, complex, specific, political, and personal. Instead of setting up an exemplum or foil he begins by improvising a pain-to-pleasure ratio. (It's a bit disconcerting and, in mathematical terms, is a zillion-to-four.) There follows a climactic pairing of pains and pleasures whose allusive terms are drawn from festival performances of music and theater with the last, and most important, item being *para prosdokian* the emptiness of the Pnyx on the occasion of the first or "sovereign" assembly (*kyria ekklesia*). The complaint and its expression are quite specific and extend in significance beyond the immediate scene into the subsequent action, both in language and in theme. Dicaeopolis is conspicuously a part of the general fabric of *Acharnians* and rather hard, as such, to separate out (at least linguistically) as a fully "bounded individual," i.e. as an individual "voice" separate from the chorus, poet, and other players. In this respect one may agree with Dover's point that Dicaeopolis does not have a "distinctive language," i.e. that Aristophanic comedy the primary dialogism of a modern realist play or novel. As we compare across comedies, however, protagonist to protagonist, chorus to chorus, this assertion becomes less convincing. Stepping away from a naturalistic (absolutist) understanding of "distinctive" it would be possible, space permitting, to make the case for relative characterization within the constraints of the system. In other words, while the figure of Dicaeopolis may not have enough linguistic and behavioral uniqueness to meet a "real

---

[78]See Goldhill, "Civic Ideology" 99-199, on the Proagon.

world" standard of distinctness, this figure is quite distinct within the specific world of Aristophanic comedy with its unusual dialogism (polyphony, improvisation, irony) and three-dimensional fiction (self-conscious network of poet~players~spectators). As we turn to the Middle Comic harangue, we lose the specificity, complexity, and individuality of Dicaeopolis' performance. Literary topos, verbal formula, and character type conspire to produce a less personal discourse which, for all its apparent generality, possesses a new potential for characterization. While the vigor and variety of Aristophanic discourse tended to overshadow the dramatic figure, the standardization of diction through the Middle period paved the way for more subtle and natural ("probable") development of character through language and behavior.

I conclude by placing this study of comic discourse in a theoretical perspective to which my approach is naturally suited. Having used the terms "dialogism" and "dialogical" several times I have implicitly engaged an important term of Bakhtinian criticism that trades in large and flexible (and often quite "fuzzy") concepts such as "carnival," "chronotope," and "memory." In his influential study of Dostoevsky (pp. 212-14), Bakhtin speaks of the general "dialogue" that informs all human discourse in the following terms:

> Dialogical interaction is the authentic realm of living language [подлинная сфера жизни языка]. All discourse [again, жизнь языка] is permeated with dialogical relations.... Since they lie in the realm of the word which is by nature dialogical, these relations are the province of metalinguistic study that transcends the boundaries of linguistics and has an independent agenda [предмет и задачи].

> Dialogical relations are not limited to (relatively) whole utterances. We may, in fact, take a dialogical approach to any [semantically] significant element of an utterance, even to a single word, if [such a word] is perceived not as an impersonal lexical item, but as a sign belonging to another's system of signification,[79] as a representative of an another's utterance; that is, if we hear in [this word] the voice of another [speaking subject].

[79]Literally "a sign (indication, token) of the semantic position of another," знак чужой смысловой позиции.

Owing to the creative efforts of scholars such as Jean-Claude Carrière, Kenneth Reckford, Wolfgang Rösler, and Dana Sutton the often problematic application of Bakhtin's notions of "carnival" to ancient genres and authors (especially Aristophanes) has been much advanced. "Dialogism" has come to the fore more recently and has its own bibliography.[80] Particularly relevant to my discussion is the recent study of lyric by Paul Allen Miller in which he emphasizes the need to distinguish between different types of dialogism when working across ancient genres. Miller suggests the term "primary dialogism" to refer to "that interplay of voices and concepts which is found in realist fiction and daily life. It designates that set of relations which governs the exchange of complete 'utterances' between individuals, social groups, and/or their fictional representatives...." Secondary dialogism, on the other hand, "represents that more subtle level of dialogical interaction which occurs not only within utterances, but within individual words." This phenomenon is dialogical in a deeper sense as it "results from the speaker's simultaneous *response* to past and *anticipation* of future utterances.... For every word we use carries with it the sights, sounds, and smells, the social and rhetorical contexts of its previous uses" (emphasis mine).[81] Miller argues persuasively that archaic lyric, whose realization was oral and public, was profoundly dialogical in this "secondary" sense: an apparently monological text whose elements, nevertheless, were dialogized by the performance situation.[82]

[80]The starting point for this line of inquiry (and most any other) must be work of Caryl Emerson, Michael Holquist (not least for their translations of, and introductions to, Bakhtin's work), and Gary Saul Morson. See Holquist, *Dialogism*; Morson and Emerson *Rethinking Bakhtin* and *Creation of a Prosaics*, and Emerson, "Irreverent Bakhtin."
[81]Miller, "Dialogism of Lyric" 183-84.
[82]Miller, "Dialogism of Lyric" 186, notes that "utterances are always other-directed, and this is particularly so in the case of public artistic performances where the audience is immediately present. Such poems are of necessity communal events, rather than closed confessions. Each new performance is a separate utterance, indissolubly linked to the moment of enunciation and so forever reinforcing the radically occasional nature of archaic lyric." The dialogue of a poet in this genre is "with both the (oral) poetic tradition and the collective ideological and social world in which it is performed" (p. 195).

The characterization of Aristophanic discourse above as complex and polyphonic clearly places it in the category of "secondary dialogism" despite the fact that the surface of the work is articulated into speaking "parts." A deep priority in political comedy, as we have seen, is its involvement in a civic agon wherein a playwright appeals to his public. From this perspective "the play as whole" of which Gould speaks (see note 62 above) *is the poem*, and it is worth emphasizing that we do not refer to ancient composers of tragedy and comedy as "poets" trivially or in quaint deference to academic usage. The poetics of playing an oral composition to a public on a ceremonial occasion is of immesurable antiquity and should prompt us to look deep within the "poem" for "dialogue" on a much smaller, or very different, scale than a mere change of speaker ("microdialogue" in Bakhtin's coinage). Thus, as Tony Edwards has recently argued, despite its position at the center of an evolving democracy, political Old Comedy was primarily in the hands of elitist writers whose agenda could diverge from that of the *demos*.[83] The clash between "democratic" and "conservative" voices in Aristophanes that has engendered so much debate is not evidence of generic schizophrenia or a temperamental incongruity; rather, it is a natural reflection of the different ideologies, social strata, and voices constituting the community. The voice singled out for attention at the beginning of this paper—that of the poet—is especially prominent here and, as such, provides a natural clue luring us on to discover the complexities of comic dialogism. A great challenge to the Aristophanic critic is to negotiate the elaborate and unresolved tension between the archaic "secondary" dialogism perpetuated by the performance context (dramatic festival), and an emerging "primary" dialogism which is one of the most vivid realizations in dramatic discourse of the "probable": strict mimesis of real conversation. From a play such as *Clouds* where we can never be

---

[83]Edwards, "Popular Grotesque" 103, speaks of "the tension between the conservative positions developed within individual comedies and the universally critical and popular tendency of the grotesque. This rift is recapitulated within comedy itself in the unwillingness of an unruly and anarchic humor to be subjected to the discipline of political arguments. Such tensions are built into the attempt to turn the grotesque to conservative and overtly political purposes."

confident that a given voice or position will coincide with a formal dramatic utterance (e.g. the notoriously unstable identity of the chorus), we progress to *Dyscolus* where "voice" and utterance are brought into close identity: the characters are stable constructs and the voice of the playwright has fallen silent.

The modified approach to Bakhtinian dialogism outlined above allows us to discern within the monologue of Dicaeopolis other voices in "microdialogue," some of which might be identified as follows:

"Aristophanes": Lines 6-8 are a potent moment of self-citation where the author situates Cleon within his own dramatic career, that is, between *Babylonians* of the past (426 BC), in which the demagogue "vomited five talents," and *Knights* of the future (424 BC) with its sustained allegorical attack. This voice is that of the individual citizen-poet who often criticizes and lampoons leaders of the *demos* such as Cleon and their policies.

"The author as κωμῳδοδιδάσκαλος" (as opposed to tragedian, dithyrambist, etc.): By quoting tragedy (lines 8 and 27), the text, as a partisan representative of κωμῳδία, points to its dialogical relationship with its sister-genre, a critical, transformational dynamic that finds fuller expression later in the usurpation of Euripides' *Telephus*. This is the voice that expresses the "carnival" spirit of comedy with its license and reversal of social hierarchies as, for example, in the epirrhema and antepirrhema of *Birds* (lines 753-768 and 785-800).

"Intellectual spectator": The criticism of festival events in lines 9-16 reveals a keen and, of course, humorous standard of excellence by which an educated Athenian *spectator* (sometimes even *reader*) evaluated the poets and performers at the City Dionysia. We learn of his disapproval of Moschus and Dexitheus and, predictably, his nostalgia for Aeschylus. This voice is heard often in fifth-century plays such as *Peace* (lines 43-48) and *Frogs* (lines 1-100 and passim).

"Dicaeopolis": This is the most obvious "dramatis persona," that of a disgruntled ἄγροικος and member of an inland deme. He has come to the ἄστυ (city center) to protest the war and to try to promote peace through the available means of active participation in politics. He is critical of the urban center, its inhabitants and way of life.

These voices might be further refined according to generic sub-divisions, social "class," gender, age, etc. It should be clear, however, that the unhomogenized variety of linguistic resources outlined at the beginning of this paper (pp. 59-61) is bound up with the "internal" dialogism of Aristophanic poetry. In dialogical terms, changes of speaker and the relative identities of various stage-figures are not given priority in such a script and often, in fact, appear to be in a sort of contrapuntal relationship with the "microdialogue" set forth here.

As the comedy evolved—and I see this process clearly in the Middle Period—the three dimensions of this fiction (poet~players~spectators) were reduced to two in the plane of a stricter dramatic illusion with striking results. To begin with, the language and action are brought into conformity with "the probable," i.e., these elements of the performance become more "natural," purged of the eccentricities, passions, personality, and imagination of the "partisan" poet and troupe playing political satire. I cite, in this connection, T. B. L. Webster's discussion of Aristotle's τὸ εἰκός: "[New] Comedy," he notes, "is a 'combination of probable incidents'; the important word is 'probable' and it can be interpreted in three ways." These are "probable sequence," "the sort of thing which happen every day," and "suitable to the character in this particular situation."[84] It is apparent from this analysis that the dynamics of the three-dimensional Old Comic agon have yielded to the very different aesthetic of mimetic realism. The polis and its life are still present, to be sure, but are embedded in a dramatic structure that precludes a crossing of boundaries between "poet," "play," and "public." Thus, as comedy loses the (quasi-fictional) persona of the poet "behind" the players and "speaking to" the spectators, there arises between "the world of the auditorium" and "the world of the play" a formidable wall

---

[84]Webster, *Later Greek Comedy*[1] 114-16: "In the first place it means that the incidents of the plot arise out of one another in a probable sequence. In this sense 'probable' refers to the technique of plot-construction, to the unity of action and the preparation and motivation of exits and entrances. Secondly 'probable' is interpreted as 'the sort of things which would happen' or, as we might say, the sort of things which do happen every day.... The realities of time and place are also carefully observed; Thirdly, 'probable' can be used in the sense of 'suitable to the character in this particular situation'."

of illusion or distance. This, of course, is quite in keeping with the new theory of τὸ εἰκός as resisting intrusions from "behind the scenes" or disruptive clashes of worlds, "fictional" and "real." New Comedy, naturally, relaxes its preoccupation with topicality and particulars of the polis. "We have seen in discussing politics," notes Webster, "that the chief point of many of the political allusions in New Comedy is simply to give a realistic contemporary reference."[85] This is, above all, a matter of performance dynamics—the modes of transaction between stage and spectators—which become palpably more generalizing and impersonal.

We find in Middle Comedy, then, a dramatic discourse from which the "poet" (as intrusive/controlling fiction) has withdrawn, leaving open new avenues of characterization. There is a paradox here: as non-political comedy assimilates to a higher standard of realism, it would seem that the dramatic figure might evolve into a more natural and bounded, i.e. separable, dramatic entity with the potential for fuller characterization in the modern sense. The evidence of Middle Comedy, however, is equivocal in confirming this expectation, as its potential for characterization appears muted by the trend toward types operating in stock-situations. In this connection I find compelling Niall Slater's suggestion (above, p. 45) that "a diverse and internationalized audience created an enormous demand for a standardized and portable product" the result of which were the "framing" of comic action (illusion) and the "abstraction of the comedy from its specifically Athenian festal setting."

It is important to proceed with caution, however, when generalizing about a genre as it evolved over time. I have been referring specifically to "Aristophanic political satire," for example, in order to avoid suggesting that the fifth century saw an undifferentiated procession of "Old" comedies, all of them political plays in the style of *Knights* and *Lysistrata*. The sub-genre of political comedy appears to have been forged by Cratinus only in the 450's—a full thirty years after Chionides' victory in the first comic competition. The next generation of this "school" which included Aristophanes and Eupolis cultivated a precarious and innovative balance between an appeal to the

---

[85]Webster, *Later Greek Comedy*[1] 114.

demos and ridicule—from a distinctly conservative viewpoint—of specific individuals and policies closely associated with the "radical" democracy. What little we know of the alternative "school of Crates," to use Norwood's term, suggests that some "middle" and "new" comic elements were being developed simultaneously by this poet who took his cue from Epicharmus.[86] "Old Comedy," in other words, was not a unitary phenomenon, but was most likely articulated by a number of "schools" and approaches.[87] We must be careful, when comparing the political satire of the 420's and fourth-century comedy, not to exclude the synchronic axis: the distinctions that one observes, say, between Aristophanes' *Knights* and Menander's *Samia* (plays separated by a full century) might be valid, to some extent, for a comparison between exactly contemporary plays of different styles such as Aristophanes' *Peace* and Pherecrates' *Savages*. It appears, however, that Aristophanes single-handedly thrust his style of political comedy into prominence for the several decades in which he was a successful competitor, and that already at the end of his career (*Wealth, Aiolosikon*) the "alternative" style—call it what you will—had claimed him as one of its own. As long as we avoid the trap of forcing our evidence into a narrow and linear model—and this is surely the problem with simplistic equations tracing the genre's evolution as a direct function of Athenian politics—it is safe to assert that the change in comic discourse outlined above is very real and important indeed.

On the other side of the Middle Comic divide which saw profound changes in the genre we find Menander's univocal figures interacting in a new way that reflects the new theory of "the probable." The script is far weaker in internal dialogism or "microdialogue," and is articulated strictly by changes of speaker and the principles of consistent character. By comparison to *Acharnians* or *Frogs, Dyscolus*, as a whole, is much less an entry

---

[86]Norwood, *Greek Comedy* 145-77. For current work on the relationship between political comedy (especially in its "iambic" aspect) see Edwards, "Popular Grotesque," and Platter, "The Uninvited Guest." "The making of plots," writes Aristotle, "originated in Sicily; of Athenian poets Crates was the first to drop the comedy of invective and frame stories and plots of a general nature" (*Poetics* 1449b5-9).

[87]On a member of Crates' "school," Pherecrates, and his place in the evolution of comedy see the essay of Dobrov and Urios-Aparisi below.

in an agon of the polis, i.e., a coherent "poem" written by a citizen-poet and played by a partisan group as a persuasive appeal to members of their own community. This departure from the archaic and "radically occasional" poetics of performance purged the new "drama of the actor" of features limiting its sphere of relevance in space and time (e.g., an integrated chorus and internal dialogism). A crucial step was thus taken toward making a legacy of this ancient genre whose popularity and longevity would remain unsurpassed.

The Continuity of the Chorus in Fourth-Century Attic Comedy*

Kenneth S. Rothwell, Jr.

Already in antiquity scholars had identified the decline of the chorus as one of the traits that distinguished New Comedy from Old.[1] The reasons given by ancient scholars for this change sometimes simply show how little evidence was available to them, but modern research has been able to pinpoint a number of factors that can rightly be thought responsible.[2] For example, comedy may have been influenced by the diminished role of the chorus in tragedy. Comic playwrights became more interested in creating a sense of illusion, unbroken by choral interaction with the actors,[3] which was in turn abetted by a growing interest in the art of the actor.[4] Another factor may have been the internationalization of the market for comedy, which would have made choral drama less exportable.[5] Innovation in dance and music, too, had repercussions for the chorus.[6] In any event, what

---

*Note: This is an expanded version of an article published in *Greek, Roman, and Byzantine Studies* 33 (1992), 209-25, and is reprinted with permission.

[1] Platonius 4.20-22, 36 (Koster, *Prolegomena* [V], 13.10ff.) and Evanthius, *De Fabula* XXV 1 (Koster, *Prolegomena* 125.78-85). Consult Nesselrath, *Mittlere Komödie*, 31, 42-43, 51, 167.

[2] Essential literature includes: Maidment, "The Later Comic Chorus"; Pickard-Cambridge, *Dramatic Festivals*, 46-51, 86-93, 232-46; Webster, *Later Greek Comedy*; Sifakis, "Aristotle, *E.N.*, IV, 2"; Hunter, "The Comic Chorus"; Nesselrath, *Mittlere Komödie*.

[3] Slater, "Fabrication of Comic Illusion" 29-45 (above).

[4] Ghiron-Bistagne, *Recherches* 173-202.

[5] Slater, "Fabrication of Comic Illusion" 39-42 (above).

[6] Nesselrath, *Mittlere Komödie* 335 notes that the anapestic tetrameter, one of the most characteristic meters of Old Comedy, virtually disappears from fragments in the fourth century; cf. Silk, "Aristophanes as a Lyric

had been an organic part of the genre in the fifth century seems to have been jettisoned in the fourth.

In this paper, however, I would like to stress that in several respects there were significant continuities at work. Much of the evidence for the fourth-century chorus has already been examined by modern critics, yet it still tends to be treated in isolation from its institutional context, the *choregia*. Moreover, its relationship to the Athenian democracy has often been misunderstood. I would like to show that (a) contrary to claims occasionally made, the fading of the comic chorus probably had little to do with a supposed loss of vigor in the fourth-century democracy at Athens, (b) the *choregia* was quite healthy and well funded for most of the fourth century, and (c) literary fragments and archaeological evidence offer hints that the chorus' diminished role did not come about abruptly.

The Chorus and the Fourth-Century Democracy

A good deal of modern scholarship on comedy frequently works from the premise that Athens entered a period of long-term decline after the defeat of 404 BC and that the evolution of comedy was a response to this. The following is representative:

> In the history of Athens choral drama and participatory democracy are coexistent: when one declines, so does the other. After the shattering defeat of the Peloponnesian War, an increasingly apathetic public removed itself from the decision-making process, and with the ascent of Macedon a centralized government imposed itself on the city-states. A parallel manifestation occurs in the theatre. Aristophanes' *Ecclesiazusae* is a comedy about voter apathy. It shows an Athens where legislative and executive procedures have broken down; where the male population has grown so lethargic that it must be bribed into attendance at the Assembly; and where women find it easy to take over. In its dramatic structure, it also marks the virtual death-knell of the chorus. Although there is still a chorus in this play, its appearances are spasmodic and perfunctory. The action, as in politics, is left to the principals. But, at its best, the Greek

---

Poet" 146ff. Webster, *Greek Chorus* 31-32, observes that innovation ceases in fourth-century depictions of dances and (on p. 198) sees few metrical subtleties in what survives. See also Lawler, *Dance* 14-21, 60-61, 97-99.

dramatic chorus bore the distinctive features of its place and time, an index of a public mentality that recognized arduous and time-consuming service to the state as a necessary component of the well-rounded life.[7]

The scenario sketched out here for the demise of the chorus can no longer be sustained. Indeed, it is *not* clear that Athens' defeat in the Peloponnesian War shattered the participatory democracy; throughout most of the fourth century the democracy was stable and Athens enjoyed a modicum of prosperity. Nor is it entirely fair to speak of the Athenians as an "increasingly apathetic public." I will discuss these issues in turn.

The interpretation of the fourth-century democracy is subject to perennial re-evaluation. On the one hand, there is unmistakable and well-documented evidence that Athens faced difficulties.[8] A few examples will serve to illustrate the problems. The loss of the imperial revenue that Athens had received from the Delian League in the fifth century had serious consequences. We know, for instance, that Athens was forced to modify the trierarchy so that the burden of that liturgy would be more widely shared.[9] Athens also faced shortfalls in the aftermath of the Social War of the mid-350's; in 349 BC Athens even temporarily ran out of money to pay the *dikastai*.[10] Politically, the Athenians lost a large measure of their independence after the battle of Chaeronea in 338 and finally the democracy itself in 322/21, when an oligarchy was imposed by Antipater.[11] Many similar episodes in the fourth century point to a city struggling not to succumb.

And yet, on the other hand, other evidence can lead us to different conclusions. The periods following the Peloponnesian War and the Social War were surely difficult, but a balanced account of the fourth century would need to acknowledge the

---

[7]Arnott, *Public and Performance* 24; cf. Lesky, *History* 643 and 658; Cantarella, "Polis e il Teatro" 54-55: "Fine della polis e fine del teatro."

[8]Representative of this view are Mossé, *La fin*; Pritchett, *Greek State at War* 456-504; David, *Fourth-Century Athenian Society* 5-20; Runciman, "Doomed to Extinction" 347-67.

[9]Recent studies of the symmory include: Rhodes, "Problems," and Ruschenbusch, "Symmorienprobleme."

[10]Demosthenes 39.17.

[11]Ferguson, *Hellenistic Athens* 1-37; de Ste. Croix, *Class Struggle* 300-6.

remarkable resilience and economic revitalization of Athens.[12] Athens was able to compensate for the loss of imperial income through energetic financial administration. M. H. Hansen has written:

> The other allegation of historians, since the middle of the nineteenth century, when interest in Athenian democracy began to be concentrated on the age of Perikles, is that the democracy was only possible because of the proceeds from Athens' naval empire—hence democracy in the fourth century was only a shadow of what it had been a century before. That assertion fits ill with the fact that the two most expensive payments, Assembly pay and the *theorika*, were only introduced in the fourth century when Athens had already lost her empire. Pay for magistrates was doubtless much less in the fourth century than in the fifth, but all in all the democracy of Demosthenes' time was far costlier than in that of Perikles, and the big daily payments of the fourth century support the very opposite assertion, that Athenian democracy was *not* dependent on the proceeds of empire.[13]

We therefore need to be quite cautious about drawing one-sided conclusions from the difficulties in fourth-century Athens; it is imperative to set them in proper context and to understand the circumstances at hand. For example, the suspension of pay to the *dikastai* was probably a temporary cash-flow problem. Cawkwell has written, "The statement ... that there was not enough pay for a jury in the latter part of 349/48 is not to be taken too seriously; there always was a temporary shortage in the later part of the year until the taxes due in the tenth prytany were paid (Dem. 24.98; Arist., *Ath. Pol.* 47.4)."[14] In the same year, moreover, Demosthenes urged the Athenians to tap the theoric fund for military expenses; if they did so they could have a larger military fund than any other nation. The impediments to this were

---

[12]Gomme, "End of the City-State"; Strauss, *Athens after the Peloponnesian War* 42-69; French, "Economic Conditions" 24-40; Isager and Hansen, *Aspects of Athenian Society* 52-55. In "La vie économique," Mossé took a more favorable view of economic activity and proposed that social and political problems of the *polis* in the latter half of the fourth century were fruits of precisely this success; see also Pečirka, "Crisis."

[13]Hansen, *Athenian Democracy* 318-19.

[14]Cawkwell, "Eubulus" 62-63.

primarily legal ones; what the Athenians faced in 349 was not so much outright poverty as a tough decision about allocating resources.[15] By 346 income had risen to 400 talents a year; between 357/56 and 330/29 the Athenian fleet grew from 283 triremes to 392.[16] Several times in the fourth century we have reports of grain crises, and these would have contributed to a sense of loss of control, yet their ultimate effect should not be exaggerated; according to one recent study there can have been no question of these crises amounting to a famine.[17] The military defeat at Chaeronea in 338 was a blow to Athenian independence in foreign affairs; paradoxically, however, it led to compensating advantages: a peaceful Aegean and an unprecedented volume of trade at Piraeus.[18] Although the processes of internal political decision-making in the fourth century were not identical with those of the fifth century (the *nomothetai*, for example, gradually acquired greater powers), the democratic institutions were on the whole remarkably stable until Antipater established more oligarchic institutions.[19] Furthermore, it may even be legitimately objected that 322/21 did not mark the "end" of the democracy but an interruption, because there were a series of democratic revivals in the decades following.[20] Whether Athens fell under the control of the Macedonians because she simply lost the battle at Chaeronea in 338 or because the democracy, despite Demosthenes' exhortations, had been fatally weakened from within, is perhaps one of the great questions of Athenian history.[21] It may be simplistic to attribute a turning point in

---

[15]*First Olynthiac* (1) 19. For the issues in question see Cawkwell, "Eubulus," esp. 57-58, and now Sealey, *Demosthenes* 256-58.

[16]Income: Theopompus fr. 166; triremes: compare *IG* ii² 1611.9, 1613.302, 1627.269. Cawkwell, "Eubulus" 62, 65.

[17]Garnsey, *Famine and Food Supply* 134-64.

[18]Burke, "Economy" 204.

[19]Rhodes, "Athenian Democracy"; Humphreys, "Lycurgus of Butadae" 201-2, on the *nomothetai* and pp. 217-19 on Lycurgus' use of *eisangelia*; for a useful checklist of differences between the fifth- and fourth-century democracies see Hansen, review of Sinclair, 71-73. The fundamental soundness of the fourth-century democracy is affirmed by Stier, *Untergang* 75, and Ober, *Mass and Elite* 334.

[20]These are detailed in Gomme, "End of the City State."

[21]Sealey, *Demosthenes* 194-219.

history to a bad day on the battlefield, and I would be reluctant to condemn the vigor of the democracy without clearer evidence.

This brings me to the view that an "apathetic public" became less engaged in political decision-making in the fourth century. This is, I suspect, an overstatement if not an outright falsehood. The view that the fourth century witnessed the emergence of individualism—*homo publicus* being replaced by *homo economicus*—is a cliché that has remained an unquestioned orthodoxy for many historians of fourth-century comedy.[22] This is too large an issue to be dealt with adequately here, but I will make two observations.

First, we should be skeptical about the assumption that the chorus represented the consensus of the community and that an active chorus could exist only in an era of devotion to the *polis* (the fifth century) but waned in an era when the individual was presumably of greater importance (the fourth century). The relationship between chorus and community was surely more complicated than this.[23] Even in the surviving fifth-century comedies of Aristophanes, with choruses composed of groups as diverse as farmers, *hippeis*, women, animals, clouds—not to mention the fact that the chorus of the *Lysistrata* is divided into two halves at odds with one another—it is difficult to assert that the chorus consistently represented the interests of anyone, much less the audience as a whole, or would have somehow symbolized vigorous and broad-based participation in the democracy.[24] Moreover, diminution of the chorus need not necessarily contribute to drama more suited to individuals. It can be argued that it is precisely by having a chorus on stage that a playwright is more easily able to isolate what is peculiarly individual about a given character; one function of the chorus is to act as a wider context against which the individual character's actions can be

---

[22]See for example: Maidment, "Later Comic Chorus" 8; David, *Fourth-Century Athenian Society* 30-32; Landfester, "Geschichte" 516-17; Ghiron-Bistagne, "Krise des Theaters." Longo, "Theater of the *Polis*" 17, at least allows that it is a complex process.

[23]Of course the question of the meaning of the chorus in society is an old one: see, for example, Silk and Stern, *Nietzsche on Tragedy* 350-53.

[24]The wide range of possible relationships between chorus and audience in Aristophanic comedy is surveyed by Thiercy, "Il ruolo del pubblico."

considered and help us measure the individual character's isolation.[25]

Second, it has been argued that traditional patriotism was less intense in the fourth century than in the fifth and that when an Athenian acted on behalf of the city he saw himself less as a citizen performing his duty than as a private benefactor (*euergetes*), offering his services as a favor, almost as if he were a foreigner; accordingly, when the wealthy citizen performed a liturgy he went out of his way to take credit for his generosity (something that becomes a familiar *topos* in fourth-century rhetoric).[26] That changes along these general lines took place seems to me to be relatively certain, though there is room for dispute as to precisely what extent the wealthy cooperated in liturgies.[27] But even if Athenians were not motivated only by selfless civic duty, the fact remains that they did continue to perform their liturgies. And this has important consequences for the fourth-century chorus.

The Fourth-Century Choregia

Against the long-standing assumption that the disappearance of the chorus stemmed to some extent from a "crisis" in the *choregia*,[28] I would like to suggest that the *choregia*,

---

[25]Goldhill, *Reading Greek Tragedy* 270-71. Menander must of course rely on a different set of conventions for delineating character.

[26]The phenomenon has been documented by Lévy, *Athènes devant la défaite* 223-57, esp. 242; Daverio-Rocchi, "Transformations de rôle" 33-50.

[27]Humphreys, "Lycurgus of Butadae" 204 and 212, notes the extent of free cooperation in supporting civic initiatives offered by Athenian upper classes during the Lycurgan period. For a harsher judgement on the upper classes see Christ, "Liturgy Avoidance." What might be more relevant would be information about the extent of popular participation in Athenian politics in the fourth century, and information about their experience as members of the audience. I suspect that Plato's complaint about a *theatrokratia* (*Laws* 701a) might actually reveal a continuing appreciation of and involvement with the theater by fourth-century popular audiences.

[28]Some of this may originate with Platonius, who wrongly thought that Athenians ceased to choose *choregoi* in the fourth century (Koster, *Prolegomena* 4.20-22); see Nesselrath, *Mittlere Komödie* 31. "Men able and willing to pay with the former lavishness for mounting tragedies and

until it was replaced with the *agonothesia* by Demetrius of Phaleron after 317 BC, actually worked rather smoothly. Of course some things would always go wrong. There were *choregoi* for whom the incentive of being honored as *euergetes* was insufficient and who were reluctant to pay or did so only with difficulty. Ischomachus, the gentleman in Xenophon's *Oeconomicus*, implies that a man who is *kalos te kagathos* should expect to be summoned into court at one time or another for an *antidosis* concerning a trierarchy or *choregia*.[29] Demosthenes' *Against Meidias* ([21] 13-18) describes how, in the case of a dithyrambic chorus, arrangements broke down in the initial selection of a *choregos*.[30]

Nevertheless we must bear in mind that we only hear about this because Demosthenes made a point of telling how he saved the day, voluntarily offering to become *choregos* so that the show could go on (*Meidias* [21] 14). Demosthenes—and Xenophon's Ischomachus—perhaps had an interest in over-stating the difficulties that they faced. It is true that some *choregoi* were stingy in the fourth century, but we also hear of stingy *choregoi* in the fifth century.[31] It should be emphasized, too, that the *antidosis* was not a phenomenon of the fourth century only; an inscription from Ikarion indicates that it was already available at that deme by the middle of the fifth century,[32] and it may simply be because no fifth-century forensic speeches survived that we do not know of specific instances of the *antidosis* in the fifth century.

Further evidence for the continuing strength of the *choregia* is the notable series of choregic monuments that were erected at

---

comedies could no longer be found," says Norwood, *Greek Comedy* 29; similarly Webster, *Later Greek Comedy* 14; Ghiron-Bistagne, "Krise des Theaters" 1344.

[29] *Oeconomicus* 7.3.

[30] See MacDowell, *Demosthenes: Against Meidias* 236-43.

[31] That Dicaeogenes came in dead last as *choregos* for tragic and Pyrrhic choruses is proof of his miserliness: Isaeus 5.36 (ca. 389 BC); Antimachus failed to provide for a proper banquet (*Acharnians* 1150-1161)—though this would hardly hamper the performance of the chorus, suggests Capps, "Later Greek Drama" 318.

[32] *IG* i^3 254 (=i^2 187) spells out provisions for two *choregoi* and *antidosis*; see Davies, *Athenian Propertied Families* xxii. In the fifth century, pseudo-Xenophon refers to *diadikasiai* with reference to the festivals (3.4).

Athens beginning around 335/34. By the time of Demetrius of Phaleron so many monuments had been set up that the areas adjacent to the precincts of Dionysus were "bristling with tripods."[33] These attest to the *philotimia* of individual *choregoi*, but they are also mute evidence of the expenses *choregoi* were willing to undertake.[34] For Aristotle these expenditures were so conspicuous that they smacked of ostentation and were morally troublesome. He specifically complained that some *choregoi* were dressing their choruses in purple cloaks for the *parodos*.[35] Aristotle also advocated removing the burden of the *choregia* from well-to-do citizens and wanted to prevent them from performing *choregiai* "even if they are willing" (καὶ βουλομένους, *Politics* 5.8 1309a17), which at least indicates that some were willing and that opposition to paying for choruses was not universal. In *Against Meidias*, Demosthenes' pride shows through when he describes the golden robe and crowns he had arranged for.[36] There were surely many such Athenians who were either genuinely proud, or at least quick to claim credit, for the liturgies they supported. In any event, however selfish or patriotic the motivations of *choregoi* were, it remains a fact that for as long as the *choregia* existed in the fourth century we do not know of a single instance in which it was not performed.[37]

It was in the fifth century, not the fourth, that the chorus suffered from financial limitations. During the Peloponnesian War the number of poets competing in the dramatic festivals was evidently reduced from five to three. In 406/5 BC, an especially trying year, the Athenians resorted to the *synchoregia*, in which

---

[33]Amandry, "Trépieds d'Athènes" 62.

[34]Humphreys, "Lycurgus of Butadae" 213. Ghiron-Bistagne, *Recherches* 84, notes that more dithyrambic monuments have survived than have dramatic monuments, but no tripod was even awarded in the dramatic contests. For this point I am indebted to Andronike Makres (Oxford), who is completing a dissertation on the *choregia*.

[35]Sifakis, "Aristotle, *E.N.*, IV, 2."

[36]*Against Meidias* (21) 16; see also Pickard-Cambridge, *Dramatic Festivals* 77, cf. 89.

[37]Pickard-Cambridge, *Theater of Dionysus* 167, misleadingly implies that *Ath. Pol.* 56.3 indicates that tribes took over the *choregia*—in fact it seems that the tribes nominated *choregoi* to the Archon; cf. Rhodes, "Problems," and MacDowell, *Demosthenes: Against Meidias* 236-37.

the financial burden was shared between two people.[38] What is notable about this improvisation is that the chorus itself was not affected: in order to insure that a chorus could be fully supported, the Athenians went out of their way to restructure the *choregia*.[39] Moreover the *synchoregia* was probably only in effect for that one year (406/5), as Edward Capps showed in 1943, thereby eliminating the *synchoregia* as a pretext for doubts about the later viability of the *choregia*.[40] We thus never hear of *synchoregiai* at fourth-century City Dionysia, at least for the years recorded in the Fasti (*IG* ii² 2318, covering the period 398-329 BC).[41] For the deme festivals about ten *synchoregiai*, involving as many as three people each, are attested in fourth century inscriptions. "Poverty is suggested" by the use of *synchoregoi*, thought Pickard-Cambridge,[42] though in three instances the three *choregoi* were a father and two sons, which means that the burden was still borne by one family, and where these *synchoregoi* are known they are found to be people of substantial wealth.[43] A clear instance of the *choregia* being fulfilled by individuals, not *synchoregoi*, is offered by a recently published dedication from Thorikos, dating from the middle of the fourth century.[44]

---

[38]In general, consult Pickard-Cambridge, *Dramatic Festivals* 74-92. The *synchoregia* is attested in Σ *Frogs* 404 of which, says Pickard-Cambridge (p. 87, note 2), "this is only a conjecture by the scholiast, and ... there is no other evidence to support it." We cannot be certain that the number of comedies performed at the festivals was reduced during the Peloponnesian War: see Luppe, "Zahl der Konkurrenten"; for a response, Mastromarco, "Guerra peloponnesiaca." It is sometimes thought that, in order to save the *choregoi* money, the frog chorus in *Frogs* was unseen and that the chorus of initiates wore ragged clothing. But the invisibility of the frogs is debatable and there are other explanations for the ragged clothing. See Dover, *Frogs* 56-57 and 62-63.

[39]Maidment, "Later Comic Chorus" 5-6.

[40]Capps, "New Fragment."

[41]Pickard-Cambridge, *Dramatic Festivals* 87, 102; consult also Ghiron-Bistagne, *Recherches* 7-27.

[42]Pickard-Cambridge, *Dramatic Festivals* 48.

[43]Pickard-Cambridge, *Dramatic Festivals* 48: *IG* ii² 3095, 3096 and 3098; on the known *choregoi* see Whitehead, *Demes of Attica* 217; Hagnias (of *IG* ii² 3098) was trierarch at least twice: Davies, *Propertied Families* 3-4.

[44]Whitehead, "Festival Liturgies" 213-20.

There is no firm evidence that the size of the comic chorus shrank from the twenty-four members common in the fifth century. Aristotle's remark that the same choristers could compose a tragic and comic chorus (*Politics* 3.3 1276b4) has been taken to mean that both choruses were fixed at the same number,[45] but it seems to me that Aristotle's point depends on a qualitative identity, not on numerical equality. A fragment of the *Orestautocleides* of Timocles (fr. 27 K.-A.) names eleven women who may constitute the chorus, but by itself this is no real indication that they represent the entire chorus or even a chorus at all.[46] We should also bear in mind that by Greek dramatic convention "a chorus of twelve (Aeschylus) can represent fifty daughters of Danaus, or a chorus of fifteen (Sophocles, Euripides) nine Muses or seven (or more accurately five) mothers of the Seven against Thebes."[47] A third-century inscription from Delphi mentions comic choruses with seven or eight members, but by then we are in a different world entirely.[48]

The fourth-century *choregia* (it has been thought) was becoming a hollow institution, carried on by mere inertia. It is true that times had changed and the *choregia* no longer meant what it had for the Athenian *polis*; during the radical democracy of the middle fifth century, satisfying aristocratic private *philotimia* and *euergesia* seems not to have been as important. And I concede that, although the simple mechanistic explanation for the decline of the chorus (that it waned as the *choregia* underwent a financial "crisis") is demonstrably wrong, it would be equally mechanistic to infer from the continuation of the *choregia* that the chorus' significance and role in drama did not alter. The remarkable thing about the fourth-century *choregia*, however, is that the institution was supported as vigorously as it

---

[45]Maidment, "Later Comic Chorus" 13.

[46]Maidment, "Later Comic Chorus" 13, thinks it a chorus, but see Hunter, "Comic Chorus." Interestingly the scholiast to *Knights* 589 claims that the comic chorus of twenty-four dancers had eleven women and thirteen men. The scholion is of highly dubious credibility, but if true, could the eleven in Timocles' fragment be the women of a twenty-four-member chorus? See Dearden, *Stage of Aristophanes* 106.

[47]Trendall and Webster, *Illustrations* 69.

[48]Sifakis, *Hellenistic Drama* 72-73, 113-35; Gentili, *Theatrical Performances* 22-25.

was. It cannot have been an anachronistic fossil from the standpoint of the audience at Athens. The chorus was alive and well, it was an entrenched fact of the Athenian festivals, and it was available. If comic playwrights decided to write plays whose plots depended on individual characters and excluded choruses from their action, that was a conscious choice on the part of the playwrights and not imposed by external circumstances.

Evidence for the Role of the Chorus in Comedy

In view of the fact that choruses were virtually being forced upon them, what use, if any, did comic playwrights put them to? This question can be addressed in several ways. By counting the number of lines spoken in the surviving plays we could chart an abrupt decline in the activity of the chorus. In the fifth-century *Acharnians* and *Birds*, for example, the chorus represents, respectively, 25% and 23% of each play. Even in the *Frogs* 23% was spoken by the chorus, but in the fourth-century *Ecclesiazusae* the role of the chorus accounts for only 8% of the play and in the *Plutus* the number drops to about 4%. In Menander the chorus has no role at all, save as a kind of *entr'acte*. The only clues to the existence of the chorus are the phrases χοροῦ μέλος (or simply χοροῦ) and characters who comment merely on the fact of the chorus's approach. At the end of the first act of the *Dyscolus* (lines 230-32), for example, Daos says that he sees some drunken worshippers of Pan coming near. Similar remarks are found in other plays.[49]

Yet these crude measurements can mislead. One of the reasons for the smaller role of the chorus in the *Ecclesiazusae* is that it has no *parabasis*, which in the fifth-century comedies accounts for as much as a quarter of the number of lines spoken by a chorus. In the opening three hundred lines of the *Ecclesiazusae* members of the female chorus carry on a spirited dialogue with Praxagora, reminiscent of comedies of the 420s. Conversely in the *Frogs* the actual level of interaction between chorus and actors can be reckoned to be qualitatively less than the numbers indicate;

---

[49]These only appear at the end of the first act; consult Gomme and Sandbach, *Menander* 172; Handley, *Dyskolos* 171-72.

the chorus acts more like passive spectators than active participants.⁵⁰ Therefore the gap separating the *Ecclesiazusae* and *Frogs* is perhaps less than appears when we take overall dramatic action into consideration. Although the level of interaction between actors and chorus is open to question, there can be no doubt that as a rule choruses appeared on stage in the fourth century.

Other indirect evidence reinforces this conclusion. The phrases χοροῦ μέλος or simply χοροῦ, which appear between "acts" in papyri of fourth-century comedy, generally (in my view) mark the location in fourth-century comedies of choral songs that were performed but unconnected with the action and felt by later editors to be expendable.⁵¹ (It is theoretically possible that the omitted choruses were not even written by the comic playwrights themselves. Nevertheless in third-century papyri we find that choruses have been cut from plays such as the *Bacchae*, whose choruses were surely written by Euripides, so the absence from papyri of choral lyrics proves nothing about their authorship.⁵²) The practice of writing choral songs that were not integrated into the plot of a play can, in part, be traced to the last decade or two of the fifth century, when Agathon is thought to have begun writing choral interludes, or *embolima*.⁵³ This lack of choral relevance is, of course, a phenomenon that has been detected in later plays of Euripides; and even earlier choruses, such as that of Euripides' *Suppliants* (of the 420's), have been accused of passivity.⁵⁴ Of course even a choral interlude that is not integrated into the action of the play at least has the positive

---

⁵⁰Zimmermann, *Untersuchungen* 134 and 252-53, sees the chorus more as spectators than as participants.

⁵¹For various views see Handley, "ΧΟΡΟΥ"; Beare, "A Reply" 49-52; Pöhlmann, "χοροῦ-Vermerke"; Perusino, *Dalla commedia antica* 68.

⁵²For the papyri, see Pöhlmann, "χοροῦ-Vermerke" 70-71.

⁵³Aristotle *Poetics* 1456a32. Agathon's death has been put at 401 BC by Lévêque, *Agathon* 73-77.

⁵⁴The ode to the Mountain Mother in *Helen* 1301-1368 is often said to have little connection to plot; on *Suppliants* see Dale, "Chorus in the Action" 210-20, esp. 211; Xanthakis-Karamanos, *Fourth-Century Tragedy* 9 and note 4. Of course Euripides' choruses have their defenders; on the Mountain Mother ode in *Helen* see Segal, "Two Worlds" 595-600.

function of structuring the play by giving weight to act-divisions.[55]

At the same time, there are hints that not all comic choral songs were expendable and that choral participation with the actors continued in the fourth century. Interaction between actors and chorus is non-existent in surviving Menander, but several fragments suggest that it cannot be excluded from other playwrights.[56] A fragment of the *Trophonius* of Alexis (fr. 239 K.-A.) makes sense if understood as spoken to a chorus: someone asks them to strip for dancing; the chorus is addressed in the second person plural.[57] This stands in sharp contrast to the *Dyscolus*, in which Daos made a loud point of clearing the stage, before the chorus entered, so as to avoid any interaction with them.[58] Two fragments from Eubulus—one from the *Anculion* (fr. 2 K.-A.) and one from the *Amaltheia* (fr. 7 K.-A.)—also seem to address a chorus directly, in preparation for dance.[59] A few fragments in lyric dactyls from Eubulus' *Stephanopolides* (fr. 102-103 K.-A.), a play evidently named for its chorus, seem to imply a conversation between the leader of the chorus and the actors.[60] Dialogue between actors and chorus is probable in Adesp. 239 Austin.[61] Aeschines, in his oration against Timarchus (1.157), mentions in passing that in a play at the rural Dionysia an actor had spoken in anapests directly to the chorus—clearly suggesting interaction. Less direct evidence is offered by Roman comedies

---

[55]Pöhlmann, "Funktion des Chors."

[56]See Hunter, "Comic Chorus." It is hard to improve on Hunter's collection of evidence, though Eubulus fr. 2 K.-A. might be given slightly more prominence; cf. Sifakis, "Aristotle, *N.E.* IV, 2" 423-24.

[57]See K.-A. II.155 for further bibliography.

[58]Sifakis, "Aristotle *N.E.* IV, 2" 421-22; Maidment, "Later Comic Chorus" 14.

[59]Hunter, *Eubulus, ad loc.*

[60]Hunter, *Eubulus* 191; Webster, *Later Greek Comedy* 62ff.; "remarkably parallel to the *Ecclesiazusae*" says Arnott, "Aristophanes to Menander" 67-68.

[61]Austin, *CGFP* 241, suggests that ἄνδρες (line 18 of Adesp. 239) may simply be an address to the audience; further examples of this use of ἄνδρες are collected in Bain, *Actors and Audience* 190-94. Nevertheless, notes Hunter, "The Comic Chorus" 37, most of these examples are in monologue and Adesp. 239 is in dialogue. Cecilia Ferrari, "Il frammento" thinks it addresses the chorus.

that are based on fourth-century Greek originals. In the *Rudens* of Plautus, in which a chorus of fishermen sing what we might call a *parodos*, the leader briefly converses with one of the actors (290-323). The *Rudens* is based on a comedy by Diphilus and it seems more likely that Plautus preserved the chorus from the original play than that he created one of his own.[62] The *Poenulus*, which is probably a reworking of the *Carthaginians* of Alexis, has a group of *advocati* who may reflect a chorus in the Greek original (578-614).[63]

Archaeological finds also point to continuity in the role of the chorus. Two fourth-century stone reliefs found in the Athenian *agora* depict contemporary comic choruses in performance.[64] Gregory Sifakis has pointed out that in one of these reliefs an actor appears to be participating with the chorus in dance and that this must represent the subject of the play, not an interlude.[65] It must also be relevant that depictions of choruses as illustrations of drama on dedications were eventually replaced by the depictions of masks—emblematic, perhaps, of a growing interest in actors—but this did not occur until the third quarter of the fourth century. One of the earliest instances is on a dedication from Aixone, probably from 340/39 BC, which has five masks in relief.[66]

It would be foolish to ignore the implications of evidence outside of Attica. Although travelling troupes of actors cannot be

---

[62]Jachmann, *Plautinisches und Attisches* 98-99 note 3.

[63]On the *Poenulus* and the *Carthaginians* of Alexis: Arnott, "Greek Original" 252-62; Flickinger, "ΧΟΡΟΥ in Terence" 26 note 2. Leo, *Plautinische Forschungen* 217 note 1, points also to the *lorarii* in the *Captivi* and the *Menaechmi*. Roman tragedy retained the chorus, even altering it to establish a closer relation between chorus and actors: see Capps, "Later Greek Drama" 298-300.

[64]Webster and Green, *Monuments* 118-19 AS 3-4; see Green, "Seeing and Depicting" 24.

[65]Sifakis, "Aristotle, E.N. IV, 2" 19. A recectly published vase of ca. 360 BC appears to show three members of the comic chorus dancing to an *auletes*: see Pingiatoglou, "Eine Komödiendarstellung."

[66]Webster and Green, *Monuments* 118, AS 2; though Pickard-Cambridge, *Dramatic Festivals* 49, thinks 313/12 BC a more likely date for the Aixone relief. In general see Green, "Dedications of Masks" 246, on the marked increase in masks in the third quarter of the fourth century; see also Green, *Theatre in Ancient Greek Society* 77.

expected to have maintained an extensive chorus, there is no reason to think that dramatic performances in the western Greek cities were slap-dash improvisations, even if the plays being performed were imported from Attica. Syracuse, for example, had a theater by the early fifth century. We know relatively little about festival arrangements, but on the face of it there is nothing to prevent an established theater in Magna Graecia from mounting a production with a full complement of twenty-four chorus members.[67] Taplin suggests that the recently published "Choregoi" vase, an Apulian bell-krater ca. 380 BC, represents a comic chorus. It shows two characters who are labelled "choregos"; these may be wealthy *choregoi* constituting a chorus in a comedy. One of them is speaking to an actor labelled "Aigisthos" and, significantly, both *choregoi* are standing not in the orchestra but on the stage, which seems to be raised up three steps.[68] Four other vases have identically dressed figures that may also represent choruses. Although none of these offers decisive evidence for choruses in comedy in the fourth century, "we have no direct evidence of any kind of drama in the west (or anywhere else) in the fourth century that did *not* have a chorus."[69]

We can also get a sense of the continuity of the choral tradition by looking at the problem from another angle: it may be that the shift from the fifth-century to the fourth-century chorus was not as abrupt as might be thought because we have overestimated its importance in the fifth century. Although the comedies of Aristophanes obviously constitute our most extensive evidence for fifth-century practice, his eleven surviving plays may have been preserved because of their political content, not because they were typical of Old Comedy in constructing and using the chorus.[70] Even within the Aristophanic corpus we can

---

[67]How many productions were held in "established" theaters we cannot say; a large number of vase-paintings depict stages that may be temporary: Trendall, "Farce and Tragedy" 162-63.

[68]Taplin, *Comic Angels* 55-63.

[69]Taplin, *Comic Angels* 56; for the identically dressed figures see pp. 75-77.

[70]Handley, *Oxyrhynchus Papyri* 81-82 and 85-86, on P. Oxy. 3540, a fragment that he identifies (hesitantly) as the prologue to the *Thesmophoriazusae II* (407/6 BC). See also Handley, "Comedy" 391-406; Sutton, "Transition to Middle Comedy" 94-95.

see experimentation and a loosening of the old structures of the chorus from the time of the *Birds* on. The *Lysistrata*, for example, has two choruses and the *parabasis* is merged into the plot.[71] Moreover the *Frogs*, by having an animal chorus that may have begun to seem old-fashioned by the end of the fifth-century and by using the *parabasis* in ways not seen since the plays of the 420's, was possibly seen as archaizing and retrospective.[72] Aristotle reported that at Athens Crates (active ca. 450-430 BC) was the first to relinquish the lampoon (ἰαμβικὴ ἰδέα) and compose "plots of general interest" (καθόλου ποιεῖν λόγους καὶ μύθους, *Poetics* 1449b8-9), thereby following the lead of Epicharmus and anticipating the attention to plot that we associate with New Comedy.[73] Needless to say even a comedy with a "plot of general interest" could put a chorus to good use, but it is less likely to need a *parabasis* if it lacks the ἰαμβικὴ ἰδέα. By one estimate just under half of the dated plays in the last two decades of the fifth century involved mythological parody,[74] which presupposes a structured plot. In this connection we should consider the testimony of Platonius, who said that the *Odysses* of Cratinus (a mythological parody of 439-437 BC),[75] like the *Aiolosikon* of Aristophanes, had neither choral songs nor a *parabasis*. This cannot be literally true, because (to reemphasize a point I have made above) the grant of a chorus was the institutional precondition for performance at a festival.[76] And some fragments of the *Odysses* do seem to be from a chorus,

---

[71]For a recent study see Hubbard, *Mask of Comedy* 182-95; McEvilley, "Development."

[72]Hubbard, *Mask of Comedy* 157-58, 200, and 201 note 123. But even here we cannot be sure that the animal chorus had entirely seen its day: Archippus' *Fishes* seems to have been written after the end of the Peloponnesian War: see Archippus fr. 27 K.-A.

[73]Clearly *Thesmophoriazusae II* (ca. 407/6 BC) had a *parabasis* (see Deichgräber, *Parabasenverse*; cf. fr. 346 K.-A.), but if it began with a prologue spoken by a divinity, then Aristophanes had introduced into comedy a key characteristic of New Comedy before the century was out.

[74]Webster, "Chronological Notes" 23.

[75]Geissler, *Chronologie* 20; the play seems to have been performed at the time of the decree of Morychides, which would limit personal attacks but there is no necessary reason why this would affect the chorus. Diminution of the chorus could be due to artistic considerations.

[76]The point was made by Kaibel, "Kratinos' ΟΔΥΣΣΗΣ" 75.

though it may be that the chorus' role did not extend beyond the *parodos*.[77] (In the fourth century, too, the chorus seems to have made its deepest impression in the *parodos* and Sifakis has argued that it is the *parodos* that is depicted on the two fourth-century stone reliefs from the *agora*.)[78] Yet the existence of a comedy with a peripheral chorus that was performed well before Aristophanes even began his career raises a serious question: Was the chorus always "the heart and soul of Old Comedy"?[79] It may be that comedy with little role for the chorus was a tradition of long standing—a tradition obscured by the surviving political plays of Aristophanes.

Conclusion

I conclude by trying to reconstruct the evolution of the chorus in the fifth and fourth centuries BC. There is a very real possibility that, decades before Aristophanes' *Ecclesiazusae* and *Plutus*, there was a tradition of comedy in which choruses were limited to the *parodos*. If Platonius was even partly correct about Cratinus' *Odysses*, action in non-Aristophanic comedy could have been left to the principal actors for some time. Furthermore, the evidence we reviewed above indicates that in at least some comedies the chorus remained a presence well into the fourth century and continued a modest level of interaction with the actors. Admittedly we cannot be confident that these choruses performed lyric songs of high quality, but at least a good deal of fourth-century comedy may have more resembled the *Ecclesiazusae* and *Plutus* than the *Dyscolus*. Menander did not incorporate the chorus into the action, but we cannot be certain that other fourth-century playwrights made the same choice. In any event I do *not* think that the defeat of 404 BC was the decisive

---

[77]That the role is limited to the *parodos* is suggested by Perusino, *Dalla commedia antica* 83; but see Bertan, "*Odyssês* di Cratino" 173-74. Cf. Hubbard, *Mask of Comedy* 24; Nesselrath, *Mittlere Komödie* 33. Händel, *Formen* 130, entertains the possibility that there were other plays with little choral involvement.

[78]Sifakis, "Aristotle, *E.N.* IV, 2" 416-17; Hubbard, *Mask of Comedy* 27, suggests that the *parados*, not the *parabasis*, was once the place for choral self-presentation. The *parodos* was the one choral form retained (p. 247).

[79]As Capps, "Later Greek Drama" 304, characterizes the chorus.

turning point it has been made out to be. In fact, the very notion of a "turning point" may not be helpful: we are dealing with trends that evolved over decades, with traditions (e.g. political satire, mythological parody, "plots of general interest") that existed side by side for generations, and with poets who wrote comedies that, should they ever be discovered, might defy categorization and surprise us with their versatility. Let me suggest, however, that if we must have turning points they came both earlier and later than 404 BC.

Of course the later turning point is a familiar one: the suspension of the democracy in 322/21. Menander's first play was in 321 and the *choregia* as we know it was eliminated after 317; I do not doubt that in these years there were profound changes in social attitudes and dramatic production. It is in this period that the chorus and actors were probably separated from one another by a high stage.[80] Although Menandrean comedy still had a chorus, evidence for interaction between actors and chorus largely disappears.

The earlier turning point would be the years around 411 BC. Politically this was an era of upheaval: the destruction of the Sicilian expedition, the occupation of Decelea, the oligarchic seizure power in 411, and the restoration of the democracy. In fact J. K. Davies treated the period 412-380 as a single unit, with 404 as simply one event in a thirty-year period of Spartan supremacy.[81] In comedy we see experimentation with the chorus on the part of Aristophanes from the time of the *Birds* (414 BC). It must have been in this period that Agathon, whose first victory was in 416 and who was so prominent in the *Thesmophoriazusae*, began to use *embolima*. Euripides seems to have recourse to these in the *Helen* and *Iphigeneia in Tauris*. Accordingly, the frog chorus of the *Frogs* may have been artistically *retardataire* by 405. The role of the chorus in comedy was surely being re-thought for some time *before* the defeat in 404 BC.

R. L. Hunter has judiciously warned that "In many matters connected with the chorus we must be content with an honest

---

[80]Pickard-Cambridge, *Theater of Dionysus* 156-68; Slater, "Transformations of Space" 5; Townsend, "Fourth-Century Skene" 435.

[81]Davies, *Democracy* 129-64; Nesselrath, *Mittlere Komödie* 334, likewise thinks that Old Comedy began to evolve more quickly after 411. See also Segal, "The φύσις of Comedy" 129-36.

profession of ignorance."[82] Nevertheless, I think we can at least sort out what is more probable from what is less probable. The trends that we find in the fourth century have precedents in the fifth, and the diminished role of the chorus may be one of these. But the stability of the *choregia* and the continuity of the chorus are factors that we neglect at great risk. The gulf separating the fifth from the fourth centuries was certainly not a vast and precipitous one.

---

[82] Hunter, "Comic Chorus" 23.

Plato Comicus and the Evolution of Greek Comedy

Ralph M. Rosen

In tracing the formal changes in comic drama from the fifth to the fourth centuries, it is common to point to such things as the waning role of the chorus and parabasis, an increasing subordination of lyric elements, and a tendency towards more coherent, unified plots.[1] But changes in subject matter, topoi, themes and tone are more difficult to ascertain, especially in light of the wholly fragmentary nature of the comedy that survives from the period between Aristophanes and Menander. Handbooks tell us that along with the decline of the Athenian polis at the end of the fifth century, such hallmarks of Old Comedy as personal invective, obscene language and political satire also disappeared. But such generalizations obviously stem from the careless assumption that fourth-century comedy must have been more like Menander than Aristophanes. In fact, when one looks at the comic fragments from the middle decades of the fourth century, it is striking just how many elements normally associated with Old Comedy appear.[2] Still, however artificial and imprecise the labels we assign to literary movements may be, most scholars would agree that they remain constructs useful for organizing the undifferentiated material history leaves us.

In the case of Greek comedy the general division between the "Old" and the "New" began at least as early as Aristotle, who could speak at *Eth. Nic.* 1128a22 of παλαιά and καινή comedy.

[1] See, for example, Norwood, *Greek Comedy* 58-60, and Schmid-Stählin, *Geschichte* 450-52.

[2] Hunter, *Eubulus* 20-30, in his concise survey of the characteristics of Middle Comedy, makes it clear that some of the crucial features of Old Comedy, e.g. political satire, tragic parody, and mythological burlesque (see below, pp. 123-26), did not suddenly disappear in the fourth century.

Exactly which poets Aristotle would include under these rubrics remains uncertain, especially since it is likely that he considered at least some of Aristophanes' plays to be "new" and it was only at the end of Aristotle's lifetime that the chief representative of our so-called "New Comedy," Menander, began his rise to prominence.[3] The tripartite division of comedy as we know it (Old: to the death of Aristophanes; Middle: early fourth century to Menander; New: Menander and beyond) probably originated in Hellenistic scholarship, but even so, as Heinz-Günther Nesselrath has meticulously discussed in his recent book on Middle Comedy, there was often considerable disagreement in antiquity about which poets belonged to what period.[4]

I would like to address here one of these disagreements, namely the question of whether the playwright Plato Comicus (hereafter simply "Plato") belonged, as a few ancient commentators have claimed, in any meaningful sense to Middle Comedy. The question, I believe, is more than just a trivial quibble about the category of literary history to which we should assign Plato. I am, in fact, less interested in what we choose to call Plato than in the nature of his poetic production and its relationship to subsequent comic drama. Focusing on Plato in this way enriches our conception of comic trends in late fifth-century Athens, a conception which is too often skewed by inferences drawn solely from the extant plays of Aristophanes. Now that Nesselrath has so thoroughly examined the history and descriptive validity of Middle Comedy as a literary-critical construct, we are well positioned to reconsider whether Plato fits squarely into the mainstream of Old Comedy, or whether he anticipated to a significant degree trends in comedy that we associate with fourth-century Middle Comedy.

---

[3]Cf. Janko, *Aristotle on Comedy* 244-49, who argues that a tripartite division of comedy existed before Menander, but that with Menander's rising fame the earlier system was reformulated to make him the representative of "new" comedy. Cf. also Nesselrath, *Mittlere Komödie* 44-45, 145-49. Nesselrath argues against Janko's position that the tenth-century *Tractatus Coislinianus* (which speaks clearly of a tripartite division of comedy) ultimately descends from Aristotle's *Poetics*.

[4]Nesselrath, *Mittlere Komödie* 45, note 39 and, in general, 1-187. For a survey of the history of modern scholarship on the concept of a "middle" comedy, cf. pp. 1-29.

From a strictly chronological point of view, of course, there can be little doubt that Plato belonged to Old Comedy. His career began in the middle of the fifth century and continued until at least the 380's, roughly paralleling the career of Aristophanes. Yet Plato has frequently been regarded as a transitional figure in the development of Greek comedy from Old to New. Some nineteenth-century scholars such as Cobet and Wilamowitz,[5] influenced by certain ancient testimonia, went so far as to proclaim Plato the inventor of Middle Comedy. Norwood even posited the notion of a distinct fifth-century school of comedy (with Crates as its putative leader) which had, he believed, affinities with Middle Comedy.[6]

Nesselrath is aware, of course, as he shows so clearly in the first half of his book, that one can define "Middle" so as to include just about anyone, as some of the scholiasts seemed to do. He has demonstrated in fact how the meaning of "Old," "Middle," and "New" tended to vary according to whatever generic teleology a commentator had in mind for comedy. Thus, for example, when a scholiast on Dionysius Thrax held that Cratinus was a quintessential representative of Old Comedy, that Aristophanes and Eupolis belonged partly to the Old, partly to the Middle, Plato to the Middle, and Menander to the New Comedy, it is

---

[5]Cobet, *Observationes*. Wilamowitz, *Thukydideslegende* 326-67 = [1969, 31]. Cf. also Oppé, *New Comedy* 42. On the development of Wilamowitz's views about Greek comedy and on his evaluation of Plato in particular, cf. Nesselrath, *Mittlere Komödie* 12-17, 34-35.

[6]Norwood *Greek Comedy* 145-77. The idea that Crates represented some sort of alternative or transitional form of Old Comedy derives, of course, from Aristotle's laconic remarks about him in *Poetics* 1449b7-9, in which he claims that Crates was the first one among the Athenians to "abandon the iambic form" (ἀφέμενος τῆς ἰαμβικῆς ἰδέας) and to "construct generalized plots" (καθόλου ποιεῖν λόγους καὶ μύθους). As reliable literary history, Aristotle's statements about Crates are problematic and hardly authorize us to posit a distinct Cratetan "school" (cf. Rosen, *Iambographic Tradition* 4, note 17; Hubbard, *Mask of Comedy* 24, note 42; Hubbard's view that "iambic form" actually refers to a loose type of plot structure is close to that of Heath, *Aristophanes and his Rivals* 143-44); on the other hand, there may very well have been differences between Crates and poets such as Aristophanes and Cratinus which anticipated literary norms more commonly associated with the fourth century. Cf. also Bonanno, *Studi su Cratete* 51-54.

because his definition of the terms turned on the amount of invective found in a play.⁷ So even though Plato had not abandoned personal abuse, we can understand how a commentator might have wished to distinguish him from his more acerbic contemporaries by placing him in a different category. Nesselrath, however, reminds us that this "Middle" Comedy is not the same as the "real" Middle Comedy, which he would have begin rather strictly around 380 BC.⁸

Nesselrath's mission of staking out the territory of the "real" Middle Comedy, however, does have the distinct disadvantage of obscuring any notions of Greek comedy as a developing organism. The nature of his task demands, of course, that he focus on what are specific, essential features of Middle Comedy rather than on its similarities with earlier comic trends, but we must at the same time avoid conceiving too rigidly of the tripartite division of Greek comedy. It is inevitable that the stricter we are about delimiting boundaries between literary periods and genres, the more likely we are to emphasize the criteria by which we *exclude* works from a given category. Nesselrath's study demonstrates well the virtues and the pitfalls of conceptualizing literary history in this way: we end up with perhaps as clear a picture as the evidence allows of what fourth-century comedy looked like, and we are given good reasons for using the term "Middle Comedy" to describe it. But discussing *similarities* between literary works of different periods tends to make generic categorizations less tidy, and so Nesselrath, no doubt unconsciously, occasionally privileges differences between periods in trying to articulate clearly the rationale for his tripartite division of comedy. In the case of Plato, as I noted above, there was something about his comedy that could lead a

---

⁷Cf. especially Nesselrath, *Mittlere Komödie* 36-39. The scholiast on Dionysius Thrax (XVIIIa Koster = test. 16 K.-A.) calls Plato a "distinguished" (ἐπίσημος; we might say "remarkable") example of Middle Comedy.

⁸Cf. in particular Nesselrath's epilogue (*Mittlere Komödie* 331-45). A first-century BC statue base from Ostia evidently accompanied a bust of Plato, and refers to him as the "poet of Old Comedy" Πλάτων ὁ τῆς ἀρχαίας / κωμῳ⟨ι⟩δίας ποιητής (= test. 18 K.-A.). This suggests at least that, outside of scholarly circles, Plato's status as a poet of Old Comedy was reasonably secure in antiquity.

commentator to consider aspects of his work qualitatively different from that of his contemporaries, and perhaps somewhat ahead of his time. Fragmentary as the evidence is, I believe that those commentators who claimed that Plato was a poet of Middle Comedy, however hyperbolically and however erroneously from a chronological point of view, correctly sensed that he played a pivotal role in the gradual evolution of Greek comedy from the Old to Middle to New.

One type of comedy that has often been seen to link Old and Middle Comedy is the mythological parody, typically a play taking its plot from a well known myth and offering a send-up version of the original. Such plays were common enough within the mainstream of Old Comedy (Nesselrath calculates a fourth or fifth of Aristophanes' plays to be of this sort, and nearly a third of Cratinus'),[9] though typically Old Comedy was characterized more as a genre of personal abuse and politically engaged satire. For whatever reasons, mythological parody became very popular in Middle Comedy, and, as Nesselrath has shown, seems to have taken on a character in this period somewhat different from that of the previous century. Nesselrath points in particular to the tendency to "rationalize" the myths more, to integrate them more seamlessly into scenes of everyday life, and to downplay explicit political satire.[10] The poets of Old Comedy, by contrast, Nesselrath argues, tended to distort the original versions more, focusing on comically absurd aspects of the myths and engaging in transparent political innuendo.

Plato's own apparent penchant for mythological parody (roughly a third of his known plays seem to fall into this category) certainly inspired a number of scholars over a century ago to credit the testimonia that claimed him as a poet of Middle Comedy.[11] Nesselrath has corrected this overstatement based on the chronological parameters that he posits, but he does not examine in great detail what it is about the nature of Plato's mythological plays that might have led ancient (and then modern) commentators to conceptualize him in this way. But let us ignore

[9]Nesselrath, *Mittlere Komödie* 204.
[10]Nesselrath, *Mittlere Komödie* 204-41, especially 239-41. See also Hunter, *Eubulus* 24.
[11]Cf. above, note 5.

mere labels for the moment and consider a few examples from Plato's mythological plays which, I believe, ally him in spirit at least with comic poets of the next generation.

Two mythological subjects in particular seemed to attract Plato, as they did many poets of Middle and New Comedy: the amorous escapades of Zeus and the life and character of Heracles. One play of his, in fact, Νὺξ Μακρά (*Long Night*), combined both subjects. This play is likely to have dealt with the conception and birth of Heracles, where "long night" referred to Zeus (disguised as Amphitryo) sleeping with Alcmene.[12] Only six meager fragments survive (fr. 89-94 K.-A.), but several of the fragments seem to come from the prologue and suggest that the play followed a traditional plot that stressed the domestic relations between Alcmene and Amphitryo, much as we find in the later Plautine version. Others have argued on the basis of Plautus' *Amphitryo* 142-145[13] that Plato fr. 90 K.-A. may be spoken by Hermes, as he tells the audience what to look for in the actors' costumes in order to distinguish between the real Amphitryo and the disguised Zeus: "he will hold a two-wicked lamp here over the tops of / his temples" (ἐνταῦθ' ἐπ' ἄκρων τῶν κροτάφων ἕξει λύχνον / δίμυξον). Fr. 93 K.-A., too, foreshadows Plautus' Mercury in 474-475: "Then, with just a few brief words, they will become reconciled" (*denique Alcumenam Iuppiter / rediget antiquam coniugi in concordiam*). Another fragment (fr. 89 K.-A.), unplaced in the play, most likely comes from a speech by Alcmene:[14] "but again, it's absurd <to suppose that> my husband / didn't give me a thought" (ἀλλ' αὖ γελοῖον ἄνδρα μου μὴ φροντίσαι / μηδέν). This is not, of course, a great deal to go on, but the fragments draw us forward in time to later Greek comedy and to Roman comedy in their suggestion that the play highlighted the domestic ramifications of a divine intervention.

Nesselrath's observation that Middle Comedy often invested traditional myths with domestic coloration typical of the fourth century holds also for several other plays of Plato. The after-dinner game of kottabos, for example, in which contestants

---

[12] The connection was first made by Casaubon, *Animadversionum* 213.29 in reference to Athenaeus 110d (= Plato fr. 92 K.-A.).

[13] Cf. Frantz, *De comoediae* 40.

[14] A suggestion of Kassel-Austin, based on fr. 93: ἥξειν ἀποφλεγμήναντας εἰς διαλλαγάς.

would try to dislodge little disks from a shaft by hurling wine drops at them (or in another version would try to sink saucers floating in a basin, as in Cratinus fr. 124 K.-A.) was especially common in Middle Comedy. While allusions to the game can be found in Old Comedy (Cratinus and Ameipsias, among others),[15] it is noteworthy that the references in Plato are set apart from these not so much in their details, as in their self-conscious, self-contained treatment, a feature that clearly foreshadows Middle Comedy.

In a fragment of Ζεὺς Κακούμενος (46 K.-A. *Zeus Afflicted*) Plato has a scene in which Heracles is about to play the kottabos game. The fragment opens with an interlocutor addressing two characters, one of whom is Heracles: "... you two play at the kottabos game until I've / fixed some dinner for you inside" (πρὸς κότταβον παίζειν, ἕως ἂν σφῷν ἐγὼ / τὸ δεῖπνον ἔνδον σκευάσω, 1-2). These lines imply that the audience will actually witness a game on stage, introducing no doubt a rather trivial, whimsical scene that places the hero in a banal, domestic setting. A discussion follows about what the kottabos-prizes ought to be, in which Heracles suggests that they play for kisses—again reflecting a fourth-century interest in amorous themes: (Heracles) "Fine, bring the mortar, fetch some water, put out / the wine-cups! And let's play for kisses!" (φέρε τὴν θυείαν, αἶρ' ὕδωρ, ποτήρια / παράθετε. παίζωμεν δὲ περὶ φιλημάτων, 4-5). Evidently, there followed an exchange in which someone (perhaps Heracles and his partner) received instruction on how to play the game properly (fr. 47 K.-A.): "...it's quite essential for you to bend back / your hand and throw the kottabos smoothly" (...ἀγκυλοῦντα δεῖ σφόδρα / τὴν χεῖρα πέμπειν εὐρύθμως τὸν κότταβον).

In another play (*Spartans* or *Poets*) we find a fragment (71 K.-A.) that distinctly foreshadows the detailed interplay between two slaves in later Greco-Roman comedy as they comment on the domestic activities of their superiors and which also features the kottabos. In the first part of the fragment, in which the slaves are discussing their duties in managing the banquet underway within the house, Slave (A) mentions that he will bring out the kottabos

---

[15] On the game of kottabos cf. Sartori, *Das Kottabos-Spiel* and Sparkes, "Kottabos" 202-6.

after the libations have been poured. In the second part, one of the slaves has evidently returned from within and describes the progress of the activities: "The libation has now been made, and they're far along in their drinking / the drinking-song has been sung, and the kottabos has been brought outside..." [16] (σπονδὴ μὲν ἤδη γέγονε καὶ πίνοντές εἰσι πόρρω, / καὶ σκόλιον ᾖισται, κότταβος δ' ἐξοίχεται θύραζε, 10-11). After three more lines, the citation breaks off, and Athenaeus says: "After these lines, I think, there was a discussion of the kottabos and its players [ἀποκοτταβίζοντες]." If we can trust Athenaeus' memory on this point, the slaves must have continued at length about the details of the game.

Both scenes in Plato are reminiscent of a similar one in the middle comic Antiphanes' Ἀφροδίτης Γοναί. Fr. 57 K.-A. of this play offers in 20 verses an elaborate set of instructions on the kottabos to an apparent novice: "I will teach you step by step..." declares one character to the other; at line 15 the instructor says, "you have to curve the fingers crab-like as if to play the aulos, pour out some wine—not too much—and then hurl" (αὐλητικῶς δεῖ καρκινοῦν τοὺς δακτύλους / οἶνόν τε μικρὸν ἐγχέαι καὶ μὴ πολύν· / ἔπειτ' ἀφήσεις). Eubulus, one of the best known poets of Middle Comedy, has a flying character in his *Bellerophon* (probably Bellerophon himself) compare himself to a tall kottabos shaft (fr. 15 K.-A.),[17] and, as I have argued elsewhere, it even seems likely that his play entitled *Ankylion* featured a character whose name reflected the bend in the wrist necessary for a successful kottabos toss.[18] Nesselrath himself has noted that the peculiar interest in the kottabos game in Middle Comedy reflected the trend toward incorporating local *Realien* into plots in general, and, more specifically, into the treatment of traditionally elevated mythological figures.[19] Plato's own references to the kottabos, I would add, herald this trend.

[16]The meaning of ἐξοίχεται is uncertain; it may mean that the kottabos apparatus has been "put away" (as we might say, "it's gone out of sight") rather than "brought outside."

[17]On this fragment cf. Hunter, *Eubulus* 108-9.

[18]Cf. Rosen, "Euboulos' *Ankylion*." For another explanation of ἀγκυλέω as it relates to the kottabos, cf. Borthwick, "Gymnasium of Bromius."

[19]Nesselrath, *Mittlere Komödie* 234.

The strongly demarcated lines between the mythological parody of Old and Middle Comedy that Nesselrath argues for, as we have seen, begin to blur somewhat in the case of Plato. But Plato is not the only fifth-century comic poet whose particular brand of mythological comedy prompted ancient commentators to reconsider how to categorize his oeuvre, despite the pressures of chronology. Cratinus too, whose reputation was fading as Aristophanes' was cresting,[20] composed a number of mythological comedies, one of which, *Odysses*, Platonius (*De diff. com.* [I] 4.29ff Koster = *PCG* IV p. 192), classified as a "Middle" comedy (τύπος τῆς μέσης κωμῳδίας), like Aristophanes' *Aiolosikon*.[21] Nesselrath in particular gives little credence to Platonius' testimony, and it is not difficult to see why. Platonius seems confused about the chronology of Cratinus, implying that *Odysses* was composed near the end of the fifth century;[22] his remark that *Odysses* had no choral lyrics is evidently contradicted by some of the fragments.[23] Still, it does not seem to follow from Platonius' inaccuracies, as Nesselrath argues, that he had no knowledge of any comedies or playwrights between Aristophanes and Menander which could serve in his own mind as representatives of Middle Comedy.[24] Nor is it entirely clear to me, even if Nesselrath were correct on this point, why he would then conclude that Platonius' ignorance of comedy between Aristophanes and Menander would necessarily lead him to date Cratinus' *Odysses* (along with Aristophanes' *Aiolosikon*) to the end of Old Comedy.[25] Indeed, Perusino had cautioned earlier that simply because Platonius' chronology is misguided need not lead

---

[20]Even allowing for comic exaggeration and conventions of rivalry among poets, Aristophanes implies as much in *Knights* 526-536 and *Peace* 700-703 (which would have us believe that Cratinus was even dead by the time of the production of *Peace*, though this has often been suspected; cf. Platnauer, *Peace* 127-28.)

[21]Scholars have quibbled over whether Platonius, in referring to Cratinus' *Odysses* as a τύπος of Middle Comedy, implies that the play in fact was a representative of the genre, or merely "like" a comedy of the middle period. Cf. Bertan, "Gli *Odyssês*" 171-78, Perusino, *Dalla commedia antica* 83; Nesselrath, *Mittlere Komödie* 33, note 15.

[22]Nesselrath, *Mittlere Komödie* 33, note 16.

[23]See Norwood, *Greek Comedy* 129, note 3 (citing Körte, *RE* 22.1653).

[24]Nesselrath, *Mittlere Komödie* 33.

[25]Nesselrath, *Mittlere Komödie* 33.

us to reject his entire testimony.[26] Perusino herself attempts to explain Platonius' remarks about the lack of choral parts in *Odysses* as follows: "dal momento che gli *Odissei* sono inseriti tra *Eolosicone* di Aristofane, che sopra è stato definito 'privo di canto corali,' e 'moltissime commedie antiche che non hanno né canti corali né parabasi,' le stesse caratteristiche debbono essere attribuite anche al dramma di Cratino." Perusino suggests, therefore, a diminished role of the chorus in *Odysses*, not a total absence, and finds it likely that the chorus' main impact occurred during the parodos.[27]

Nesselrath is understandably uncomfortable with what can only remain speculation on Perusino's part, given the lack of further evidence, but Perusino's willingness to give Platonius' testimony some credence, I believe, is appropriate. As I have stressed in the case of the problematic testimony about Plato's status as a potential forerunner of Middle Comedy, we can only assume that the ancient commentators who sensed features of Middle Comedy in obviously fifth-century poets must have been responding to some literary idiosyncrasies or anachronisms in the texts that they had at hand. Nesselrath would conclude from the various demonstrable errors in the testimonia that *all* their remarks must be tainted. But it seems just as likely that such inaccuracies may originate, as Perusino implies, in the commentators' zeal to account for very real elements in Old Comedy that seemed somewhat alien to their own conception of what Old Comedy was supposed to be.[28] This does not mean that any fifth-century play "was" in any technical sense an example of

---

[26]Perusino, *Dalla commedia antica* 81.
[27]Perusino, *Dalla commedia antica* 83.
[28]Platonius also mentions, for example, that *Odysses* contained no personal abuse—a mark of Middle Comedy, to his thinking—but rather travesty of the *Odyssey* (οἱ γοῦν Ὀδυσσεῖς Κρατίνου οὐδενὸς ἐπιτίμησιν ἔχουσι, διασυρμὸν δὲ τῆς Ὀδυσσείας τοῦ Ὁμήρου, *De diff. com.* [I] 5.51-52 Koster = Cratinus, *PCG IV* p. 192). This remark occurs right after he appears to misdate the play to the late fifth century. Do we repudiate his observation about the lack of personal abuse simply because he misdates the play? I should think, again, that a true observation that the play seemed surprisingly free of invective for a work of Old Comedy, could easily and (forgivably) account for a desire to date it as late as possible.

Middle Comedy, but it may very well reveal distinct steps in a continuous development of Greek comic drama.

Nesselrath is, however, willing to give Platonius a hypothetical benefit of the doubt, when he carefully discusses the fragments of *Odysses* to see whether the commentator, in spite of himself, might have been right to identify anachronistic elements in the play. Nesselrath's treatment of this subject follows his painstaking analysis of mythological burlesque in the fragments of Middle Comedy, about which he concludes that such plays

> ...neigen dazu, die märchenhaften Züge zu rationalisieren und so das ehemals Wundersame weitgehend zu eliminieren, und sie durchsetzen den Mythos stark mit Elementen aus dem zeitgenössischen attischen Leben; dabei entstehen Situationen und Konstellationen, die denen späterer Nea-Komödien weitgehend gleichen, nur dass die Figuren nicht die Namen athenischer Bürger, sondern die mythischer Götter und Helden tragen.[29]

When he examines the fragments of Cratinus' *Odysses*, however, he observes that the treatment of the myth offers no "vestiges of rationalizing or the downplaying of Odysseus' adventure with the Cyclops, or any attempt at all to give the scene an Attic ambience in any form," and he concludes that "in the treatment of myth [in *Odysses*] so many clear differences appear that Middle Comedy—at least on this issue—cannot be considered a real continuation of Old Comedy."[30]

While Nesselrath has been able to isolate superbly many salient features of the mythological plots of Middle Comedy, it seems to me that he is too hasty and categorical in reaching his conclusions about their relationship with earlier comedy. For one thing, in the case of *Odysses* we are dealing with a deplorably small amount of evidence. Kassel-Austin collects some fifteen

---

[29]Nesselrath, *Mittlere Komödie* 236.

[30]Nesselrath, *Mittlere Komödie* 239. Nesselrath notes as well that another type of mythological comedy can be seen in Cratinus' *Dionysalexandros*, though this too, with its political allegory and focus on the parody of a myth, is similarly unlike anything he has detected for Middle Comedy. But see my reservations about how useful such observations can be for assessing the essential nature of comedies that are known to us only in a few fragments, p. 131 below.

fragments, which offer barely twenty-five disconnected verses. Nesselrath is probably right to conclude from the fragments that Cratinus maintained the same basic portrait of Polyphemus in the play and the same general setting that we find in the Homeric version of the story,[31] and on these points there can be little doubt that the play was very much in the tradition of Old Comedy. But the handful of scattered lines in the play hardly allows us to make any real judgments about its details or generic character. It may be true that the treatment of the Cyclops in the play was essentially Homeric in its plot, and that the play's humor depended heavily on a point-by-point distortion of the Homeric narrative, but any number of individual episodes within this structure—all now lost to us—could have afforded opportunities for the poet to craft a mythological comedy that anticipated in any number of ways the sort of rationalizing and domesticization that Nesselrath regards as a defining feature of mythological comedy in the Middle period.[32] Nesselrath, therefore, ultimately

---

[31] Nesselrath, *Mittlere Komödie* 239.

[32] Fr. 150 K.-A. may provide an example of a theme that underwent further development in later Greek comedy. Here the Cyclops threatens to cook up Odysseus' companions and eat them (lines 2-5):

φρύξας χάψησας κάπανθρακίσας κωπτήσας,
εἰς ἅλμην τε καὶ ὀξάλμην κᾆτ' ἐς σκοροδάλμην
χλιαρὸν ἐμβάπτων, ὃς ἂν ὀπτότατός μοι ἁπάντων
ὑμῶν φαίνηται, κατατρώξομαι, ὦ στρατιῶται

Obviously the notion that the Cyclops would actually take the trouble of cooking the men before devouring them is a comic emendation of the Odyssean version (in which he ate them raw), and the culinary details he offers—he mentions roasting, baking, grilling and several forms of pickling—are very much in keeping with similar jokes elsewhere in Old Comedy. But cooks and cooking became quite popular and highly developed motifs in Middle Comedy, especially in connection with dithyrambic "parody" (see below, pp. 132-35), as Nesselrath shows in his lucid treatment of the subject (*Mittlere Komödie* 297-309; see also the essay of Dobrov and Urios-Aparisi below). Although Nesselrath, *Mittlere Komödie* 297, note 31 (citing with approval A. Giannini, *La figura del cuoco nella commedia greca* [Acme, 1960] and H. Dohm, *Mageiros. Die Rolle des Kochs in der griechisch-römischen Komödie* [München, 1964]) observes that in earlier comedy we cannot really speak of the μάγειρος as a distinct comic "type," he does not pursue the matter. But a scene in

seems to repudiate Platonius' testimony on the basis of *argumentum ex silentio*: nothing in the fragments of *Odysses* looks like Middle Comedy; therefore Platonius, in addition to his chronological errors, must also have been wrong to characterize the play as representing a τύπος τῆς μέσης κωμῳδίας.

In attempting to soften the rigid division Nesselrath posits between Old and Middle Comedy, I am not suggesting that we conceptualize Old Comedy differently than we are used to. Changes in cultural norms, political climate, and theatrical conditions certainly conspire to effect literary evolution, and such changes no doubt account for the fact that a comedy from the middle of the fourth century looked quite different from one of Aristophanes' fifth-century plays. I am not convinced, however, that there is enough evidence to conclude, along with Nesselrath, that the mythological comedy we know of from Old Comedy must have had such a completely different φύσις from that of its fourth-century incarnations that we must regard them as virtually unrelated literary phenomena. Plato, at any rate, as I have argued, has given us some cause to imagine a real transition from the mythological comedy of the fifth century to that of the fourth, and I strongly suspect that if we had a better sampling of other mythological comedies of Old Comedy, including Cratinus, we would find even more affinities between the two periods that would make the task of assigning even approximate dates to the transition between them even more problematic.

So far our discussion has focused on Plato's mythological comedy and whether it might help us chart the evolution of comedy from the Old to the Middle periods. This question is easily framed (if less easily answered) mainly because this comic sub-genre was extremely popular in Old and Middle Comedy

---

Cratinus' *Odysses* featuring Polyphemus calling attention to his cooking skills might easily have been developed in a direction that anticipated the cook's "role" in Middle Comedy. My point is not that we must assume that Polyphemus as cook was an important and well articulated theme of *Odysses*, but simply that our evidence from the fragments of Old Comedy is truly too insubstantial to allow us to draw major conclusions about the genre based on what is *not* to be found in them. And when such a line of argument leads scholars to condemn ancient testimonia that offer something *positive* for a change, such as Platonius, it would appear that we need to rethink that particular point anew.

alike. But this is not the only area in which Plato appears as the transitional figure for which some of his commentators have argued. Two of our longest fragments of Plato Comicus, both from his *Phaon*, also suggest other connections with later comedy and deserve our attention. This play treated the myth of Phaon, the ferryman of Lesbos, who was rewarded by Aphrodite with a magical ointment for carrying her—disguised as an old woman—free of charge to the mainland. The ointment, of course, once applied daily, caused all the women to fall in love with Phaon. The fragments, I believe, clearly point to a transitional play, and not surprisingly we can even assign a rather late date to it (391 BC), based on a scholium on Aristophanes' *Wealth* 179.[33]

In fr. 188 K.-A. of this play, Aphrodite seems to address a throng of women who passionately desire Phaon. She begins on a note familiar from Old Comedy, making jokes about women's universal bibulousness (lines 1-4), and proceeds over the next seventeen lines to list all the things the women must do in order to get to Phaon. This minor *tour de force* is, in form at least, not alien to Old Comedy, where we often find humorously protracted lists of items. What makes this particular list somewhat more in keeping with Middle Comedy, however, is its sustained interest in esoteric aspects of religion, specifically the worship of minor erotic deities:

>   πρῶτα μὲν ἐμοὶ γὰρ Κουροτρόφῳ προθύεται
>   πλακοῦς ἐνόρχης, ἄμυλος ἐγκύμων, κίχλαι
>   ἑκκαίδεχ' ὁλόκληροι μέλιτι μεμιγμέναι,
> 10 λαγῷα δώδεκ' ἐπισέληνα. τἆλλα δὲ
>   ἤδη †ταῦτ' εὐτελέστατα·† ἄκουε δή.
>   βολβῶν μὲν Ὀρθάννῃ τρί' ἡμιέκτεα,
>   Κονισάλῳ δὲ καὶ παραστάταιν δυοῖν
>   μύρτων[34] πινακίσκος χειρὶ παρατετιλμένων·
> 15 λύχνων γὰρ ὀσμὰς οὐ φιλοῦσι δαίμονες.
>   †πυργης τετάρτης† Κυσί τε καὶ Κυνηγέταις,
>   Λόρδωνι δραχμή, Κυβδάσῳ τριώβολον,
>   ἥρῳ Κέλητι δέρμα καὶ θυλήματα.
>   ταῦτ' ἐστι τἀναλώματ'. εἰ μὲν οὖν τάδε

---

[33]Cf. Geissler, *Chronologie* 72-73.

[34]For "myrtle" as a euphemism for the female genitalia, cf. *PCG* on Plato fr. 188 (line 14), Henderson, *Maculate Muse* 134-35. Cf. *Lysistrata* lines 838 and 1004.

20   προσοίσετ', εἰσέλθοιτ' ἄν· εἰ δὲ μή, μάτην
     ἔξεστιν ὑμῖν διὰ κενῆς βινητιᾶν

>   first you must offer to me, the Goddess who nurtures
>   children
>   a well-hung bit of cake, a tart made with the best flour,
>   sixteen birds intact and soaked in honey,
> 10   twelve crescent-shaped dainties. And there are also
>   these additional items which are the cheapest. Listen:
>   three sacks of bulbs for Orthannes,
>   and for Konisalos and his two attendants,
>   a platter of myrtle berries plucked by hand
> 15   (since divinities don't like the smell of burning off hair);
>   a quarter pound of wheat for the Dogs and the Hunters,
>   a drachma for Lordon, three obols for Kybdasos,
>   a leather hide and sacrificial cakes for the hero Keles.
>   This is what it will cost you. So if you bring them all out,
> 20   then you can go in <and see Phaon>. Otherwise you're
>   wasting
>   your time—you'll be hot for a fuck for no purpose.

All the names for these obscure figures are, of course, obscene: Orthannes and Konisalos are otherwise attested names for the deified Phallos worshipped in Athens,[35] while Lordon, Kybdasos and Keles seem to refer to various positions of copulation.[36] More than a passing interest in such deities or quasi-deities is clearly evident from the fragments of Middle Comedy. Eubulus composed an entire play called Ὀρθάννης and, although the few fragments do not allow us to speculate about its plot, one fragment (75 K.-A.), written in the dithyrambic style that Nesselrath has shown to be so common in Middle Comedy, describes elaborate culinary preparations that may indicate preliminaries to a celebration of the phallic god.[37] Xenarchus composed a play entitled Πρίαπος and Timocles a play called Κονίσαλος (the same "deity" mentioned in the *Phaon* fragment).

That such humorous themes of ithyphallism were at least recurrent in, if not central to, Plato's *Phaon* can be seen in fr. 189 K.-A., in which one character reads to another from what he

---

[35]Cf. Herter, *De dis Atticis*, and Hunter, *Eubulus* 165-66.
[36]For references cf. *PCG*, ad loc.
[37]Hunter, *Eubulus* 166-67.

claims to be a new cookbook by Philoxenus (Φιλοξένου καινή τις ὀψαρτύσια, 4):

   ἐγὼ δ' ἐνθάδ' ἐν τῇ ἐρημίᾳ
   τουτὶ διελθεῖν βούλομαι τὸ βιβλίον
   πρὸς ἐμαυτόν. (Β.) ἔστι δ', ἀντιβολῶ σε, τοῦτο τί;
   (Α.) Φιλοξένου καινή τις ὀψαρτυσία.
5 (Β.) ἐπίδειξον αὐτὴν ἥτις ἔστ'. (Α.) ἄκουε δή.
   ἄρξομαι ἐκ βολβοῖο, τελευτήσω δ' ἐπὶ θύννον.
   (Β.) ἐπὶ θύννον; οὐκοῦν †τῆς τελευτ† πολὺ
   κράτιστον ἐνταυθὶ τετάχθαι τάξεως.
   (Α.) βολβοὺς μὲν σποδιᾷ δαμάσας καταχύσματι δεύσας
10 ὡς πλείστους διάτρωγε· τὸ γὰρ δέμας ἀνέρος ὀρθοῖ.
   καὶ τάδε μὲν δὴ ταῦτα· θαλάσσης δ' ἐς τέκν' ἄνειμι
   οὐδὲ λοπὰς κακόν ἐστιν· ἀτὰρ τὸ τάγηνον ἄμεινον,
   οἶμαι
   ὀρφῶν αἰολίαν συνόδοντά τε καρχαρίαν τε
15 μὴ τέμνειν, μή σοι νέμεσις θεόθεν καταπνεύσῃ,
   ἀλλ' ὅλον ὀπτήσας παράθες· πολλὸν γὰρ ἄμεινον.
   πουλύποδος †πλεκτὴ δ' ἂν ἐπιλήψῃ† κατὰ καιρόν,
   ἐφθὴ τῆς ὀπτῆς, ἢν ᾖ μείζων, πολὺ κρείττων·
   ἢν ὀπταὶ δὲ δύ' ὦσ', ἐφθῇ κλαίειν ἀγορεύω.
20 τρίγλη δ' οὐκ ἐθέλει νεύρων ἐπιήρανος εἶναι·
   παρθένου Ἀρτέμιδος γὰρ ἔφυ καὶ στύματα μισεῖ.
   σκόρπιος αὖ (Β.) παίσειέ γε σου τὸν πρωκτὸν ὑπελθών

  (A:) I'd like to read this book to
  myself as I sit here alone.
  (B:) And what book is that, I ask you?
  (A:) It's the "nouvelle cuisine" of Philoxenus.
5 (B:) How 'bout a sample? (A:) OK, then, listen:
  I'll start with "b" for *b*ulbous vegetables, and I'll take it up to
  "t" for *t*una fish.
  (B:) To tuna fish?! Then surely it's by far the
  best thing to be stationed in the last position.
  (A:) (*reading aloud*) "Tame the bulbs with ashes, douse them
   in sauce
10 and then consume as many as you can: this'll straighten up a
   man's cock."
  That's it for that recipe; now I'll move on to the "children of
   the sea... "

* * *

> ... and the frying-pan isn't bad either, though the sauce-pan is better,
> I think...
> (*reading on*) "Don't cut up the perch, the trout, the bream
> 15 the saw-tooth, unless you want heaven's wrath to breathe down on you,
> but cook it up, and serve it up whole; that's much better.
> If you tenderize the tentacle of the octopus at just the right moment,
> it is far better boiled than baked, at least if it's a large one.
> But if two are baked, then to hell with the boiled one.
> 20 The red mullet doesn't usually help tense up the "nerve,"
> since that fish really comes from the virgin goddess Artemis and hates hard-ons.
> And now the scorpion... " (B:) "... might sneak up and sting you right in the asshole!"

This alleged excerpt from a cookbook may be a parody of the poem known as the Δεῖπνον by the dithyrambist Philoxenus of Leucas (remarkably well preserved by Athenaeus; and cf. *PMG* 836), although even Athenaeus had trouble distinguishing this Philoxenus from a roughly contemporary dithyrambist of the same name from Cythera. As Nesselrath has carefully argued, allusions to dithyrambic poetry, though common enough in Old Comedy, became less explicitly parodic in the period of Middle Comedy and more integrated into the diction of the plays (a development he even traces through the career of Aristophanes).[38] "Parody" of course can be an elusive term, but I would argue that the focus of the scene in Plato's fr. 189 K.-A. is not so much on parodying Philoxenus as on the humorous lucubrations about achieving an erect phallus, as indeed the statement regarding bulbs ("this'll straighten out a man's cock") at line 10 above and the low opinion of the red mullet at line 20 suggest.

Indeed it even seems likely that the recurrent detail of the aphrodisiac bulb (mentioned at fr. 188 K.-A., line 6: "bulbs for Orthannes" and fr. 189 K.-A., line 9: "tame the bulbs, douse them in sauce") foreshadows another obsession typical of Middle Comedy. It is in fact striking that in his disquisition on bulbs at 63d-64f, Athenaeus draws the bulk of his poetic examples from

---

[38]Nesselrath, *Mittlere Komödie* 241-66.

fourth-century comedy, citing Eubulus, Alexis, Xenarchus and Philemon. Of all the various authorities he quotes in this passage, both scientific and literary, it is curious that only in the comic excerpts are the aphrodisiac properties of the bulb revealed. In Eubulus' *Amaltheia*, another of the many popular "Heracles" plays of the period, Heracles includes bulbs as one of the foods he studiously avoids in favor of beef and pork (fr. 6 K.-A.), no doubt because of their unheroic associations. Alexis, according to Athenaeus, "stressed the aphrodisiac power of bulbs" in an unknown play, at fr. 281 K.-A.: "if anyone in love with a hetaira should find other drugs more useful than these... " (τούτων ἄν τις εὕρῃ φάρμακα / ἐρῶν ἑταίρας ἕτερα χρησιμώτερα, 3-4), and the single extant citation from Xenarchus' Βουταλίων (fr. 1 K.-A.) describes paratragically how even the bulb cannot save the master of the house from his terminal impotence:

ἄστυτος οἶκος κοὐδὲ βυσαύχην θεᾶς
Δηοῦς σύνοικος, γηγενὴς βολβός, φίλοις
ἑφθὸς βοηθῶν δυνατός ἐστ᾽ ἐπαρκέσαι· (4-6)

The house can't get it up, and the stubby-necked
companion of Demeter, earth-born bulb—a real help to
friends when boiled up—cannot even now do any good.

In itself, forging a link between Plato and later comic poets by means of bulbs may perhaps seem a tenuous exercise, but we should remember that these passages in Plato reflect other trends emblematic of the transition from Old to Middle Comedy, including an interest in dithyrambic language, religious esoterica, sustained erotic scenes, and possibly even in the fourth-century parody of philosophical schools.[39]

In discussing elements in Plato that suggest his affinities with later Greek comedy, I have, of course, downplayed those fragments which serve to secure his "rightful" status as a poet of Old Comedy. His interest in political satire and personal abuse, at all events, certainly affirm that his comedy can be classified as belonging to the "Old" period.[40] Still, even if we exclude Plato

---

[39]On which, cf. Nesselrath, *Mittlere Komödie* 228; Hunter, *Eubulus* 228-29.

[40]For a balanced survey of Plato's literary characteristics, cf. Schmid-Stählin, *Geschichte* 145-54. The author is keenly aware that the fragments

from the traditions of Middle and New Comedy for the sake of chronological consistency, I hope to have shown that we may at least sympathize with those ancient scholars who were confounded by some of the anachronistic and possibly even avant-garde tendencies of his comedies and applaud their basic intuitions about the importance of Plato Comicus in the transition from Old to Middle Comedy.

---

of Plato leave us with a somewhat ambivalent impression of the poet. Though some of his titles would appear to indicate plays in the politically vituperative tradition of Old Comedy, e.g. *Hyperbolus*, *Cleophon*, and *Peisandros* (he may even have been the first to signal his strong commitment to κωμῳδεῖν ὀνομαστί in the very title of his plays, though this remains speculation in the absence of better evidence), politics and obscenity do not seem to pervade the fragments that do survive. It is, of course, impossible to gauge accurately from the fragments what role such features played in Plato's comedies, but Schmid-Stählin are quick to note the impression that, as I have discussed in this paper, Plato seemed to anticipate later comedy as much as he reflected the conventions of his own time.

The Maculate Music: Gender, Genre, and the *Chiron* of Pherecrates

Gregory W. Dobrov and Eduardo Urios-Aparisi

Throughout this century the study of Greek comedy has been furthered by significant papyrus finds and improved editions of surviving texts. Recent work on the comic fragments based on Kassel and Austin's magisterial *Poetae Comici Graeci* has prompted us to reconsider Pherecrates, a controversial fifth-century figure who may be compared with other playwrights more productively than is often supposed. Our preliminary review of the claims handed down by tradition, though inconclusive, leads to an oblique evaluation of Pherecrates from the perspective of comedy's evolving response to the dithyramb. At the heart of our project is a new reading of the substantial fragment 155 K.-A. (*Chiron*) in terms of its gender and sexual thematics. A juxtaposition of this excerpt with other dithyrambic passages, such as the Cinesias scene in Aristophanes' *Birds* and the parodos of *Wealth*, is then used to adjust the characterization of Pherecrates as a genuine representative of Old Comedy whose work, nevertheless, anticipated important changes evident in the first quarter of the fourth century. We hope, in the process, to suggest that the evidence for composers other than Aristophanes and Menander might still be used to challenge what M. Davies ("Monody" 52) has called "the tyranny of the handbook."

At the dawn of dramatic criticism Pherecrates was already associated with Crates, who avoided personal ridicule and emphasized plot-construction in contrast to Cratinus and the next generation of political satirists such as Eupolis and

Aristophanes. This view is expressed well in the anonymous treatise on Comedy (with Norwood's translation):[1]

Φερεκράτης 'Αθηναῖος. νικᾷ ἐπὶ Θεοδώρου (Dobree: θέατρον codd.)· γενόμενος {ὁ} δὲ ὑποκριτὴς ἐζήλωσε Κράτητα, καὶ αὖ τοῦ μὲν λοιδορεῖν ἀπέστη, πράγματα δὲ εἰσηγούμενος καινὰ ηὐδοκίμει, γενόμενος εὑρετικὸς μύθων.

Pherecrates of Athens was victorious in the archonship of Theodorus (437) and emulated Crates, whose actor he was. Further, he refrained from abuse, and gained a reputation for introducing new topics, showing himself fertile in plots.

Pherecrates, as far as we can tell, had in common with his mentor[2] an apprenticeship in the productions of other playwrights.[3] Dobree's widely accepted emendation of θέατρον to Θεοδώρου (vs. Capps' Πυθοδώρου = 431) places Pherecrates' first victory in 437, twelve years before his younger contemporary's prize-winning *Acharnians*. A joke in *Lysistrata* (line 158) suggests that Pherecrates and his work were current enough in 411, and it is reasonable to suppose that he lived until the end of the century.[4] For the performance of *Savages* ("Άγριοι) we have a secure date of 420, this being the only other point of chronological certainty in the poet's career.[5] Although the number of known titles (between seventeen and nineteen) suggests that he was not especially prolific by comparison with other playwrights, his *oeuvre* exhibits a certain breadth, in illustration

---

[1] Pherecrates test. 2a K.-A. (= Koster, *Prolegomena* [III] 8.30). Norwood, *Greek Comedy* 3, and Nesselrath, *Mittlere Komödie* 45, agree in regarding this text as a valuable ancient testimonium.

[2] Storey, "Dating" 3, notes that ἐζήλωσε suggests a "vertical relation between poets."

[3] So the Anonymus: Κράτης 'Αθηναῖος, τοῦτον ὑποκριτὴν φασι γεγονέναι τὸ πρῶτον, ὃς ἐπιβέβληκε Κρατίνῳ, πάνυ γελοῖος καὶ ἱλαρὸς γενόμενος, καὶ πρῶτος μεθύοντας ἐν κωμῳδίᾳ προήγαγεν. τούτου δράματά ἐστιν ἑπτά. "Crates of Athens. This man, they say, began as an actor. He succeeded Cratinus, was extremely funny and witty, and was the first to introduce drunken persons into comedy. There are seven plays by him" (adapted from Norwood's translation).

[4] The interpretation of the three-line supplement to fr. 155 (lines 26-28) as referring to Philoxenus requires Pherecrates to see the turn of the century. See note 12 and pp. 142-44 below.

[5] On the authority of Plato *Protagoras* 327d.

of which we suggest the following thematic categories: utopia, contemporary manners, politics, and mythological burlesque.[6] Judging roughly by their first victories and the length of their careers we estimate that Pherecrates' closest contemporaries were Callias, Teleclides, Phrynichus and Hermippus.[7]

Questions of style and dramatic technique are more difficult. The tradition, reflected in the testimony of *Poetics* (1449b5-9, on Crates) and the Anonymus, insists on several characteristics distinguishing the "school" of Crates and Pherecrates: an attenuation of mockery and obscenity and the advancement of a new dramatic concept involving mannerism. Although the division between iambic and non-iambic comedy is Aristotelian, subsequent ancient scholarship singled out ὀνομαστὶ κωμῳδεῖν, "to ridicule by name," as the dominant criterion for the former.[8] The issue of obscenity and λοιδορία—however defined—is second in importance only to that of plot and dramatic design. An impressive showing in *PCG* (120 pages) notwithstanding, the lack of a single complete script puts us entirely at the mercy of our secondary sources in this fundamental area. It appears more productive, therefore, to emphasize the *comparative* potential of what remains, as this dimension of Pherecrates' contribution is far from having been exhausted.

Fragment 155 K.-A., from *Chiron*, is valuable for an appreciation of Pherecrates' craft in several respects: it is one of the longest (28 lines); it contains ridicule of specific individuals and may thus shed light how he "τοῦ λοιδορεῖν ἀπέστη"; it

---

[6]The authorship of some plays is debated. In general the utopian comedies are Ἄγριοι, Κραπάταλοι, Μεταλλῆς, Πέρσαι; the comedies of manners include Ἀγαθοί, Δουλοδιδάσκαλος, Λῆροι, Μέτοικοι, with a subset of hetaira-comedies: Ἐπιλήσμων ἢ Θάλαττα, Ἰπνὸς ἢ Παννυχίς, Κοριαννώ, Πετάλη (see below, pp. 157-60); two political plays: Γρᾶες, Τυραννίς; and the mythological-fantastic: Αὐτόμολοι, Ψευδηρακλῆς, Ἀνθρωφηρακλῆς, Μυρμηκάνθρωποι, Χείρων. Such a classification is, of course, speculative and cannot serve as the basis for unequivocal judgements in the style of Norwood, *Greek Comedy* 165, for example.

[7]Callias' first victory was in 446 (see Storey, "Kallias' *Pedetai*") and Teleclides had his first in 441. Phrynichus won in 436 for the first time and *Mousai* was performed in 405. Hermippus won in 435 and *Artopolides* was performed in 420/19.

[8]See the introductory discussion in Rosen, *Iambographic* Tradition, Degani, "Aristofane," and Carey, "Comic Ridicule" (and pp. 150-52, below).

belongs to a mature stage of the poet's life; and, lastly, it exhibits a metaphorical virtuosity (music in terms of sex) that harmonizes with the representation of Pherecrates' style in Aristophanes.[9] Owing to its status as a key testimonium for the study of Greek music,[10] however, fr. 155 K.-A. is seldom considered for its literary value as an excerpt from a delightful script.

Chiron

Despite conflicting testimonia on the issue of authorship,[11] there is no firm basis for doubting the attribution of *Chiron* to Pherecrates. The main argument *contra* is the rather weak assumption that he could not have lived long enough for Timotheus and Philoxenus to figure as κωμῳδούμενοι in his work (fr. 155 K.-A., lines 26-28).[12] Körte argues sensibly, however, that Pherecrates could well have lived fifteen or twenty years after his

---

[9]The contemporary reference to Pherecrates by Aristophanes at *Lysistrata* 158 (τὸ τοῦ Φερεκράτους, κύνα δέρειν δεδαρμένην) has been much discussed. The scholiast at this point offers no help (ἐν τοῖς σῳζομένοις Φερεκράτους τοῦ κωμικοῦ τοῦτο οὐχ εὑρίσκεται, cf. Schmid, *Geschichte* IV 100, note 8). The expression τὸ τοῦ Φερεκράτους would appear to designate something *characteristic* of the poet (cf. *Wasps* 1525 τὸ Φρυνίχειον, Aristophanes fr. 347 K.-A., and Cratinus fr. 32 K.-A.). Rehrenböck, *Pherekrates-Studien* 259 ff., argues that the joke is based on multiple ambiguities. Aristophanes may be paying tribute to the way in which Pherecrates contextualized the proverb for obscene effect, i.e., the simple notion of "skinning the skinned dog" (futile activity) becomes a reference to female masturbation: with the ὄλισβος (so Henderson, *Lysistrata* 86, *ad loc.*) or without (so Henderson, *Maculate Muse* 133, §117).

[10]The fullest discussion of musical problems is found in Restani, "Il *Chirone*." Düring, "Studies," Borthwick, "Notes," and Zimmermann, "Comedy's Criticism," are also valuable.

[11]Athenaeus 9.368b refers to *Chiron* as τὸν εἰς Φερεκράτην ἀναφερόμενον and in 8.364a he attributes it to Νικόμαχος ὁ ῥυθμικός (see also 14.653f).

[12]Philoxenus lived from 435 to 380 (Marmor Parium A.1.2). Geissler, *Chronologie* 42, Wilamowitz, *Die Perser* 75, and Nesselrath, *Mittlere Komödie* 250 (especially note 22), record doubts about the attribution on the basis of the late date. As a member of an older generation, Pherecrates is often assumed to have died before 415. Düring, "Studies" 177, argues in favor of Pherecratean authorship (rejecting the three-line final supplement).

first victory. (Aristophanes' debut and his last plays are separated, after all, by a good four decades.)[13] The evidence for Phrynichus' life affirms the possibility that Pherecrates could have seen Philoxenus into his fourth decade of life. From time to time, moreover, there arises the problem of internal evidence as the authenticity of fr. 155 K.-A. is impugned on the basis of allegedly late subject-matter and language.[14] This line of inquiry has proven inconclusive, however, and we are left little reason to doubt that *Chiron* belongs to Pherecrates, one of his last pieces produced when Philoxenus' career was in the ascendant.

The other seven fragments which remain of *Chiron* are insufficient for a reconstruction of the plot. Certain characters and scenes do emerge, however, from the scattered pieces ranging in length from one to thirteen lines. Although Chiron himself is not mentioned explicitly, he was probably portrayed in the traditional manner, as we may infer from the disquisition on hospitality in fr. 162 K.-A. and the wisdom that comes with old age (rather pedagogical in tone) in fr. 156 K.-A. One may fill in the details from other sources: the famous centaur was skilled in medicine and music and taught remarkable pupils including Peleus, Asclepius, Jason, and Achilles. On a contemporary level he was doubtless an idealization of Athenian elitist pedagogy.[15] As a protagonist, however, Chiron was probably drawn realistically with the typical features of a comic *senex*, a detail suggested by the ψόγοι γήρως in fr. 156 and fr. 162 K.-A., where a speaker laments the lapse from standards of the past. This

---

[13]Körte, "Pherekrates" 1989, notes that "das letzte Datum, das wir für P[herekrates] besitzen, ist (s.o.) 415, aber warum soll der Dichter nicht...länger gelebt und gewirkt haben? Aristophanes hat noch 40 Jahre nach seinem ersten Dionysiensieg sein letztes Stück geschrieben, es wäre also keineswegs auffallend, wenn P[herekrates] 30 Jahre nach dem Dionysiensieg den *Chiron* verfaßt hätte."

[14]Athenaeus' skepticism noted above (note 11) may have been inspired by Eratosthenes who had doubts on the basis of vocabulary (see Pherecrates fr. 113 and 116 K.-A. and Eratosthenes fr. 46 Str.). Körte ("Pherekrates" 1988.52–89.27) argues, however, that this is simply a bit of hypercriticism based on minor metrical and linguistic difficulties.

[15]Cf. Jouan, *Euripide et les légendes* 92. For Chiron the pedagogue see Plato *Republic* 3.391c, Xenophon *Symposium* 8.23, *Cyropaedia* 1.1.2 and 1.1.5, and the Χείρωνος ὑποθῆκαι of Hesiod (cf. Merkelbach-West, *Fragmenta Hesiodea* 143ff.).

characterization anticipates the fourth-century Chiron depicted on a well-known Apulian bell-crater in the British Museum (F151). Similar travesty is suggested by fr. 159 K.-A., where Achilles refuses the "prostitutes" from Lesbos offered by Odysseus in exchange for Briseis (so Meineke). Similar travesty of mythical figures is found in Μυρμηκάνθρωποι (*Ant-men*), where Deucalion and Pyrrha—an ordinary elderly couple[16]—undertake the famous flood-journey (on a boat made of domestic articles) and encounter a chorus of human ants. The precedent of Cratinus' Χείρωνες (with a centaur chorus?) complicates the task of assessing the degree of Pherecratean innovation.[17] Although the fragments yield little more concerning the plot and the eponymous figure of our play, fr. 155 K.-A. contains many details of linguistic and dramatic interest to which we shall return.

In fr. 155 K.-A. we have either an opening scene[18] or comic agon involving a harangue spoken by Μουσική (the instrumental *and* verbal aspects of lyric poetry) to Δικαιοσύνη.[19] Harangues occur in Aristophanic prologues and often figure at the outset to define the motivations of the characters and themes of the play (e.g. *Acharnians* 1-42; see pp. 58-61, above). In the women's plays the harangue against men is honed to a fine art, exemplified by the tirade against Euripides at *Thesmophoriazusae* 383-432. Other well-known examples of outbursts devoted to leading themes are found in *Lysistrata* (women against war) and *Ecclesiazusae* (mismanagement of the polis).[20] Although the tone and language of fr. 155 K.-A. are redolent of a tragic exordium (e.g., the paratragic lines 1-3), we can only speculate about its

---

[16]Cf. fr. 119, 122, and 125 K.-A.

[17]Cratinus' play preceded that of Pherecrates (its terminus ante quem is 423 when we know that Cratinus' last play Πυτίνη was performed). Cratinus fr. 247, 248, 254 K.-A. show that music played a role in Cratinus' play (see *PCG* IV 245). For other references to Chiron in comedy, see Plato Comicus fr. 207 K.-A. and Aristophanes fr. 239 K.-A.

[18]Schmid, *Geschichte* I.4 106, and Pianko, "comico contributo" 56–62. Pianko's further attempts at reconstruction are less compelling, e.g. a second scene involving an agon between Timotheus, representative of dithyrambic music, and "Terprando o Arione o Alcmane o ancora qualche altro autore di ditirambi" ("comico contributo" 60).

[19]For a discussion of personification see pp. 157-58, below.

[20]Such passages are, among other things, a fascinating response to the topos of ψόγοι γυναικῶν on which see pp. 66-67, above.

position (initial vs. medial), as we must for most other aspects of the play, with the possible exception of the exodus.[21] Pianko's suggestion, on the evidence of fr. 157–158 and 162 K.-A., that *Chiron* ended with a banquet, is attractive.[22] A concluding festivity of some sort is common enough in comedy and a symposium would provide a particularly plausible context for the discussion of μουσική (cf. the final banquet of Aristophanes' *Clouds* and *Gerytades* of the same, fr. 161 K.-A.). Let us now consider the text itself ([Plutarch] *Moralia* 1141d-42a):

ὡς καὶ Φερεκράτη τὸν κωμικὸν εἰσαγαγεῖν τὴν Μουσικὴν ἐν γυναικείῳ σχήματι ὅλην κατῃκισμένην τὸ σῶμα· ποιεῖ δὲ τὴν Δικαιοσύνην διαπυνθανομένην τὴν αἰτίαν τῆς λώβης καὶ τὴν Ποίησιν λέγουσαν

ΜΟΥΣ. λέξω μὲν οὐκ ἄκουσα· σοί τε γὰρ κλυεῖν
ἐμοί τε λέξαι θυμὸς ἡδονὴν ἔχει.
ἐμοὶ γὰρ ἦρξε τῶν κακῶν Μελανιππίδης,
ἐν τοῖσι πρῶτος ὃς λαβὼν ἀνῆκέ με
5   χαλαρωτέραν τ' ἐποίησε χορδαῖς δώδεκα.
ἀλλ' οὖν ὅμως οὗτος μὲν ἦν ἀποχρῶν ἀνὴρ
ἔμοιγε – ∪ – ∪ πρὸς τὰ νῦν κακά.
Κινησίας δέ ⟨μ'⟩ ὁ κατάρατος Ἀττικός,
ἐξαρμονίους καμπὰς ποιῶν ἐν ταῖς στροφαῖς
10 ἀπολώλεχ' οὕτως, ὥστε τῆς ποιήσεως
τῶν διθυράμβων, καθάπερ ἐν ταῖς ἀσπίσιν,
ἀριστέρ' αὐτοῦ φαίνεται τὰ δεξιά.
ἀλλ' οὖν ἀνεκτὸς οὗτος ἦν ὅμως ἐμοί.
Φρῦνις δ' ἴδιον στρόβιλον ἐμβαλών τινα
15 κάμπτων με καὶ στρέφων ὅλην διέφθορεν,
ἐν πέντε χορδαῖς δώδεχ' ἁρμονίας ἔχων.
ἀλλ' οὖν ἔμοιγε χοὖτος ἦν ἀποχρῶν ἀνήρ·
εἰ γάρ τι κἀξήμαρτεν, αὖτις ἀνέλαβεν.
ὁ δὲ Τιμόθεός μ,' ὦ φιλτάτη, κατορώρυχε
20 καὶ διακέκναικ' αἴσχιστα. (ΔΙΚ.) ποῖος οὑτοσὶ
⟨ὁ⟩ Τιμόθεος; (ΜΟΥΣ.) Μιλήσιός τις πυρρίας.
κακά μοι παρέσχεν οὗτος, ἅπαντας οὓς λέγω
παρελήλυθεν, ἄγων ἐκτραπέλους μυρμηκιάς.
κἂν ἐντύχῃ πού μοι βαδιζούσῃ μόνῃ,
25 ἀπέδυσε κἀνέλυσε χορδαῖς δώδεκα

[21] Meineke's idea (*CGF* I 79) of joining Pherecrates fr. 157 (fr. 168 K.-A.) with fr. 155 K.-A. is attractive, but of minor consequence. On paratragic color, see the comments of Restani cited in note 25 below.
[22] Pianko, "comico contributo" 61.

καὶ Ἀριστοφάνης ὁ κωμικὸς (fr. 953 K.-A.) μνημονεύει Φιλοξένου καί φησιν ὅτι εἰς τοὺς κυκλίους χοροὺς * * * μέλη εἰσηνέγκατο. ἡ δὲ Μουσικὴ λέγει ταῦτα·

ἐξαρμονίους ὑπερβολαίους τ' ἀνοσίους
καὶ νιγλάρους, ὥσπερ τε τὰς ῥαφάνους ὅλην
καμπῶν με κατεμέστωσε

So the comic poet Pherecrates put Music on stage in the disguise of a woman, her whole body displaying signs of ill-treatment. He then makes Justice ask what caused this outrage, and Music answers:

"I'll tell you willingly: the story will be a pleasure for me to tell and for you to hear. Melanippides started my troubles. He was the first of them: he grabbed me and pulled me down and loosened me up with his countless notes. For all that, the man was tolerable enough, compared with my current troubles. That damned Cinesias of Attica has done me so much damage with the 'exharmonic' twists he makes inside the strophes, that you'd mistake his 'left turn' for his 'right' in his performance of the dithyrambs and shield-dance. Still, I could put up with him. Then Phrynis shoved in his own peculiar screwbolt all his own, bending and twisting me into a total wreck—he had twelve ways of tuning his pentachords. All the same, even he was bearable: he went wrong, but he made up for it later. But Timotheus is another matter. He's shoveled me into the earth, my dear, and ground me down disgustingly!" (Justice asks) "Who is this Timotheus?" (Music replies) "Some red-head from Miletus. The things he did to me were worse than all the others put together, with those perverted ant-crawlings he went in for. And when he found me out for a walk by myself, he stripped me and unraveled me with his innumerable notes."

The comic poet Aristophanes also mentions Philoxenus and says that he introduced... songs into cyclic choruses. Music speaks the following words:

"... exharmonic high-pitched blasphemous warbles—he stuffs me like a cabbage, (rolling me up) with wriggling caterpillars."[23]

---

[23] Translation based on Barker, *Musical Writings* I 236–37.

We imagine a scenario in which a distressed and disheveled woman comes on stage[24] and begins her tirade with mock formality.[25] She relates her grievances to Justice bemoaning the ill-treatment she has suffered from her partners, real practitioners of the citharodic nomos and dithyramb. Melanippides was the beginning of her troubles—extensions of the musical vocabulary—which do not appear to have overshadowed his overall decency, however (ἦν ἀποχρῶν). Music then berates Melanippides' pupil, Cinesias (lines 8-13), who subjected her to "exharmonic twists," despite which he was still bearable.[26] In lines 14–18 we hear of Phrynis. In contrast to his contemporary, Melanippides, the abuses of this citharist lay in the area of new modulations or tunings. "Screwbolts," "bending," and "twisting" notwithstanding, Music claims that she could put up with him as well. Timotheus (lines 19-25), mentioned next, is accused of having done greater damage with chromatic melodies (μυρμηκιαί) and (ab)use of the traditional configuration. The *communis opinio* sensibly places pseudo-Plutarch's three-liner as a final supplement to fr. 155 K.-A. The subject here must be Philoxenus of Cythera (so Kaibel arguing from the wider context). Two teachers have so far been paired with their students: Melanippides and Cinesias, Phrynis and Timotheus. With Philoxenus the speech completes the pattern, priamel-style, towards "a subject of ultimate interest,"[27] and we are justified in expecting a fifth person to surpass them all.

---

[24]Note the langauge of pseudo-Plutarch's introduction above.

[25]See K.-A. ad loc. Restani, "Il *Chirone*" 143, notes the following characteristics: "litote iniziale οὐκ ἄκουσα v.1, anafora tra l'inizio dei due succesivi vv. 2–3, ἐμοί τε λέξαι.../ ἐμοὶ γὰρ ἦρξε, complicata da un poliptoto a partire della metà del verso iniziale, σοί τε γὰρ κλύειν / ἐμοί τε λέξαι ed arrichita da un parallelismo strutturale: pronomi-congiugazione-verbo all'infinito."

[26]A stumbling-block in the interpretation of this passage has been the clause καθάπερ ἐν ταῖς ἀσπίσιν, ἀριστέρ' αὐτοῦ φαίνεται τὰ δεξιά. Borthwick ("Notes" 65) suggests a reference to the Pyrrhic dance; Zielinski (*Gliederung* 267, note 2) understands it as a mirror where right and left are confused (so also Düring, "Studies" 185–86, and Zimmermann, "Comedy's Criticism" 40).

[27]Race, *Classical Priamel* 15; see also pp. 7ff. and 86. Race speculates, in fact, that the passage parodies a priamel by Timotheus (fr. 788 *PMG*).

Κωμῳδούμενοι

The first issue we encounter, then, is that of ὀνομαστὶ κωμῳδεῖν and the alleged difference between Pherecratean comedy and the political satires of Aristophanes. While Music describes the sexual behavior of Melanippides and Phrynis in rather general terms, she sharpens her description of Cinesias and Timotheus. As the latter two (along with Philoxenus) were in the public eye at the time, we assume that personal details in their case would have been more effective than for those who, by then, were retired or deceased. Cinesias is called κατάρατος, "damned"— an epithet common enough in comedy[28]—but the term Ἀττικός conjoined to it carries the special, derogatory, sense of "born in Attica (but *not* a citizen)."[29] Thus Cinesias says of himself in *Birds* (lines 1403-1404) ταυτὶ πεποίηκας τὸν κυκλιοδιδάσκαλον / ὅς ταῖσι φυλαῖς περιμάχητός εἰμ᾽ ἀεί; "Is this how you treat me, the trainer of cyclic choruses, whom the tribes are always fighting to have?"[30]—on one reading, a jab at a reputation confined to the Attic backwater.[31] Timotheus is similarly rejected as an outsider and contemptuously referred to as "some red-haired Milesian," Μιλήσιός τις πυρρίας (line 21)[32]— an insult set up by Justice who claims not to know him: ποῖος οὑτοσὶ / ⟨ὁ⟩ Τιμόθεος, "Timotheus ... who?" (cf. Timotheus fr. 791, line 29). Such lampoons are natural enough, of course, in Old Comedy *precisely* in the case of individuals of some repute,[33] and are rather mild examples of invective *ad hominem*. The terms applied to Cinesias are common,[34] while the xenophobic ridicule

---

[28]Cf. Pherecrates fr. 76.3 K.-A. and Aristophanes *Lysistrata* 530.
[29]Düring, "Studies" 183, who cites Plato, *Laws* 626d.
[30]Sommerstein's translation.
[31]Cf. *IG* ii² 3028. Pherecrates' point may be a contrast between Cinesias and the foreigners such as Timotheus. The *dramatis locus* may not be Athenian, i.e. either Thessaly (chez Chiron) or Olympus, where Music would have gone to complain to divine Justice. Cf. *PCG ad loc.*
[32]For πυρρίας referring mainly to slaves, see Dover, *Frogs* 283 (line 730 *ad loc.*)
[33]For a profile of Cinesias (*PA* 8438) see Sommerstein, *Birds* 289. The epigraphic and literary evidence (especially *IG* ii² 18 and 3028, Lysias 20.21 and fr. 53) suggests a prominent and eccentric figure.
[34]See above on κατάρατος Ἀττικός.

of Timotheus exemplifies a well-worn convention (cf. the ongoing joke in *Birds* 11, 31, 764, 1527).

To expand the range of our search, we find mention of only several other performers and public figures in Pherecrates. Two citharists (Meles, son of Peisias, and Chaeris) are singled out as "the worst" in fr. 6 K.-A. (*Savages*),[35] no doubt as part of the running joke in which Athens' "worst" turned out to be delightful by contrast with the horrors of the "natural" (ἄγριος) community and its lifestyle.[36] The riddling jab from the same play at the sons of Carcinus (fragment 15 K.-A.) has the ring of a comic topos, recalling passages such as *Peace* 781-790 and the exodus of *Wasps*.[37] Lycurgus (tradesman, politician and grandfather of the orator) is satirized in xenophobic terms (fr. 11 K.-A.)[38] while in fr. 164 K.-A., Alcibiades is mocked as effeminate and philandering.[39] A simile in fragment 143 K.-A. (*Petale*) repeats another topos by comparing a carrier pigeon to that stock Old Comic effeminate, Cleisthenes.[40] The reference in fr. 64 to the mortgaging of Pulytion's house suggests a connection with the events of 415[41] and the wealthy businessman's role as host to scandalous parody of the Mysteries.[42] Finally, a certain Smicythion—perhaps

---

[35] We know little about Meles. For Chaeris see *Acharnians* 16, 866 and *Peace* 851.

[36] Pherecrates fr. 6 K.-A.

[37] *Wasps* 1501ff. where they may appear on stage. Cf. also *Peace* 864.

[38] Cf. also Cratinus fr. 32 K.-A. and the scholion to *Birds* 1294: "It appears that they considered Lycurgus 'Egyptian' either by extraction or character" (*PCG ad* Pherecrates fr. 11).

[39] Cf. Aristophanes *Acharnians* 716, *Wasps* 44-46, *Frogs* 1422, fr. 205, 244, 556 K.-A. and Archippus fr. 48 K.-A. The image of Alcibiades is well attested in the anecdotes explained by Athenaeus (12.534b ff.) and Plutarch in his life of Alcibiades. See Dobrov, "Tereus" 196 (note 16), and Ellis, *Alcibiades* 17.

[40] Cf. Aristophanes fr. 422 K.-A.

[41] If the mortgaging (οἰκίαν κειμένην ὑπώβολον) was somehow connected with the confiscation from Pulytion as a condemned ἀσεβής, the play Ἰπνός (or Παννυχίς) would be dated after 415. For supporting argumentation see MacDowell, *Andocides* (ad 1.12), and Geissler, *Chronologie* 52. For views *contra*, see Sommerstein, "Decree of Syrakosios" 105-106, Atkinson, "Curbing the Comedians" 63 (note 59), and Dover, *Frogs* 27 (note 46).

[42] See Andocides 1.12 and Isocrates 16.6.

identical with the sycophant in *Wasps* 401[43]— is depicted in fr. 37 K.-A. as a mercenary and food-supplier for the army. Our catalog, thus, contains only 1) a pair of politicians ridiculed by way of rather apolitical topoi; 2) Cleisthenes and Alcibiades (again) as effeminate types; 3) Pulytion, a corrupt businessman and 4) Smicythion, a parasite; and, conspicuously, 5) a list of decadent musicians and performers.

No stranger to invective topoi, Pherecrates does not give us a single original, *political* comment[44] and seems to have preferred the criticism exemplified by the final category above.[45] Even Music's harangue in the *Chiron* fragment does not, in fact, trade in serious attacks *ad hominem*, as we realize from the point of the complaints. In each instance, the personal value of the invective is subordinated to the purpose of the oblique, allegorical humor. The tirade is organized as a climactic pairing of abuses and their perpetrators in which the language mirrors the intensity of the crimes. Thus, while ἀπολώλεχ' and διέφθορεν (lines 10 and 15) are relatively bland synonyms roughly equivalent to "did me in" and "ruined me," κατορώρυχεν and διακέκναικ' αἴσχιστα (lines 19-20) are more colorful and suggestive: "shoveled me into the earth" and "ground me down disgustingly."[46] The sexual violence implicit here, quite unpleasant in and of itself, is made palatable and even amusing by being veiled in the allusive (and quite repetitious) terms of the citharodic nomos.

---

[43]This is an interesting passage for the use of the word ἐπισίτιος. As in Cratinus fr. 37 K.-A., it probably designates an official figure whose role was already identified with some sort of parasitism (cf. the invariably pejorative sense of "sycophant"; and perhaps also the προτενθαί in Pherecrates fr. 7 K.-A.). In Middle Comedy this word is also found in Eubulus fr. 20 and Timocles fr. 31 K.-A.

[44]That is, the λοιδορία implicit in the passage of the Anonymus cited on p. 140 above is confined, in our evidence, to spheres other than political views and action.

[45]This raises the much-debated question whether personal abuse in the poets of Old Comedy was a serious contribution to political discourse or harmless and politically inert convention. See Rosen, *Iambographic Tradition* 5 (with note 21), Degani, "Aristofane," and Carey, "Comic Ridicule," on this issue.

[46]The text does not follow a chronological organization of the musicians. "To the Greeks the relation master-disciple was by far the most natural sequence" (Düring, "Studies" 180).

The force of the personal ridicule in our fragment is further attenuated by topoi—elements less *ad hominem* owing to their commonplace nature. The scornful image of Timotheus' "perverted ant-crawlings" in line 23, for example (ἄγων ἐκτραπέλους μυρμηκιάς), is found in connection with the music of other musicians in Pherecrates (e.g., fr. 31 K.-A.) and Aristophanes (*Thesmophoriazusae* 100, *Clouds* 1003).[47] Although we cannot identify the source of this topos with any certainty, it had obviously gained some currency in the last decades of the fifth century as an item in the comic poets' arsenal against the new music and musicians. Along with the "ant-paths" we must also recognize as topoi most of the images and expressions for "making twists" and "loosening up" which refer, in a general way, to new trends in the citharodic nomos and dithyramb. Thus only two passages appear to have an explicitly *ad hominem* value: lines 9-13 with the allusion to Cinesias' Pyrrhic dance, and the στρόβιλον of the next line denoting some sort of innovation by Phrynis in dance or citharody. On the whole, as we have noted, the musical elements are simplified and obscured throughout by means of figural and repetitive language in the service of sexual imagery.[48] The metaphorical screen distracts us with the pretense of a harangue against *musicians* and their craft while intimating a very different discourse. Having followed the speech to the end we realize, however, that we have been led on by a master of comedy: what appears, in this metaphor, to be the tenor (sex) and vehicle (music) are, in fact, reversed as we confront the allegory as whole! Μουσική, after all, is not a real woman, and the point of the speech is to rake modern music over the coals of a favorite comic theme.

The mask of the music critic

Though difficult as a testimonium for precise technical details, the *Chiron* fragment is interesting for its more general implications about music, especially the citharodic nomos. "The

---

[47]For further references to this comic topos see *PCG ad loc.*, Borthwick, "Notes" 69, and Restani, "Il *Chirone*" 178.

[48]This imagery goes beyond simple ribaldry, as we argue below, to involve the play in an unusual study of comedy's relationship to the dithyramb and new music.

avant-garde" notes Bernhard Zimmermann, "Comedy's Criticism" 41,

> tried to enrich the music and to make it more colorful (*poikilos*) by enlarging the scale of sounds, by the addition of extra strings, by introducing chromatic scales and making modulations from one genus to another, by changing rhythm in an unexpected way (*metabolai kata rhythmon*) and even producing mixtures of the different harmonies and finally by enriching their compositions by means of coloratura arias. As a result of these innovations the traditional triadic or antistrophic structure was also abandoned, and *astropha* (songs without any metrical responsion) were introduced.

By singling out musicians who dared to innovate and to change fundamentals of the traditional tetrachord system, Pherecrates strikes a conservative pose which had become a comic topos in its own right. (Popular aversion to music involving twelve-tone rows and microtonality[49] comes to mind as a modern correlate.) Though originally identified with the strings of the lyre,[50] the tetrachord remained the basis of tonal organization in Greek music even as the instrument's range was extended by musicians such as Timotheus and Phrynis. The main affront to tradition, as Zimmermann implies, was the introduction of *poikilia* on the level of the modes, a modern term used somewhat anachronistically to denote the ancient Greek scales each of which had a different pattern of intervals, a different tonal center, and a unique ethical character (in certain sectors of the l'imaginaire grec, at any rate). Allowing for considerable eccentricity in Plato's well-known comments on the subject (*Republic* 398c-399d; *Laws* 653d-673a, 795a-812e) it would appear that individual modes could be invested with a certain power to affect the emotions and even, perhaps, to shape character.[51] It is

---

[49]See Anderson, *Ethos and Education* 16-7, and Chailley, *musique grecque* 25ff.

[50]See Abraham, *History of Music* 29.

[51]Cf. Chailley, *musique greque* 107: "[un mode] est aisément reconnaissable et acquérit une personnalité qui permet de lui attribuer un rôle social ou religieux, voir magique: d'où cette notion d'éthos (ἦθος) qui tient une si grande place dans l'éthique platonicienne et que connaissent à peu près toutes les musiques orientales (râgas Hindous, etc.): un mode

not hard to understand, therefore, why innovation in this area might be feared as having negative social and religious consequences. Indeed, *poikilia* and ethics have never mixed!

At certain moments, Pherecrates' critique concentrates on the choral and performative dimension of the dithyramb. Cinesias appears to receive special censure for his innovations in dance, as Borthwick has argued.[52] On the other hand, the prepositional phrase ἐν ταῖς ἀσπίσιν may mean "(like) a reflection in a shield" (so Barker, *Musical Writings* 236-37), the point of which would be to lament the destruction of strophic symmetry of the dithyramb and its performance[53]—an interpretation strengthened by τῆς ποιήσεως, potentially both "composition" and "performance." Choral dance appears to have lost some of its dignity, moreover, if we accept the interpretation of Phrynis' στρόβιλον (line 14) as an irregular or hectic gyration. Timotheus' innovations (lines 23–25) are related to the introduction of citharodic "nomes," or solo-songs, in the genre. This was an important development in format (e.g., the introduction of *astropha*) attended by changes in language and musical accompaniment which could overwhelm the text, upsetting the "traditional equilibrium between the three elements of a poem, between the music, dance and song" (Zimmermann, "Comedy's Criticism" 43). The final blow to lady Music, however, was dealt by Philoxenus whose "Cyclops" is featured in the parodos of Aristophanes' last extant play (*Wealth* 290-321) where Cario, playing the lead part, imitates the Dorian strains of the cithara. The burlesque "θρεττανελό" of the Cyclops and the comic chorus exemplifies the *poikilia* criticized so vehemently by Plato at *Laws* 700a-701b: "In a Bacchic frenzy ... the poets mixed lamentations with hymns and paeans with dithyrambs, imitated aulos songs with their cithara songs, and put everything together with everything else." (Zimmermann tr.)

---

caractérise un sentiment, une heure de la journée, une catégorie sociale." For the Greek modes in their cultural context see Nagy's chapter "The Panhellenization of Song" (*Pindar's Homer* 82-115).

[52]Thus, on Borthwick's reading of the "exharmonic twists" and the phrase ἐν ταῖς ἀσπίσιν (see note 26 above).

[53]Borthwick, "Notes" 62ff. On this view, Music laments the loss of responsion in *astropha* and the resulting change in dance (lines 9-12).

Although such innovations cannot have been inconsequential (as music was a central element of traditional religion and education), criticism of the sophists and the new musicians for their disruption of tradition was a common elitist posture in Old Comedy which poets such as Aristophanes were often at pains to reconcile with the popular "carnivalesque" aspects of their appeal to the demos (see above pp. 92-93). Pherecrates was quick to learn and assimilate the language of the dithyramb, in fact, as we see from a number of fragments (e.g., fr. 113, 114, 138 K.-A.). Aristophanes was also greatly influenced by the new trends of his time in a way that suggests a healthy skepticism towards the comic surface of his and his contemporaries' work. The agenda of comedy was necessarily at variance with a serious appreciation of Cinesias and Philoxenus as artists, innovators whose priorities, in retrospect, appear very modern indeed: originality in fundamental areas such as harmony and rhythm, greater range of expression and mimesis, the incorporation of new instruments, etc. (cf. Pherecrates fr. 6, 31, and 47 K.-A.).[54] In the *Chiron* fragment, then, the poet assumes a moral posture, a comic mask, that playfully engages ideas asserted more earnestly elsewhere (e.g., *Laws* 653a ff. which, however, looks back a century to the views of Damon).[55] This particular mask fits well with the ideological profile—elderly, elitist, conservative—we have assumed for the eponymous figure of *Chiron* whose part in the play (and relation to Μουσική) must remain shrouded in mystery.[56]

---

[54]See Borthwick, "Notes" 71, and Restani, "Il *Chirone*" 154.

[55]See Barker, *Musical Writings* I 100 and 168–69. For a detailed and illuminating study of various "masks" assumed by the comic poet, see Hubbard, *Mask of Comedy* (especially 41-49 on the various masks of Dicaeopolis in *Acharnians*).

[56]As we suggest above (pp. 143-44), the figure of Chiron was probably a composite of several different elements such as "pedagogue" and "elitist."

Playing the female body

The *Chiron* fragment is intent on deploying the terminology of citharody and dance in a sexual sense.[57] This is accomplished, we argue below, by means of a clever allegory that projects the figure of a κιθαρίστρια (a hetaira proficient in music) into a more abstract embodiment of her skills: the active performance of music and passive submission to intercourse are fused and *her body becomes a lyre*. This allows for the sustained exercise in double entendre that begins in lines 4-5. In musical terms, for example, χαλαρωτέραν τ' ἐποίησε χορδαῖς δώδεκα refers to the addition of new notes or strings (χορδαί is used for both) with which Melanippides modified the traditional Greek modes. The adjective χαλαρός can denote modal slackness (χαλαραί cf. Plato, *Republic* 398e) that was opposed to the traditional Dorian tautness (in the popular imagination at least, cf. *Clouds* 968). The erotic connotations of χαλαρός, on the other hand, resonate with the generalizing δώδεκα meaning "many," "countless," and χορδή which, taken as "sausage," has obvious sexual potential. The repetition of χορδή with its numbers thus connotes *multae fututiones*.[58] We find a related type of comic polysemy in the phrase Φρῦνις δ' ἴδιον στρόβιλον ἐμβαλών τινα (line 14). As a *terminus technicus*, στρόβιλον can mean "pirouette" and may refer here to "an innovation in the dithyrambic ἀγωγή," according to Borthwick who pictures "an irregular rotary motion, which

---

[57] The metaphorical aspects of Pherecrates' script have not attracted as much attention as the specifics of the musical terminology dominant in the work of Düring, Restani and the others cited above (note 10).

[58] E.g., δωδεκαμήχανον used of a versatile prostitute in criticism of Euripides at *Frogs* 1327 (cf. also Plato Comicus fr. 143 K.-A.). See Taillardat, *Images* §785, note 4, and Borthwick, "Notes" 69. For χορδή in a sexual sense, cf. *Frogs* 338-39: Xa.: "Wow! I caught a sweet whiff of pork!" Dion.: "Hold it, will 'ya? If you want to get your hands on some sausage!" Dover, *ad loc.*, has this comment: "The sexual reference of χοιρείων κρεῶν is reinforced by χορδῆς, 'sausage' (R. Seager, CQ NS 31 [1981] 250). This is not attested in the sense 'penis,' but a sausage is so like a penis (as recognized in a simile ὥσπερ ἀλλᾶντα—another word for 'sausage'—in Hipponax 84.17) that it is hard to believe that the audience would not see a double meaning in 339, whether it implies that Xanthias will be buggered (an insult, implying that he would welcome it) or that he will lay hands on a boy's penis (not an insult; cf. Av. 142 and Dover [1978] 94-7)."

disturbed the prevailing pattern of the κύκλιος χορός with a violent whirling."⁵⁹ A more concrete interpretation of this line would extend the simple meaning of στρόβιλον ("whirling top" or "shaft") to denote a crude *capotasto* invented by Phrynis for quick tuning changes in the manner of a modern pedal-steel guitar. The word ἐμβαλών would then sharpen the erotic force of βάλλω to make the phallic imagery more concrete and vivid.⁶⁰

Each musician is abstractly sketched and the references to technical innovations are presented in simple images by means of imprecise and repetitive language (e.g., the χορδαί with their respective numbers). Thus Μουσική characterizes Melanippides' extension of his tonal palette as "loosening" (χαλαρωτέραν τ' ἐποίησε etc.) while the innovations of Phrynis and Cinesias cause ruin (ὅλην διέφθορεν and ἀπολώλεχ'). Further repetition is seen in the use of the expressions for "bending," and the like. The modulations of Cinesias (mode to mode, diatonic to chromatic) involve "exharmonic twists inside the strophes" (ἐξαρμονίους καμπὰς ποιῶν ἐν ταῖς στροφαῖς); Phrynis is described as κάμπτων με καὶ στρέφων, "bending and twisting (me into a total wreck)"; and, with Elmsley's emendation in line 28 (καμπῶν for κάμπτων), the description of Philoxenus' technique punningly mixes trills (καμπαί) with caterpillars (κάμπαι): καμπῶν με κατεμέστωσε, "fills me up (stuffs me, rolling me up) like a cabbage with wriggling caterpillars."⁶¹ The changes rung on the notions "loose" or "to make loose" are another focal point that exploits the wide semantic range of the oppositions χαλαρός (ἐπανειμένος) ~ σύντονος (ἐντεταμένος) and ἀνιέναι ~ ἐντείνειν.⁶² Of Melanippides Music uses the expression ἀνῆκέ με; Cinesias is said to "loosen" her: χαλαρωτέραν τ' ἐποίησε, while Timotheus "strips and undoes": ἀπέδυσε κἀνέλυσε χορδαῖς δώδεκα.

---

⁵⁹Borthwick, "Notes" 67–68. Another example of the disturbance of balance and harmony.

⁶⁰See Düring, "Studies" 187, and the entry in Henderson, *Maculate Muse* 170-71 (§301).

⁶¹Elmsley's emendation would restore to the uncertain text a compelling reason for the phrase ὥσπερ τε τὰς ῥαφάνους...κατεμέστωσε (Borthwick, "Notes" 71).

⁶²Besides the obvious reference to string tension and tuning, the latter, for example, may mean to "cast in metrical form," "set to music," or "pitch one's voice" (*Clouds* 968, Dover *ad loc*). See Nagy, *Pindar's Homer* 93-94.

Pherecrates' conspiracy of metaphor, vagueness, repetition and comic topoi continues to engage students of Greek music such as Düring, Borthwick, Barker, and Restani who have advanced a variety of conflicting interpretations.

Both characters in the *Chiron* fragment participate in the Old Comic mode of personification exemplified by Aristophanes' antithetical Logoi (the agon of *Clouds*) and the figure of War (*Peace*). Δικαιοσύνη is doubtless a comic take on the Δίκη of archaic poetry[63] while the principal speaker of the harangue personifies τέχνη μουσική, a woman whose lovers and whose very body signal her complex literal and metaphorical association with the cithara. The formal opening, the repeated use of the first person singular (lines 2, 3, 7, etc.), and the priamel-sequence impart to her speech a shade of arrogance enhanced by the willful imprecision noted above. Her dismissal of three sexual partners alternately as ἀποχρῶν ("sufficient," "worth the trouble") and ἀνεκτός ("bearable"), moreover, is tinged with condescension. It is likely that even Timotheus was finally deemed ἀποχρῶν or ἀνεκτός in the rhetorical crescendo towards the summit of abomination, Philoxenus.

On the basis of her tone and relation to the men characterized as ἀποχρῶντες (ἀνεκτός), we submit that Μουσική was *presented as a hetaira* and that her speech is a catalog of professional experiences with different "clients." The curious attitude towards inconvenience and trouble—a mixture of outrage and professional resignation (ἀνεκτός implies a necessary evil)—is best understood, then, as belonging to the world of Athenian courtesans and their comic representation recently outlined by Heinz-Günther Nesselrath and Madeleine Henry for Middle and New Comedy, respectively.[64] Our hypothesis finds support in the frequent and abusive nature of Music's experiences and her condescending acquiescence in them. A striking feature that distinguishes Pherecrates' Lady Music

---

[63]For Dike see Hesiod *Works and Days* 259-264 and Aeschylus fr. 281a (cf. Fraenkel, *Kleine Beiträge* I 260f.). Körte's theory that the delegation in Aristophanes' *Gerytades* was sent to bring back Archaic Poetry (a female personification) is interesting, if impossible to prove (see Norwood, *Greek Comedy* 290-91).

[64]See Nesselrath, *Mittlere Komödie* 318-25, and Henry, *Menander's Courtesans*. See also Konstan, *Greek Comedy and Ideology* 94, 120, 135.

from other comic women is the utter absence of desire for her partners whom she regards, at the very best, as something to be endured.[65] Far from simply implying "bad sex" between Music and her men, this attitude has the symbolic force of designating the relationship, from the hetaira's perspective, as "business," i.e., as distinct from conjugal relations or other voluntary erotic liaisons. The nonchalant εἰ γάρ τι κἀξήμαρτεν, αὖτις ἀνέλαβεν, moreover, suggests a potentially lasting reciprocity. Although the line is commonly translated "he went wrong, but made up for it later" (cf. ἀναλαμβάνω LSJ II.2), the second clause is ambiguous and may just as naturally be understood with the main speaker as direct object: "received (me) back again," "took up (with me) again" (LSJ II.5), or even "won me over" (LSJ IV).[66] This tumultuous mixture of trouble and reconciliation fits well into the context of relations between a courtesan (especially a ἑταίρα μεγαλόμισθος) and her client. By contrast, Timotheus' behavior is especially outrageous in its violation of fundamental respect and the hetaira-client "contract": ἅπαντας οὓς λέγω παρελήλυθεν. Finally, we must wonder about the wider frame of the conversation: a scenario in which two professionals (as opposed to παρθένοι or wives) compare notes is arguably the only social context in which the exchange of fr. 155 K.-A. would be compelling, even acceptable.

From the evidence for hetaira-plays such as *Petale* and *Corianno,* Nesselrath (*Mittlere Komödie* 319) concludes that Pherecrates had an obvious predilection for this topic. We digress for a moment, in this connection, to consider a brief example that has relevance to the thematics of the body in the *Chiron* passage.

---

[65]On various representations of female desire in Greek literature see Dean-Jones, "Politics of Pleasure" 67-68. She notes, for example, that "the functional model of female sexual appetite [articulated, e.g., by the Hippocratic corpus] rationalized and integrated the cultural belief that women constantly desired intercourse with the societal need for obedient and chaste wives who yet were always ready to produce heirs and citizens." For a study of the tragic thematics of language and desire in Euripides' *Hippolytus* see Goff, *Noose of Words*.

[66]Note that the more common translation is weakened by the absence of the noun ἁμαρτία to be governed by ἀνέλαβεν. Our suggestion is simply to propose an equally viable candidate (με) instead of deriving an implicit object (ἁμαρτίαν) from κἀξήμαρτεν.

Combining the topoi of female resourcefulness and lust for drink,[67] fr. 75 of *Corianno* (continued in fr. 76?) features the entrance of a woman who says that she is back from the baths and needs a drink.[68] Another character offers her something in a small glass which she rejects as a nauseating reminder of medicine. At the punch line she produces her own, much larger, vessel with the order, "fill 'er up!"

>   ἐκ τοῦ βαλανείου γὰρ δίεφθος ἔρχομαι,
>   ξηρὰν ἔχουσα τὴν φάρυγα. (Β.) δώσω πιεῖν.
>   (Α.) γλίσχρον γέ μούστὶ τὸ σίαλον νὴ τὼ θεώ.
>   (Β.) †εἰ λάβω κυρισοι† τὴν κοτυλίσκην.[69] (Α.) μηδαμῶς
> 5 μικράν γε. κινεῖται γὰρ εὐθύς μοι χολή,
>   ἐξ οὗπερ ἔπιον ἐκ τοιαύτης φάρμακον.
>   ἐς τὴν ἐμὴν νῦν ἔγχεον τὴν μείζονα

> (A) I'm back from bathing, broiling, my throat parched.
> (B) Well, how 'bout a drink?
> (A) Please! My spit's even sticky, by god!
> (B) I have a little glass for you here ...
> (A) That small one? No way! Ever since I had to take medicine from a thing like that, the very sight of one makes me sick. Fill my personal mug here, this nice BIG one.

The language of the first few lines (δίεφθος, "I'm broiling"; τὴν φάρυγα, "gullet"; γλίσχρον σίαλον, "sticky saliva") is explicit and bold. The woman, perhaps the eponymous hetaira back from working the baths, is characterized by being made to swagger

---

[67] For this topos see also Pherecrates fr. 152 K.-A., Aristophanes, *Lysistrata* 200 and fr. 364 K.-A., and, in later comedy, Eubulus fr. 42 K.-A., Epigenes fr. 4 K.-A.

[68] The fact that the speaker announces that she has come from the public baths is significant and supports the view that she is, in fact, Corianno of the title. Respectable women were generally not to be seen at the baths (cf. Diels-Kranz, *Fragmente* II 407.1.22–4), while a prostitute would have business there (cf. Athenaeus 13.590f.). It is possible, as Ginouvès suggests (*Balaneutiké* 220ff.), that the public baths were open to women for a few hours a day. Aristophanes' *Knights* 1400–1401 implies a close association between baths and prostitutes (although the passage is a paratactic catalogue).

[69] The text is corrupt here. Kock's emendation, no doubt, captures the spirit of what Pherecrates wrote: τί λάβω κεράσαι σοι; (Kaibel: τί λάβω; κεράσω σοι).

with a confidence bordering on ἀναίδεια. The clever play with the dynamics of fluid in almost "clinical" terms places familiar topoi such as the gendered oath, νὴ τὼ θεώ, and ladies' love of liquor in an original thematic context. Corianno (let us assume) has bathed externally (with *water*) and is now dry within (her *saliva* is sticky); she will drink nothing (certainly not *medicine*) that disgusts her (stirs the *bile*) but must fill her own cup with her own "medicine" (indulge her lust for *wine*). Both the *Corianno* and *Chiron* fragments involve their women in a comic exhibition of the body deployed variously to organize a joke, a scene, perhaps even a longer dramatic sequence. Play with language is a primary accomplice in this exhibition and stands out as an Old Comic hallmark. Our passages, brief as they are, resonate with female voices that are resourceful, articulate and funny.[70]

The recent surge of interest in how various meanings, aesthetic, sexual, political, etc., are inscribed into the "body" (as object and sign) has uncovered a symbolic field of enormous breadth and depth.[71] As the vehicle of our existence and consciousness, the body is the locus of our deepest (and most common) experience and, as such, is the cornerstone of all systems of signification and transference (allegory, metaphor, etc.).[72] It is a special challenge, of course, to sufficiently defamiliarize the body in order to appreciate its semiotic potential as it is paradoxically invisible (unseen, taken for granted) *and* the totality of our being. The allegory with which we have been concerned invites us to inquire beyond the narrative surface into the thematics of Pherecrates' unusual constructed

---

[70] Our best surviving example of female characterization in Old Comedy is, of course, Aristophanes' *Lysistrata*. See Henderson, *Lysistrata* xxv-xxxvi, and Taaffe, *Aristophanes and Women* 1-23, 48-73, 134-46.

[71] For a "(partial) archaeology of the field" see Stanton, *Discourses of Sexuality* 1-46. A representative publication (from the new historicist camp) is the Spring 1986 issue of *Representations* (no. 14) edited by Catherine Gallagher and Thomas Laqueur entitled *The Making of the Modern Body: Sexuality and Society in the Nineteenth Century*.

[72] A cursory review of a study such as Lakoff, *Metaphors*, will reveal how deeply the body informs metaphor formation (and all discourses for that matter). The explosion of theoretical studies of the physical and visual aspects of sign language in the wake of Klima, Bellugi et al., *Signs of Language*, has brought to light the fundamental physicality of language, language as essentially a product of the body and its senses.

body. What might we learn, for example, from the way the poet's (already complex) criticism of music is inscribed into the female body—that of a hetaira—positioned at a specific, economically mediated, boundary between men and women outside the *oikos*? How does his bold fusion of comic elements transcend the sum of the parts which include an example of the "good" courtesan,[73] obscene imagery, a priamel-style harangue, and stock criticism of the new music from a conservative point of view? The theatrical appropriation and transformation of the latter is especially interesting for the way it is incarnated in a hetaira's body positioned before the male gaze of the polis.

Commenting on film narrative, Lauren Taaffe, *Aristophanes and Women* 16, notes that it "posits an ideal male spectator and then...manipulates the spectator's gaze to replicate and reinforce cultural images and assumptions about women, men, and male-dominated society." She expands with Jill Dolan's observation that "film offers visual pleasure by objectifying the women in the narrative for the active male protagonist with whom the male spectator is meant to identify. Women are also fetishized as objects to be looked at, thereby decreasing the threat of their sexual lack." This insight into the "construction" of the spectator as *male* maps effectively onto the Athenian festival genres which exhibited almost no concern for a female constituency among the θεαταί (if, in fact, there was one). We should at the outset, then, draw special attention to the way Pherecrates' criticism of music is complicated along gender lines: In the context of the overwhelmingly male gaze of the polis and festival, two male actors playing "women" (feminine nouns concretized) discuss five specific musicians whose innovations are allegorized as sexual relations between them as male "clients" and the hetaira, Μουσική. The *Chiron* fragment, read in the context of this gender polarity, *reveals an alliance between the male demos and the clients of Lady Music.* Pherecrates, by constructing the spectator of his play as exclusively male, invites the demos to identify with Phrynis, Timotheus and the other innovators who purchase the right to ravish tradition, as it were. Innovation is articulated in terms of male desire, pleasure, and

---

[73]See Nesselrath, *Mittlere Komödie* 318-25, for a review of the hetaira-character from Old to Middle Comedy.

power—driving forces within the polis. The superficial harangue against the new music is deconstructed by the deeper configuration of gendered elements—the female speakers, the male clients, the spectators—which structure the progressive violation of tradition as a fundamental (male) appetite and its lawful gratification.

The relationship between the traditional music (of *comedy* among other things!) and individual innovators is now a *two-way transaction*: "clients" such as Cinesias and Timotheus, with whom the male spectator will identify, are free to desire Μουσική as a "free (female) agent" in the polis whose sexual favors they must buy. They purchase their right to "play" which is, by definition, invasive, perhaps even perverse. Μουσική, for her part, expects fair "pay" which may be the subject of negotiation between several clients.[74] We have noted the thoroughgoing allegorization of new musical trends in terms of sexual intercourse. Traditional music is thereby revealed to be a sphere in which *innovation is fundamental,* just as sex is the basis of a hetaira's "business." The humor of fr. 155 K.-A., which has little to do with ethical absolutes, playfully exploits the problem of degree, implying that some clients are more "kinky" than others. Second, Μουσική will be vitally dependent on selling favors to such clients: "My (male) *philoi*," to quote the hetaira's words to Socrates (Xenophon *Memorabilia* 3.11.4), "and the contributions they choose to make *are* my livelihood."

As for the erotic surface of the text, there is little that is appealing. "Not one pleasant word survives ... about the sex" noted K. Lever[75] of Middle Comedies involving hetairai. The prevalent misogyny of Old and Middle comic hetaira-contexts, reviewed by Nesselrath (*Mittlere Komödie* 322) is especially palpable in the lurid scenario where Timotheus κατορώρυχεν / καὶ διακέκναικ' αἴχιστα, "shoveled [Music] into the earth and ground [her] down disgustingly" (connoting forced intercourse).[76]

---

[74] As illustrated, for example, on an early fifth-century cup in the British Museum ("Douris" style, E 51) showing three men bartering for the sexual favors of two women. The central male figure has three fingers raised while the woman with whom he is negotiating has four!

[75] Cited in Nesselrath, *Mittlere Komödie* 322, note 105.

[76] See Henderson, *Maculate Muse* 168 (§292).

The alterity of Athenian popular and legal attitudes[77] taken with the evidence of iconography[78] is a sobering reminder that modern sensibilities are a poor guide indeed to the obscene discourse of Old Comedy. It is important to remember, however, that we are dealing here with allegory—a mode in which the limits of the admissible surpass those constraining "direct" representation. The conceptual sophistication of Pherecrates' critique, moreover, transcends ground-level ribaldry to reveal a decidedly progressive side of his craft in which the meanest material mutates to serve an idea.

Bernhard Zimmermann ("Comedy's Criticism" 40) has recently emphasized the "paradox that on the one hand we find harsh criticism in Aristophanes of these musical innovations while on the other we often find the very same musical innovations being imitated in his own comedies." By embedding a discussion of music in a matrix of hetaira-client relations, Pherecrates engages this paradox in a clever and self-conscious way. We discern an admission (by one intimately involved with music himself) of what might be called a "co-dependency:" the comic poet and his production rely critically on the talents and innovations of progressive musicians whose influence was deep, pervasive and often accepted without comment or critique. At the same time, the playwright—*as comic poet*—reserves the right to lampoon his sister-genre and to isolate eccentricities for ridicule. Thus Pherecrates can simultaneously bemoan Cinesias' "exharmonic twists" in one passage and tout an invention of his own in another (fr. 84 K.-A., *Corianno*, presenting the "Pherecratean"):[79] ἄνδρες, προσέχετε τὸν νοῦν / ἐξευρήματι

---

[77]Cf. Lysias 1.33 and Just, *Women* 68–70. In the fourth century, of course, "rape" (usually in the context of religious festivals) became a common element underlying the comic plot as in Menander's *Samia* and *Epitrepontes*. If the *Chiron* fragment does, in fact, belong to a prologue, it may have had bearing on the plot (a precedent for a New Comic topos?)

[78]Cf. Keuls, *Reign of the Phallus* 180–83.

[79]Such innovation for innovation's sake is censured by Aristophanes at *Wasps* 1052. For novelties announced to the audience see *Clouds* 575-577 and *Ecclesiazusae* 577.

καινῷ, / συμπτύκτοις ἀναπαίστοις, "gentlemen, check out a new discovery: folded anapests!"[80]

The *Chiron* fragment, as we have seen, uses the *forms* of ὀνομαστὶ κωμῳδεῖν deconstructively, i.e., by investing considerable ingenuity and innovation in a scene supposedly directed *against* innovation! This strategy extends further to the ethical sphere as the *target* of the passage (the decadence of new practices) and its *technique* (interest in trendy music expressed in terms of gender) appear to conflict.[81] In what follows we shall consider "Zimmermann's paradox" more carefully by suggesting a diachronic context for the *Chiron* fragment. Though rooted in Old Comic agonistic ribaldry, Pherecrates' experiment looks forward to the reception of dithyramb adumbrated in the late work of Aristophanes. We find ourselves somewhere between the direct criticism and literal enactment prominent in *Clouds* and *Birds*, on the one hand, and the full "absorption" of dithyrambic discourse outlined by Nesselrath, *Mittlere Komödie* 241-80, on the other. Zimmermann's paradox—the tension between criticism and mimesis of dithyramb—is gradually resolved in the Middle Comic assimilation of the genre during the second quarter of the fourth century.

The dithyramb in comedy: from criticism to mimesis

From the political satires of the 420's through the Middle Comic period we can trace a variety of theatrical responses to the new music and dithyramb. We begin by identifying distinct endpoints that frame this evolving interaction between genres: in the early stages of Aristophanes' career the new music is a concrete, *external* object of ridicule on a level with a host of other targets. Thus, at *Peace* 829, when asked if he had seen any other man "wandering about the heavens" during his flight, Trygaeus replies, "not really, unless you count the shades of two or three dithyrambists." He goes on to explain that they were "flitting

---

[80]The word προσέχετε (*PCG* text) conforms to common Aristophanic usage (but cf. Hermann's πρόσσχετε, based on the reading πρόσχετε, which would be suitable for the rigidity of the metre).

[81]For a cautious approach to Aristophanic imitation of dithyramb see Dover, *Frogs* 362 (with bibliography), and Zimmermann, *Untersuchungen* (passim, especially on *Birds* 227-62).

about collecting ideas for some preludes (ἀναβολαί) of the air-haunting-swiftly-soaring kind." At the other end of the spectrum is the full absorption of dithyrambic discourse in Middle Comedy in which parody of the genre was subordinated to a variety of other dramatic purposes. Nesselrath's outline of this evolutionary moment, *Mittlere Komödie* 265, is worth quoting in full:

> Rätselspaß, absurdes Bravourstück und sprachliches Medium gerade der frechesten und sozial am weitesten unten stehended Bühnencharaktere—diese drei Funktionen haben das Dithyrambisieren in der Mittleren Komödie offenbar zu einem wichtigen Mittel der Komik werden lassen; und die Anwendung dieses Mittels scheint in der Tat weitgehend auf die Mese beschränkt zu sein. Die Alte Komödie hatte zwar schon die Dithyrambendichter selbst als Zielscheibe, noch nicht aber die Seltsamkeiten ihrer Sprache als Mittel der komischen Stilisierung von bestimmten Bühnenfiguren entdeckt; und als die Neue Komödie sich endgültig herausgebildet hatte, war der jüngere Dithyrambos schon wieder weitgehend aus dem öffentlichen Interesse verschwunden.

An important aspect of this transition from explicit criticism to creative mimesis is the gradual loss of interest in the performance of the dithyramb and its individual practitioners. In the mature phase of Middle Comedy the dithyramb survives almost exclusively in the verbal sphere as a peculiar type of poetry. Nesselrath's three functions, in fact, are achieved with a fairly narrow range of linguistic tools, e.g., ubiquitous descriptive participles, cryptic periphrases for familiar things, complex adjectival morphology, asyndetic relative clauses and appositives, bold metaphors, etc. The progressive assimilation of the dithyramb can be traced through a series of overlapping "modes," variously represented in the extant plays of Aristophanes and comic fragments:

1. Direct lampoons of the genre and its representatives: Next to the contemptuous joke about διθυραμβοδιδάσκαλοι cited above (*Peace* 829), we might place any number of specific jabs at the dithyramb and individual musicians such as the scorn heaped on Chaeris in the opening monologue of *Acharnians* (line 16) and the election of Meles and the same Chaeris as Athens' worst citharists in Pherecrates fr. 6 K.-A. (see above, p. 149). The contrast between the "good old days" and the horrible new music was evidently quite fashionable in the 420's, as we gather from passages such as this (*Savages*, produced in 420) and virtually every one of Aristophanes' first five extant plays. Approval of the old musical education in the agon of *Clouds* (lines 963-972), for example, is contrasted with Phrynis' new style with its καμπαὶ δυσκολοκάμπτοι, "(technically) torturous flourishes," that "extinguish the Muses." The results of the new education are enacted as Pheidippides rejects his father's request for a respectable "old" song and recites lewd Euripides instead (lines 1371-1372).

2. The dithyrambist onstage: This step involves bringing a musician onstage as a *dramatis persona* and having him take part in the action, thereby embedding him and his genre more deeply into the fabric of the play. The fullest representative of this heightened theatricalization are two intruder-scenes in *Birds* that feature, first, an unnamed lyric poet (lines 904-959), and, second, the famous Cinesias (lines 1373-1409). Comedy's reaction to the dithyramb and its poets appears now (414 BC) noticeably more complex: the first intruder's bogus claims and (partially) dithyrambic prattle manage, somehow, to win Peisetaerus' sympathy. Though Cinesias is caricatured more forcefully, Aristophanes has obviously invested some effort in portraying the man and imitating his style. Peisetaerus greets him with a funny imitation that plays on the critical terms "cyclic" and "foot": τί δεῦρο πόδα σὺ κυλλὸν ἀνὰ κύκλον κυκλεῖς; "Why have you come here circling circles with halting foot?" To which Cinesias replies that he *must* become a bird in order to "procure from the clouds new air-whisked, snow-swept preludes" (again, the "flighty dithyramb" topos, lines 1378-1385). His entire art "depends on [clouds]," he explains, "The most brilliant of dithyrambs are misty, murky, black-rayed, wing-whisked. You'll know when you hear them!" At this Cinesias lunges into a spirited performance which Peisetaerus struggles to interrupt. The punch line of the scene is Peisetaerus' invitation "to train [dithyrambic choruses] here for Leotrophides, a chorus of flying birds, a tribe of the Corncakers" (Κρεκοπίδα φυλήν, with Kock's emendation). Cinesias is made to answer Comedy on behalf of his genre, as it were: "You're obviously mocking me!" He dances off nonchalantly, however, with the promise, "But I won't stop, I assure you, until I sprout wings and run right through the airs!" This enactment of a confrontation between genres betrays a close study of the dithyramb and is more playful than critical.

3. **The dithyramb as drama:** On the way towards the full "absorption" of the dithyramb in mature Middle Comedy, we find dramatic moments in which the genre is reconfigured more thoroughly as part of a play: Agathon's monody in *Thesmophoriazusae* and the exchange between Cario and the chorus at *Wealth* 290-321 reveal different aspects of this progressive theatricalization. A distinguishing feature of these two improvisations on the dithyramb is an explicit "frame" that identifies them as such. Agathon's slave, for example, spins a bombastic prelude whose style and dithyrambic buzzwords prepare us for Agathon's metrically and musically modern aria: μέλλει . . . δρυόχους τιθέναι δράματος ἀρχάς. / κάμπτει δὲ νέας ἀψῖδας ἐπῶν, "[my master] is about to lay the foundation-timbers for a drama. He's *twisting* words into new structures" (lines 52-53); and χειμῶνος οὖν ὄντος, / κατακάμπτειν τὰς στροφὰς οὐ ῥᾴδιον, "it's not easy to *turn and twist his strophes* in the winter" (lines 67-68). A reference to the familiar "ant-paths" specifies the nature of the Kinsman's irritation (the new music "bugs" him, so to speak): μύρμηκος ἀτραπούς, ἢ τί διαμινύρεται; "Is he warbling ant-paths, or what?" (line 100). "The *metabolai kata rhythmon* [of Agathon's song]," notes Zimmermann, "Comedy's Criticism" 45, "guarantee a certain internal structure by dividing the song in small units." The oxymoron παράρυθμ' εὔρυθμα (line 121) underscores the paradox "that the monody is composed in a rhythm which at the same time both suits the song and dance and contradicts them." Though a comic exaggeration, this aria in the dithyrambic mode ("Phrygian," lines 120-22) is not inconsonant with the impression we get from Aristotle who notes Agathon's innovations in the areas of plot (*Poetics* 1451b18-23) and format (*Poetics* 1456a27-32). Aristophanes' caricature works, in fact, as a distorted demonstration of one of Agathon's "trademark" interludes showcasing fancy composition and performance. We note, in passing, that Agathon's song and its "effeminate" delivery initiate the gender-game that informs so much of

Thesmophoriazusae.[82] It is as if the mimesis of dithyrambic discourse entails appropriate changes in a man's very nature: ὅμοια γὰρ ποιεῖν ἀνάγκη τῇ φύσει, "a man must compose according to his nature" (line 167).

The second of our examples of the dithyramb as drama—and certainly one of the most intriguing—is found in Aristophanes' last extant play, *Wealth*, produced in 388. Cario, Chremylus' *servus callidus*, summons his master's friends, the chorus of poor rustics, who improvise with him a variation on Philoxenus' *Cyclops*. This famous dithyramb was written, according to an anecdote in Athenaeus (1.6e ff.), as an autobiographical court-allegory:[83]

> Dionysius [I] enjoyed drinking with Philoxenus. But when he noticed that [the poet] was attempting to seduce his beloved Galatea, he cast him into the quarry. There Philoxenus composed *Cyclops*, basing the plot on the calamity that befell him and representing Dionysius as the Cyclops, the flute-girl as Galatea, and himself as Odysseus.

Although details of the anecdote vary from source to source,[84] there can be little doubt that the literary myth of Polyphemus and Galatea has its origins in the allegorical dithyramb.[85] The fame of this influential composition has a great deal to do with its experimental nature. In his *Cyclops*, Philoxenus appears to have extended the mimetic potential of choral lyric into a sort of "drama" involving

> the insertion of actual solo-passages into [the] dithyramb so that monody and even dialogue-passages (still presumably in lyric meters) as well as instrumental solos were interspersed with the choral poetry performed by the traditional round

---

[82]See the classic exposition of the gender thematics of *Thesmophoriazusae* in Zeitlin, "Travesties" 169-217. Taaffe, *Aristophanes and Women* 74-102, is a valuable recent contribution to the study of the play.
[83]On Philoxenus' *Cyclops* see, most recently, Sancho Royo, "Analisis," and Sutton, "Dithyramb as Drama," with full bibliographies.
[84]See Sutton, "Dithyramb as Drama" 37.
[85]Sancho Royo, "Analisis" 48, puts it this way: "With Philoxenus the narrative, dramatic and epic aspects of the myth died, as it were, leaving only the romance and love between Polyphemus and Galatea."

chorus... The *Cyclops* would still be a recognizable dithyramb but might nevertheless merit the designation δρᾶμα. It would be more than a purely choral lyric production although something less than a true play. Modern terminology has words for such works of intermediate nature, such as oratorio and masque.[86]

The attention lavished on Philoxenus in *Wealth* is not surprising, given Aristophanes' tendency to single out the innovative aspects of his contemporaries' work for parody, refashioning and other types of response.[87] On a technical level, Aristophanes recreates Philoxenus' experiment by foregrounding the self-aware mimesis of soloist and chorus in vigorous interaction. The ease with which a segment of the dithyramb grafts into this comic context highlights the capacity of the two genres for formal and thematic interaction. There is a price to pay, however, and we note a transformation whereby polymetric variety of the model yields to simple iambic strophes and the mythical narrative is subordinated to the "coarse pleasantry of Athenian rustics."[88] We must not be too quick, however, to dismiss the thematic relevance of Philoxenus' *Cyclops* to Aristophanes' play. A.M. Bowie (*Aristophanes* 287), for example, has recently suggested that Cario's performance intimates a Cyclopean world in which Penia and her arguments are rendered powerless. Indeed, the clash of genres and the (potential) clash of worlds in the parodos work together to make the interlude an arresting and effective turning point in the play. Cario, announcing his transition from one fiction to another (Polyphemus, Circe, then back to "himself"), represents the dithyramb as a rival genre in a direct confrontation with a typical comic chorus. The latter participates in the exchange as a comic and utopian subset of the demos that appropriates the μῆτις of the Homeric Odysseus[89] to hypothesize a strategic victory over the wild and anti-social figures imported, mimetically, from the dithyramb. Everything remains in the realm of the potential, signaled verbally and gesturally but not enacted with any further permanence.

[86]Sutton, "Dithyramb as Drama" 42.
[87]See Dobrov, "Tereus," for an Aristophanic response to Sophoclean innovation in *Tereus*.
[88]Rogers, *Plutus* 33; See also Zimmerman, *Untersuchungen* I 159.
[89]For Odysseus' μῆτις see Pucci, *Odysseus Polutropos* 16-17, 243-44.

Comedy frames its mimesis of the dithyramb with appropriate gestures and language. As the dialogue trimeter is about to yield to the lyrics, for example, the rustics announce their role in the forthcoming exchange by responding to Cario's news in self-reflexive choral terms (line 288): ὡς ἥδομαι καὶ τέρπομαι καὶ βούλομαι χορεῦσαι, "I'm delighted! I'm so happy I think I'll dance!" Cario then marks his song as a dithyramb with the onomatopoetic "θρεττανελό"—a significant bit of sound-symbolism alluding to the Doric strains of a cithara. The dancer describes his dance and announces the first in a sequence of fanciful transformations, experiments in competitive shape-shifting (lines 290-291):

> καὶ μὴν ἐγὼ βουλήσομαι θρεττανελὸ τὸν Κύκλωπα
> μιμούμενος καὶ τοῖν ποδοῖν ὡδὶ παρενσαλεύων
> ὑμᾶς ἄγειν.
>
> Now I'll imitate the Cyclops—twang!—and lead the way, dancing, moving my feet like this!

On our reading, the original court allegory has mutated to represent the interplay of genres in the "potential" mood. Cario secures his identity as Philoxenus' character with a direct quotation: ἀλλ' εἶα τέκεα θαμίν' ἐπαναβοῶντες, "Come on, all my little ones, with incessant clamor."[90] The choristers reject the subordinate role assigned to them by the uncouth Cyclops and assume the aggressive mask of Odysseus and, by metonymy, his comrades. They describe their enemy in "dithyrambic" terms as carrying a wallet and herbs—features of Philoxenus' production[91]—and relate how they will overcome him in his sleep and drive a stake into his eye (Aristophanes cleverly substitutes his own sound symbolism, σφηκίσκον ἐκτυφλῶσαι, for Homer's famous σίζ[ε] at *Odyssey* 9.394). The players of comedy demonstrate their mastery over the dithyramb by outwitting Philoxenus' character and, implicitly, his composition. If we trust the anecdote of Athenaeus, the dithyrambist has been shifted

---

[90]This line and the θρεττανελό of line 290 are identified by the scholiast as coming from the original by Philoxenus.
[91]So the Scholiast: Φιλοξένου ἐστὶ παρηγμένον καὶ τοῦτο τὸ ῥητόν· τοιοῦτον γὰρ τὸν Κύκλωπα εἰσάγει, πήραν ἔχοντα καὶ ἐπὶ ταύτῃ λάχανα ἄγρια.

from his role as Odysseus in the model to that of the dumb Cyclops in the comedy!

Cario then changes both his form and the allegorical reference: "I'll now assume the role of that Circe who, of late in Corinth, concocted drugs and made the comrades of Philonides, as pigs, eat shit-cakes which she kneaded herself" (lines 302-306). The reference is set up earlier in the play when Chremylus says to the daimon Wealth: "And doesn't [the hetaira] Lais love Philonides thanks to you?" A popular target of ridicule, Philonides[92] is often lampooned in terms of women: he is Lais' dupe, his mother was a camel, etc. The characteristics of the leader are again transferred to the comrades and Circe-Lais gloats at their humiliation and caprophagous travesty of xenia (lines 304-305): ἔπεισεν ὡς ὄντας κάπρους μεμαγμένον σκῶρ ἐσθίειν, αὐτὴ δ' ἔματτεν αὐτοῖς. The chorus respond to the scatological taunt in kind by stripping off the mask and attacking the actor: "We'll now play Odysseus and string you up by your balls and rub your nose, as if it were a goat's, in shit!"[93]

The allegory has been dismantled and the dithyrambic inspiration exhausted. Cario anticipates the end of the interlude with the final and most explicit metatheatrical comment. He links the transformation induced by Circe's drugs with the travesty of genre (lines 316-317):

> ἀλλ' εἶα νῦν τῶν σκωμμάτων ἀπαλλαγέντες ἤδη
> ὑμεῖς ἐπ' ἀλλ' εἶδος τρέπεσθ',
>
> And now, set aside the travesty and
> assume the other form (i.e. return to your *genre*)

Cario signals his return to himself and his genre by replacing Circe's active kneading (μάττω) with his own stealthy consumption (μασώμενος: he will steal food and continue working while *chewing*). The window of possible fictions is closed as the action resumes with Chremylus' entrance.

As we move into the fourth century, then, we see a shift away from bald criticism of the dithyramb to its mimesis on the levels of technique (meter, music), performance, character,

---

[92] For ridicule of Philonides see Philyllius fr. 22 K.-A.; Plato (Comicus) fr. 65 K.-A., Nicochares fr. 4 K.-A., Theopompus fr. 5 K.-A.

[93] For Aristyllus and the "μίνθος incident" see *Ecclesiazusae* 646-648.

theme, and language. The latter category will eventually prevail as interest in the others wanes. Before its final "absorption," however, the dithyramb is drawn more deeply into the fabric of comedy for creative improvisations on its many aspects such as we have seen in Agathon's aria and the parodos of *Wealth*. The shift from lampoon to study appears, in a sense, to be an admission of a long-standing involvement with the new music and its trends.

4. The dithyramb as "strange language": In the second quarter of the fourth century the range of comedy's responses to, and assertions of difference from, other genres narrowed considerably. The fragments of mature Middle Comedy attest to the final stage in our evolutionary scheme in which the dithyramb loses most of its musical, metrical, and performative characteristics to be absorbed into the comic arsenal as an odd sort of poetry, a style comprising a rather narrow inventory of techniques: bold metaphors, an abundance of descriptive participles, new and complex adjectives, asyndetic relatives and appositives, and odd periphrases for ordinary things. Commenting on an interesting example of the latter from the *Milesioi* of Alexis (spoken by a cook) Norwood, *Greek Comedy* 43, notes that it "rises at the end into queer poetry":

> 15 ἑστήκαθ' ὑμεῖς, κάεται δέ μοι τὸ πῦρ,   (fr. 153 K.-A.)
> ἤδη πυκνοὶ δ' ἄττουσιν Ἡφαίστου κύνες
> κούφως πρὸς αἴθραν, οἷς τὸ γίγνεσθαί θ' ἅμα
> καὶ τὴν τελευτὴν τοῦ βίου συνῆψέ τις
> μόνοις ἀνάγκης θεσμὸς οὐχ ὁρώμενος.

> There you stand. My fire burns
> and already the hounds of Hephaestus
> flit in a nimble shower airwards: for
> them alone birth and death are enfolded
> in the same instant by an invisible
> ordinance of necessity.

> (adapted from Norwood)

This distillation to a riddling and highly "other" style spoken incongruously by lowly characters is understandable in light of the importance which music and performance had for the dithyramb as a whole: reduced to a formless stream of language (without the rhythm, music and delivery), the bare script of a piece such as Timotheus' *Persae* would indeed have difficulty standing on its own.[94] A paradox in the evolution of comedy's response to the dithyramb, then, is that the highly genre-conscious experiments with dithyramb as drama in the transitional period (approximately 410-390) resulted in the gradual appropriation of dithyrambic discourse with an attendant disappearance of the literary agon,[95] that contest animated by a self-conscious spirit of rivalry exemplified, above all, by *Frogs*.

Conclusion: Pherecrates' Dramatization of Dithyramb

The implication of the ancient testimonia that Pherecrates belonged to a forward-looking, alternative "school" (i.e., distinct from Eupolis, Aristophanes, et al.) is difficult to evaluate. Although our brief review of the most important parameter—that of personal invective—does not *contradict* Aristotle or the Anonymus, it offers little in the way of positive support for assertions, such as Norwood's (*Greek Comedy* 165), that Pherecrates was "more notable than Crates as an exponent of the urbane side of Old Comedy" and that he "belongs even more than Plato or Phrynichus to the Middle Comedy."

Our reading of fr. 155 K.-A. (*Chiron*) has suggested an indirect approach to Pherecrates from the perspective of comedy's evolving response to the dithyramb. The conceptual and verbal sophistication of the *Chiron* fragment place it squarely in our third category above—"the dithyramb as drama"—i.e., much closer to the *Wealth* of Aristophanes than to his *Clouds*. The dithyramb has been dismantled, as it were, and reconfigured as a play thematized along gender lines: the field of Music is personified as a hetaira, prominent musicians are represented as her clients, and musical terminology is used to express the business between them. The sexual innuendo that deceptively imparts to the passage an Old Comic color is, in fact, part of a

---

[94] As would a Wagnerian libretto (Nesselrath, *Mittlere Komödie* 265).
[95] For a stimulating study of agon and its thematics from lyric into drama, see Nagy, *Pindar's Homer* 382-413 (Chapter 13): "The Genesis of Athenian State Theater and the Survival of Pindar's Poetry."

subtle exposition of comedy's ambivalence towards the new music and dithyramb. Fr. 155 K.-A. is less an exercise in direct criticism than it is a reflexive study of "Zimmermann's paradox" (see p. 163) and the terminology of the new music. Like Agathon's monody in *Thesmophoriazusae* and the parodos of *Wealth*, the *Chiron* fragment exhibits deep interest in, and study of, the dithyramb—qualities of late Old Comic theatricalization that laid the groundwork for the Middle Comic "fad" outlined by Nesselrath. We can thus catch another glimpse of Pherecrates' craft and how he contributed to the evolution of his genre.

Beyond Aristophanes

Jeffrey Henderson

Our attestation of Greek comedy includes a wider range of composers, and covers a longer continuous period of time, than any other Greek poetic genre. Yet scholarship has tended to concentrate almost exclusively on the extant remains of only two composers, Aristophanes and Menander, leaving their contemporaries, and the composers who bridged their eras, relatively unexplored. Nesselrath's *Die attische Mittlere Komödie: Ihre Stellung in der antiken Literaturkritik und Literaturgeschichte* (1990) was the first comprehensive treatment of the intermediate era in 152 years. As often happens, scholarly neglect has bred contempt, an attitude well illustrated in this case by Gilbert Norwood's summary judgment (*Greek Comedy* 38):

> Middle Comedy is a backwater; the fourth century is a century of prose: many single pages of Plato and Demosthenes are worth all these remnants. Between the excitingly varied landscape of Old Comedy and the city of Menander stretches a desert: therein the sedulous topographer may remark two respectable eminences, and perhaps a low ridge in the middle distance, or a few nullahs, and the wayfarer will greet with delight one or two oases with a singing bird or so; but the ever-present foreground of his journey is sand, tiresome, barren and trickling.

Yet this is the period when comedy became truly international and professional, and when even a huge supply of original comedies could scarcely keep up with demand. Had comic and poetic standards really fallen so low so fast? If the entire Greek-speaking world from Italy to the Black Sea seems to have been well pleased with their comic poets, on what basis have we the right to condemn their judgment? If Thalia's heart had indeed been broken, as Norwood proclaims in the ironic epigraph to

Dobrov's introduction, it seems best to ask her about it directly: the texts themselves are our only sure basis.

Happily, the ongoing and gratifyingly rapid publication of the Kassel-Austin *PCG* is rekindling interest in these overlooked stretches of the comic terrain, and the present book, along with Nesselrath's, are but the first of what will surely be a new series of maps for wayfarers eager to journey beyond Aristophanes and to take a fresh look at what they see. Our editor to be congratulated for creating this opportunity for a team of scholars to focus its attention on some of the productive new approaches now underway. They have left precious little for this commentator to add, other than to underline some key ideas and discoveries and to suggest what seem to be promising directions for further exploration.

The greatest impediment to the study and appreciation of Middle Comic composers is their entirely fragmentary attestation—the reasons for which would be interesting to know—and the consequent difficulty of reconstructing their plots, assessing the character of their plays and identifying trends. But Nesselrath's essay on the *gonai*-plays, which exemplify but one thematic trend from the transitional phase of Attic comedy so impressively identified and surveyed in his book, shows how much our fragments and testimonial sources can tell us if we attend to them with care and imagination. The essay calls attention to the major role played by myth in the history of Greek comedy and reminds us how much work remains to be done in that area, not only for the Middle Comic period but for earlier periods as well, in Athens and elsewhere. Because all of our extant plays from the fifth century happen to be topical comedy should not blind us to the comparable importance of mythical comedy. For it is a fact that no less than half of the plays datable to the period of Aristophanes alone were mythological, and the popularity of myth as a comic subject remained only slightly diminished from that level until the 350's at the earliest. Myth may well turn out to be important in tracing the prehistory of Attic comedy as well, to judge from its prominence in Epicharmus and in the neighboring genres of tragedy and dithyramb. If the Middle Comic period was innovative, there were still important elements of continuity, among them perhaps even re-stagings of the more exportable Attic Old Comedies, as Taplin's *Comic Angels* argues from the iconographic record.

At the same time we must be cautious in determining the corpus of mythological comedies. Didascalia and titles can be treacherous guides: were these all that remained of Aristophanes' *Acharnians*, *Thesmophoriazousae* and *Wealth*, or of Menander's *Sicyonians*, for example, we would be unable to discern the vital roles played by myth in them. Such plays also raise the complex issue of parody and the cyclical pattern of its targets: Nesselrath's *gonai*-plays seem to feed mostly on epic/hymnic sources; Aristophanes prefers tragedy (especially Euripides) and practically ignores epic; while a generation earlier epic parody seems prominent in the plays of Cratinus. So are these *gonai*-plays a novelty or a reversion to an earlier style, or some of both? A full answer will have to include tragedy and dithyramb as well as comedy, and that of course means dealing with the fragmentary record as well as with our extant examples. It also means asking not merely *how* comic poets parodied other genres but *why*: no easy task even in the plays of Aristophanes, where we have plots, contexts and some extant targets. In this connection we look forward to the publication of Dobrov's book *Tropics of Play: Fictions of Theater, Genre, and Society in Greek Drama*.

There is also the problem of attribution. *CGPF* 215, attributable to one Philiscus, is an impressive piece of writing, but because Philiscus is "an obscure writer active for (it seems) only a couple of years around 400, of whom next to nothing is otherwise known" (p. 25, above). Nesselrath is inclined to award the fragment to Antiphanes, and Kassel-Austin plan to relegate it to the *Adespota*. But can we be sure that Philiscus' obscurity is not merely a product of transmission? And even if he *was* as obscure as the record suggests, we must remember that the annals of the arts are replete with excellent works whose authors created little or nothing else of note.

"Transition" traces a development *from* something *to* something, and the essays by Rosen, Dobrov, and Urios-Aparisi are salutary reminders that we should not be too confident that we have a solid picture of Old Comedy to start with. Concentration on Aristophanes' extant plays has created a misleadingly narrow picture of the genre. Certainly some trends that seem prominent in the Middle Comic period begin already in the fifth century, so that we should not at the outset be over-strict when postulating chronological boundaries or areas of characteristic emphasis in a given era. We should bear in mind also the revue-like character of the exant examples of Old Comedy, where diverse elements, some traditional and some novel, are combined into one plot. If we had only quotations from the second half of *Acharnians* or *Frogs*, for example, we should never guess what the first half had been like. Rosen has shown that Plato's comedies look more Middle Comic than those of his contemporary, Aristophanes, while Dobrov and Urios-Aparisi reveal a Pherecrates whose character as Old Comic or Middle Comic composer seems to lie in the eye of the beholder, or on what feature is being beheld. The same may well be true of other Old Comic poets, and even of the non-extant work of Aristophanes himself. Nor should we overlook, for the fifth century, the vibrant *western* comic tradition of poets like Epicharmus, which Aristotle says had begun to influence Attic poets like Crates in the generation *before* Aristophanes. In this connection we keenly await the western installment of the *PCG* and, on the iconographic side, follow-up on the hunches put in play by Taplin's *Comic Angels*.

In the work of tracing the diversity and evolution of comedy we must be as alert to those features that continued to be productive as we are to those that seem to be new. I suggest that the successful approaches already developed for the evaluation of Hellenistic poetry (including techniques for teasing context out of fragments) might turn out to be useful also for evaluating the development of fourth-century comedy.

Conversely, we should not be too quick to postulate what was "characteristic" of one or the other period. Political satire is a good example. Since most of our attested Old Comedy is confined to the relatively small number of plays composed in the period *c.* 430-410, what we might call the demagogic phase of the Peloponnesian War, our impression of the centrality of political satire in Old Comedy may to some extent be a false emphasis resulting from the selection of plays made for posterity by the Alexandrians. I have already mentioned the evidence for substantial production of mythological comedy alongside political satire in the Old Comic period, and one could add the domestic comedies said to be "characteristic" of Crates and Pherecrates (though the fragments of the latter's *Chiron*, under the scrutiny of Dobrov and Urios-Aparisi, tell a different tale than his testimonial reputation has led us to expect). The same cautions apply to our impression of the *absence* of political satire in the Middle Comic period. There is very little in the fragments, but Isocrates in 355 could still complain about the irresponsibility of political satire in comedy (*On the Peace* 8.14), as does Plato some years later (*Laws* 935e), and Aeschines could still invoke the "evidence" of satirical comic anapests in his prosecution of Timarchus (1.157). The fragments of Timocles, whose career overlapped with Menander's, are similarly suggestive.

Ken Rothwell's essay moves us from thematic to structural aspects of evolution by reopening the question of the supposedly vanished chorus. He is right to stress that the sheer vitality of the comic theater after 404 undercuts the view that changes in comic drama are evidence that Athens' loss of a war and an empire ushered in an era of distressed impoverishment, and he is right to remind us that the institution of the *choregia* remained alive and well through most of the fourth century. Rothwell's association of the comic chorus with the degree of audience engagement is fascinating, though I have doubts about a simple contrast between fifth-century activism vs. fourth-century apathy. After all, it was in 425 that Aristophanes portrayed assemblymen as having to be herded into the Assembly, while it was in the fourth century that the Theoric Fund enabled everyone to attend the theater and when a dual career as actor and politician became feasible.

I am skeptical, too, about the assumption that the changes affecting the chorus in the fourth century indicate that the chorus somehow went into decline. This assumption is based on the virtual absence of choral poetry in our fourth-century texts. Yet, as Rothwell says, there is plenty of external evidence for the chorus in that century, and one could easily multiply his examples. What we can say for certain is that not many choral passages are *transmitted* to us, but it does not necessarily follow that the chorus had lost its vitality or its importance in the dramatic performances, or that choruses were expendable or no longer connected with the plot. *Something* happened in those spots where we now read χοροῦ. That we do not have the choral texts may mean simply that the poets less frequently wrote the choral parts themselves, so that they were not transmitted to posterity as the poet's own work. This phenomenon is apparent already in the plays of Aristophanes, several of which contained choral performances of traditional texts that are not transmitted in our manuscripts.

It may well be that in the fourth century choral writing, like acting, became more professionalized, with fewer poets able to write both dialogue and choruses. Developments that may have forced such specialization are the greater demand for plays in this era, reflected in the huge output of poets like Antiphanes, and the greater sophistication of choral writing, reflected in the complexities of the New Dithyramb that so annoyed and intrigued the aging Aristophanes. A changed theatrical landscape may also have played a role in the separation of choral from dramatic texts: for a touring company (as opposed to a local festival troupe) a chorus may well have been optional, depending on local conditions, so that dramatic texts had to be stageworthy with or without a chorus and adaptable to more than one kind of choral component. In these conditions it is not surprising that the texts that reached Alexandria for transmission to posterity will have contained only dialogue.

If that is so, then for all we know fourth-century choruses may have been vastly superior musically and choreographically to their fifth-century predecessors, who after all had been local amateurs, some pressed into service, who competed in a single festival. And for all we know fourth-century choruses may have been just as well integrated into the drama as fifth-century ones. In this connection, we should reconsider what exactly we mean by "integrated" or "important to" the plot, and we should begin with the late fifth-century plays by Aristophanes, Sophocles and Euripides whose choruses we do possess: how "integrated" are these choruses, and in what ways? What difference would it make if these choruses were not transmitted?

When we come to the issue of plot and aesthetics we find that Dobrov and Slater exhibit a stimulating complementarity. For Slater, the developing illusionism of fourth-century comedy did not depend on processes internal to the comic tradition, such as as the influence of tragedy or heroic myth, but was rather an adaptation to the requirements of a diverse and internationalized audience that demanded a more standardized and portable product. For Dobrov, the polysemous Old Comic "character" gives way to a homogeneous verbal mask, the stock type, and the Old Comic situational farrago gives way to a more naturalistic discourse as the result of processes both internal to the comic tradition and external to it (especially the changing social dynamics of the dramatic festivals).

No doubt both of these insights provide part of the answer to our questions about the evolution of the comic mythos. But the very persuasiveness of each account suggests that we need more fine-tuning of both our critical and our evolutionary models. If illusionism and stock types were really the product of a new internationalism, what of those plays by Menander that were written for local Attic production? Was Old Comic polysemy an feature internal to the genre or was it prompted by a linguistic environment peculiar to the fifth century? At what point did the local festivals begin to absorb the new international style? And was internationalism primarily a fourth-century development? After all, tragedy was already a highly exportable commodity in the days of Aeschylus, and possibly even before, since the conviction of Phrynichus in 493/92 forbade *reperformance* (where?) of his *Capture of Miletus*. As for comedy, Aristophanes claims (no later than 417) to have privileged the Athenians by producing his *Clouds* for them first (this is the clear import of *Clouds* 522-523), and Taplin has shown that Old Comedy had indeed made its way west by the early fourth century. So perhaps it was only the more *topical* fifth-century plays that tended to remained a local product and to keep to the old styles of festive competition, while all along the more adventuresome poets would occasionally write for a wider audience. An early parallel for this sort of career is Pindar, who mastered both an international style and intimate local ones, depending on the circumstances of his contract.

In this scenario, we should look rather for dominant trends, or a range of possibilities, in a given era rather than for a series of revolutionary changes. The proliferation of international venues for drama in the fourth century surely encouraged the development of more universal, and perhaps more illusionistic, styles of drama, but at the same time the development of these styles must have originated within the traditions of character and plot that were internal to the dramatic genres and that had their roots in the traditional festivals, which of course still continued to thrive. In a sense we have a chicken-and-egg problem, with changes in the genre and the expectations of new audiences going hand-in-hand.

In its critical approach Dobrov's discussion of linguistic characterization raises some complex issues that would more suitably be handled in a seminar than in a brief thumbnail sketch, so I will simply touch on some of its basic points here.

On the connection of the "imagist" style of Old Comedy with parodic force in references to mythical characters I would be prepared to argue for more nuance. Dicaeopolis, as Dobrov notes, often incorporates or assimilates the language and even the personae of tragedy without calling attention to his external sources, as in his opening harangue. Tragic language and situation thus seem to have become part of a discourse common to tragedy and comedy—what we might, with Dicaeopolis, call *trygedy*. Was the same sort of thing true of the relationship of Middle Comedy to the new dithyramb? The examination by Dobrov and Urios-Aparisi of the Pherecratean attitude toward dithyramb establishes points of contact with the late Aristophanes and suggests that, in comedy, initial hostility to the new dithyramb has been leading to integration, or better, comic incorporation or usurpation, like a python circling, capturing and finally digesting a rabbit. Somehow, the digestion of tragedy helped turn Old Comedy into New Comedy; what did the digestion of dithyramb lead to? The novel and suggestive conclusion of the essay by Dobrov and Urios-Aparisi points to much work yet to be done in this area; Nesselrath's *Mittlere Komödie* collects much of the relevant material for analysis, and we now have a new book on the dithyramb by Zimmermann.

Dobrov connects the development of an illusionistic theater with the poet's withdrawal from the world and the language of his play noting that the engagement of poet with polis was essential to one particular type of play, the topical satire. In plays that did not set out to satirize local politics—mythological plays, for example, or plays addressed to an international audience—there would ordinarily be no particular need for a poet to insert himself into the play. Hence the importance of connecting the role of the poet with generic as well as evolutionary processes in order to include consideration of a play's social and political environment alongside aesthetic considerations. Comedy is always on some level a participatory experience.

Finally, though Dobrov is right to say that there is some degree of linguistic distinctiveness as we move from one Aristophanic play to the next, on the whole Aristophanic characters achieve uniqueness more by their situation than by their language, and in this sense each is just as unique as any tragic character, with the typology of social background standing in for the typology of heroic myth. The problem with tracing these features of comic characterization from the fifth to the fourth century is of course our ignorance of Middle Comic plots: were the situations as "typical" as the characters seem to be? When did the "typical" plot characteristic of Menander begin, and by what stages?

Bibliography

Abel, Lionel. 1963. *Metatheatre: A New View of Dramatic Form*. New York.
Abraham, Gerald. 1979. *The Concise Oxford History of Music*. Oxford.
Allen, T. W., W. R. Halliday, and E. E. Sikes. 1936. *The Homeric Hymns*. Oxford.
Amandry, Pierre. 1976. "Trépieds d'Athènes: I, Dionysies." *Bulletin de Correspondance Hellénique* 100.15-93.
Anderson, W. D. 1966. *Ethos and Education in Greek Music*. Cambridge, Mass.
Arnott, Peter D. 1989. *Public and Performance in the Greek Theater*. New York and London.
Arnott, W. Geoffrey. 1959. "The Author of the Greek Original of the *Poenulus*." *RhM* 102.252-62.
Arnott, W. Geoffrey. 1972. "From Aristophanes to Menander." *G&R* 19.65-80.
Arnott, W. Geoffrey. 1989. "Studies in Comedy, I: Alexis and the Parasite's Name." *GRBS* 9.161–68.
Arnott, W. Geoffrey. 1993. "Comic Openings." in Slater and Zimmerman. *Intertextualität* 14-32.
Atkinson, J. E. 1992. "Curbing the Comedians: Cleon Versus Aristophanes and Syracosius' Decree." *CQ* 42.56–64.
Austin, Colin, ed. 1973. *Comicorum Graecorum Fragmenta in Papyris Reperta* [*CGFP*]. Berlin and New York.
Bain, David. 1977. *Actors and Audience: A Study of Asides and Related Conventions in Greek Drama*. Oxford.
Bain, David. 1993. "A Misunderstood Scene in Sophokles, *Oidipous* (*O.T.* 300-462)." in Ian McAuslan and Paul Walcot, edd. *Greek Tragedy*. Greek and Rome Studies II. Oxford. 81-94.
Bakhtin, Mikhail. 1979. *Problemy Poetiki Dostoevskovo*. (referred to as *Dostoevsky's Poetics*). 4th ed. Moscow.

Baldry, H. C. 1953. "The Idler's Paradise in Attic Comedy." *G&R* 22.49–60.
Barker, Andrew, ed. 1984. *Greek Musical Writings I: The Musician and his Art*. Cambridge.
Barthes, Roland. 1970. "L'ancienne rhetorique." *Communications* 16.170-97.
Beare, W. 1955. "χοροy in the *Plutus*: A Reply to Mr. Handley." *CQ* 5.49-52.
Bertan, M. 1984. "Gli *Odyssês* di Cratino e la testimonianza di Platonio." *Atene e Roma* 29.171-78.
Bierl, Anton. 1990. "Dionysus, Wine, and Tragic Poetry: A Metatheatrical Reading of *P. Köln* VI 242A = *TrGF* II F646a." *GRBS* 31.353-91.
Boettiger, Karl A. 1837. *Kleine Schriften*. vol. 1. Leipzig.
Bonanno, M. G. 1972. *Studi su Cratete comico*. Padua.
Bonanno, M. G. 1987. "Paratragodia in Aristofane." *Dioniso* 57.135-67.
Borthwick, E. K. 1964. "The Gymnasium of Bromius—a Note on Dionysius Chalcus, fr. 3." *JHS* 84.49-53.
Borthwick, E. K. 1968. "Notes on the Plutarch *De musica* and the *Cheiron* of Pherecrates." *Hermes* 96.60–73.
Bowie, A. M. 1982. "The Parabasis in Aristophanes: *Prolegomena, Acharnians*." *CQ* 32.27-40.
Bowie, A. M. 1993. *Aristophanes: Myth, Ritual and Comedy*. Cambridge.
Bowie, E. L. 1988. "Who is Dicaeopolis?" *JHS* 108.183-85.
Bremmer, J. M. 1991. "Pindar's Paradoxical ἐγώ and Recent Controversy about the Performance of His Epinikia." in Slings, *The Poet's "I"* 41-58.
Browning, Robert. 1958. "Greek Abstract Nouns in -sis -tis." *Philologus* 102.60-74.
Burke, Edmund. 1992. "The Economy of Athens in the Classical Era: Some Adjustments to the Primitivist Model." *TAPA* 122.199-226.
Burnett, A. 1989. "Performing Pindar's Odes." *CP* 84.283-93.
Cantarella, R. 1965. "Atene: La Polis e il Teatro." *Dioniso* 34.39-55.
Capps, Edward. 1895. "The Chorus in the Later Greek Drama with Reference to the Stage Question." *AJA* 10.287-325.

Capps, Edward. 1943. "A New Fragment of the List of Victors at the City Dionysia." *Hesperia* 12.1-11.
Carey, C. 1994. "Comic Ridicule and Democracy." in R. Osborne and S. Hornblower edd. *Ritual, Finance, Politics: Athenian Democratic Accounts Presented to David Lewis.* Oxford. 69-83.
Carey, C. 1989. "The Performance of the Victory Ode." *AJP* 110.545-65.
Carey, C. 1991. "The Victory Ode in Performance: The Case for the Chorus." *CP* 86.192-200.
Carrière, Jean-Claude. 1979. *Le Carnaval et la politique.* Paris.
Cartledge, Paul. 1990. *Aristophanes and His Theatre of the Absurd.* Bristol.
Casaubon, I. 1621. *Animadversionum in Athenaei Dipnosophistas libri XV.* Lyons.
Càssola, F. 1975. *Inni Omerici, a cura di F. Càssola.* Florence.
Cawkwell, G. L. 1963. "Eubulus." *JHS* 83.47-67.
Chailley, Jacques. 1979. *La musique grecque antique.* Paris.
Christ, Matthew. 1990. "Liturgy Avoidance and *Antidosis* in Classical Athens." *TAPA* 120.147-69.
Cobet, K. G. 1840. *Observationes criticae in Platonis comici reliquias.* Amsterdam.
Csapo, Eric and William J. Slater. 1995. *The Context of Ancient Drama.* Ann Arbor.
Dale, A. M. 1969. "The Chorus in the Action of Greek Tragedy." in T. B. L. Webster and E. G. Turner, edd. *Collected Papers of A. M. Dale.* Cambridge. 210-20.
Daverio-Rocchi, Giovanna. 1978. "Transformations de rôle dans les institutions d'Athènes au IVe siècle par rapport aux changements dans la société." *Dialogues d'Histoire ancienne* 4.33-50.
David, E. 1984. *Aristophanes and Athenian Society of the Early Fourth Century BC. Mnemosyne* Supplement 81. Leiden.
Davies, J. K. 1971. *Athenian Propertied Families.* Oxford.
Davies, J. K. 1978. *Democracy and Classical Greece.* Stanford.
Davies, M. 1988. "Monody, Choral Lyric, and the Tyranny of the Handbook." *CQ* 38.52-64.

Dean-Jones, Lesley. 1992. "The Politics of Pleasure: Female Sexual Appetite in the Hippocratic Corpus." in Domna Stanton, ed. *Discourses of Sexuality: From Aristotle to AIDS*. Ann Arbo. 48-77.
Dearden, C. W. 1976. *The Stage of Aristophanes*. London.
Degani, Enzo. 1993. "Aristofane e la tradizione dell' invettiva personale." in J. M. Bremmer and E. W. Handley, edd. *Aristophane*. Fondation Hardt pour l'étude de l' antiquité classique. Entrétiens 38. Vandoeuvres.
Deichgräber, K. 1956. *Parabasenverse aus Thesmophoriazusae II des Aristophanes bei Galen*. Berlin.
DeJean, Joan. 1987. "Fictions of Sappho." *Critical Inquiry* 13.787-805.
DeJean, Joan. 1989. *Fictions of Sappho: 1546-1937*. Chicago.
DeJean, Joan. 1989. "Sappho, c'est moi, selon Racine: Coming Of Age In Neo-Classical Theater." *Yale French Studies* 76.3-20.
Del Corno, D. 1974. "Alcuni aspetti del linguaggio di Menandro." *Studi classici e orientali* 23:13-48.
Deubner, Ludwig. 1932. *Attische Feste*. Berlin.
Diels, Hermann and Walther Kranz, edd. 1951-1952. *Die Fragmente der Vorsokratiker*. vols. 1-3. 6th ed. Berlin and Zürich.
Dieterich, F. 1893. *Nekyia*. Leipzig.
Dillon, Matthew J. 1985. "Aristophanes' *Ploutos*: Comedy in Transition." dissertation, Yale.
Dobrov, Gregory W. 1988. "The Dawn of Farce: Aristophanes." in J. Redmond, ed. *Themes in Drama 10: Farce*. 15-31. Cambridge.
Dobrov, Gregory W. 1990a. "Aristophanes' *Birds* and the Metaphor of Deferral." *Arethusa* 23.2.209-33.
Dobrov, Gregory W. 1990b. Introduction to G. W. Dobrov, ed., *Aristophanes' Birds and Nephelokokkugia: Charting the Comic Polis*. Papers of the APA Seminar. Syracuse, NY. 3-7. (N.B.: this seminar has been incorporated and expanded in Section I of *The City As Comedy*, listed below).
Dobrov, Gregory W. 1990c. "The Dramatic Sources of Nephelokkokygia." in G. W. Dobrov, ed., *Aristophanes' Birds and Nephelokokkugia: Charting the Comic Polis*. Papers of the APA Seminar. Syracuse, NY. 17-26.

Dobrov, Gregory W. 1993. "The Tragic and the Comic Tereus." *AJP* 114.2.189-234.
Dobrov, Gregory W., ed. (forthcoming). *The City As Comedy: Society and Representation in Athenian Drama.*
Dobrov, Gregory W. (forthcoming). *Tropics of Play: Fictions of Theater, Genre, and Society in Greek Drama.*
Dodds, E. R. 1973. *The Ancient Concept of Progress.* Oxford.
Dohm, H. 1964. *Mageiros: Die Rolle des Kochs in der griechisch-römischen Komödie.* Munich.
Dolan, Jill. 1988. *The Feminist Spectator as Critic.* Ann Arbor.
Dover, K. J. 1963. "Notes on Aristophanes' *Acharnians.*" *Maia.* 15.6-25.
Dover, K. J. 1968. *Aristophanes' Clouds, Edited with Introduction and Commentary by K. J. Dover.* Oxford.
Dover, K. J. 1972. *Aristophanic Comedy.* Berkeley and Los Angeles.
Dover, K. J. 1987. "The Style of Aristophanes." in *Greek and the Greeks: Collected Papers.* vol. 1. Oxford. 224-36 .
Dover, K. J. 1987. "Language and Character in Aristophanes" in *Greek and the Greeks: Collected Papers.* vol. 1. Oxford. 237-48.
Dover, K. J. 1993. *Aristophanes' Frogs, Edited With Introduction and Commentary by K. J. Dover.* Oxford.
Duclos, Gloria Shaw. 1984. "Thomas Wentworth Higginson's Sappho." *The New England Quarterly* 57.403-11.
Dunbar, Nan. 1995. *Aristophanes' Birds, Edited with Introduction and Commentary by Nan Dunbar.* Oxford.
Düring, Ingemar. 1945. "Studies in Musical Terminology in the 5th Century Literature." *Eranos* 43.176–97
Easterling, Patricia. 1990. "Constructing Character in Greek Tragedy." in Pelling, *Characterization and Individuality* 83-99.
Edmonds, J. M. 1959. *The Fragments of Attic Comedy.* vol. 2. Leiden.
Edwards, Anthony. 1993. "Historicizing the Popular Grotesque: Bakhtin's Rabelais and Attic Old Comedy." in Ruth Scodel, ed. *Theater and Society in the Classical World.* Ann Arbor. 89-117.
Ellis, W. M. 1989. *Alcibiades.* London.

Emerson, Caryl. 1993. "Irreverent Bakhtin and the Imperturbable Classics." *Arethusa* 26.3.123-40.
Feneron, J. 1974. "Some Elements of Menander's Style." *BICS* 21.81-95.
Ferguson, W. S. 1911. *Hellenistic Athens*. London.
Ferrari, Cecilia. 1948. "Il frammento del papiro berlinese 11771 e la trasformazione del coro da Aristofane a Menandro." *Dioniso* 11.177-87.
Fisher, N. R. E. 1993. "Multiple Personalities and Dionysiac Festivals: Dicaeopolis in Aristophanes' *Acharnians*." *G&R* 40.1.31-47.
Flashar, Helmut. 1975. "Zur Eigenart des Aristophanischen Spätwerks." in Hans-Joachim Newiger, ed. *Aristophanes und die alte Komödie*. Wege der Forschung. Band 265 Darmstadt. 425-28.
Flickinger, Roy C. 1912. "χοροy in Terence's *Heauton*, the Shifting of Choral Roles in Menander, and Agathon's ʽΕΜΒΟΛΙΜΑʼ." *CP* 7.24-34.
Flury, Peter. 1968. *Liebe und Liebessprache bei Menander, Plautus und Terenz* (Bibliothek der klassischen Altertumswissenschaft. n.f. 2.25). Heidelberg.
Foley, Helene P., ed. 1982. *Reflections of Women in Antiquity*. New York.
Forrest, W. G. 1963. "Aristophanes' *Acharnians*." *Phoenix* 17.1-12.
Fraenkel, Eduard. 1950. *Agamemon*. vols. 1-3. Oxford.
Fraenkel, Eduard. 1964. *Kleine Beiträge I*. Rome.
Frantz, G. 1891. "De comoediae Atticae prologis." dissertation, Argent., Aug. Trev.
French, A. 1991. "Economic Conditions in Fourth-Century Athens." *G&R* 38.24-40.
Frost, K. B. 1988. *Exits and Entrances in Menander*. Oxford.
Gallagher, Catherine and Thomas Laqueur edd. 1986. *The Making of the Modern Body. Representations* 14 (Spring).
Gamberale, L. 1967. "L'inizio proverbiale di Menandro fr. 333 K.-Th." *RFIC* 95.162-64.
Garnsey, Peter. 1988. *Famine and Food Supply in the Graeco-Roman World*. Cambridge.
Gauly Bardo, *et al.*, edd. 1991. *Musa Tragica*. Göttingen.

Geissler, Paul. 1925. *Chronologie der altattischen Komödie*. Berlin.
Geissler, Paul. 1979. *Chronologie der altattischen Komödie*. revised edition. Berlin.
Gentili, Bruno and R. Pretagostini. 1986. *La musica in Grecia*. Rome and Bari.
Gentili, Bruno. 1979. *Theatrical Performances in the Ancient World*. Amsterdam.
Gentili, Bruno. 1988. *Poetry and its Public in Ancient Greece*. A. T. Cole, tr. Baltimore and London.
Ghiron-Bistagne, P. 1974. "Die Krise des Theaters in der griechischen Welt im 4. Jahrhundert v. u. Z." in C. Welskopf, ed. *Hellenische Poleis*, vol. 3. Berlin. 1335-71.
Ghiron-Bistagne, P. 1976. *Recherches sur les acteurs dans la Grèce antique*. Paris.
Giannini, A. 1960. *La figura del cuoco nella commedia greca*. Acme.
Ginouvès, Rene. 1962. *Balaneutiké: Recherches sur le bain dans l' antiquité grecque*. Paris.
Goff, Barbara. 1990. *The Noose of Words: Readings of Desire, Violence, and Language in Euripides' Hippolytos*. Cambridge.
Goldberg, S. M. 1980. *The Making of Menander's Comedy*. London.
Goldhill, Simon. 1986. *Reading Greek Tragedy*. Cambridge.
Goldhill, Simon. 1990. *The Poet's Voice*. Cambridge.
Goldhill, Simon. 1990. "Character and Action: Representation and Reading Greek Tragedy and its Critics." in Pelling, *Characterization and Individuality* 100-27.
Gomme, A. W. 1937. "The End of the City-State." in *Essays in Greek History and Literature*. Oxford. 204-48.
Gomme, A. W. and F. H. Sandbach. 1973. *Menander: A Commentary*. Oxford.
Gould, John. 1978. "Dramatic Character and 'Human Intelligibility' in Greek Tragedy." *PCPS* 24.43-67.
Green, J. R. 1982. "Dedications of Masks." *Revue Archéologique* 237-48.
Green, J. R. 1995. *Theatre in Ancient Greek Society*. Routledge.
Green, J. R. 1991. "On Seeing and Depicting the Theatre in Classical Athens." *GRBS* 32.15-50.

Green, J. R. 1991. "Notes on Phlyax Vases." *Quaderni Ticinesi di Numismatica e antichità classiche* [= *NumAntCl*] 20.49-56.
Greenberg, Robert A. 1991. "Erotion, Anactoria, and the Sapphic Passion." *Victorian Poetry* 29.79-87.
Greenblatt, Stephen. 1980. *Renaissance Self-Fashioning: From More to Shakespeare.* Chicago.
Gregory, Eileen. 1986. "Rose Cut in Rock: Sappho and H. D.'s Sea Garden." *Contemporary Literature* 27.525-52.
Gubar, Susan. 1984. "Sapphistries." *Signs* 10.43-62.
Gulick, C. B. 1941. *Athenaeus, The Deipnosophists.* vol. 7. London and Cambridge, Mass.
Halliwell, Stephen. 1989. "Authorial Collaboration in the Athenian Comic Theatre." *GRBS* 30.515-28.
Händel, Paul. 1963. *Formen und Darstellungsweisen in der aristophanischen Komödie.* Heidelberg.
Handley, Eric W. 1985. "Comedy." in P. E. Easterling and B. M. W. Knox. *Cambridge History of Classical Literature.* vol. 1. Cambridge. 355-425.
Handley, Eric W. 1953. "χοροy in the Plutus." *CQ* 3.55-61.
Handley, Eric W., ed. 1965. *The Dyskolos of Menander.* Harvard.
Handley, Eric W. 1970. "The Conventions of the Comic Stage and their Exploitation by Menander." *Entretiens Fondation Hardt* 16.3-26.
Handley, Eric W. 1983. *Oxyrhynchus Papyri.* vol. 50. London.
Hansen, M. H. 1989. review of R. Sinclair, *Democracy and Participation. CR* 38.69-76.
Hansen, M. H. 1991. *The Athenian Democracy in the Age of Demosthenes.* Oxford.
Harvey, Elizabeth D. 1989. "Ventriloquizing Sappho: Ovid, Donne, and the Erotics of the Feminine Voice." *Criticism* 31:115-38.
Heath, Malcolm. 1988. "Receiving the κῶμος: the Context and Performance of Epinician." *AJP* 109.180-95.
Heath, Malcolm. 1989. "Aristotelian Comedy." *CQ* 39.344–54.
Heath, Malcolm. 1990. "Aristophanes and his Rivals." *G&R* 37.2.143-58.
Heath, Malcolm and Mary Lefkowitz. 1991. "Epinician Performance." *CP* 86.3.173-91.

Henderson, Jeffrey. 1987. *Aristophanes' Lysistrata, Edited with Introduction and Commentary by Jeffrey Henderson.* Oxford.
Henderson, Jeffrey. 1990. "The Demos and the Comic Competition." in Winkler and Zeitlin, *Nothing to do with Dionysos?* 271-313.
Henderson, Jeffrey. 1990. *The Maculate Muse.* 2nd ed. Oxford.
Henderson, Jeffrey. 1991. "Women and the Athenian Dramatic Festivals." *TAPA* 121.133-47.
Henry, Madeleine M. 1985. *Menander's Courtesans and the Greek Comic Tradition.* Frankfurt am Main and New York.
Herter, Hans. 1926. *De dis Atticis Priapi similibus.* Bonn.
Herter, Hans. 1954. "Priapos." *Paulys Real Encyclopädie der classischen Altertumswissenschaft* [RE]22.2.1917.48-1918.4.
Holquist, Michael. 1990. *Dialogism: Bakhtin and His World.* London and New York.
Holstun, James. 1987. "'Will You Rent Our Ancient Love Asunder?': Lesbian Elegy in Donne, Marvell, and Milton." *ELH* 54.835-67.
Holzinger, Karl. 1940. *Kritisch-exegetischer Kommentar zu Aristophanes' Plutos.* SAWW Band 218. Vienna and Leipzig.
Hubbard, Thomas. 1991. *The Mask of Comedy: Aristophanes and the Intertextual Parabasis.* Ithaca.
Humphreys, Sally. 1985. "Lycurgus of Butadae: An Athenian Aristocrat." in J. Ober and J. W. Eadie, edd. *The Craft of the Ancient Historian.* Lanham, MD. 199-252.
Hunter, R. L. 1979. "The Comic Chorus in the Fourth Century." *ZPE* 36.23-38.
Hunter, R. L., ed. 1983. *Eubulus: The Fragments.* Cambridge.
Hunter, R. L. 1985. *The New Comedy of Greece and Rome.* Cambridge.
Isager, Signe and Mogens H. Hansen. 1975. *Aspects of Athenian Society in the Fourth Century BC.* Odense.
Jachmann, Gunther. 1931. *Plautinisches und Attisches.* Berlin.
Jacques, J. M. 1978. "Mouvement des acteurs et conventions scéniques dan l'acte II du *Bouclier* de Menandre." *Grazer Beiträge* 7.51-52.
Janko, Richard. 1984. *Aristotle on Comedy: Towards a Reconstruction of Poetics II.* Berkeley and Los Angeles.
Johnstone, Keith. 1979. *Improvisation and the Theatre.* London.

Jouan, Francois. 1966. *Euripide et les légendes des Chants Cypriens, des origines de la guerre de Troie a l'Iliade*. Paris.
Just, Roger. 1989. *Women in Athenian Law and Life*. London and New York.
Kaibel, G. 1895. "Kratinos' ΟΔΥΣΣΗΣ und Euripides' ΚΥΚΛΩΨ." *Hermes* 30.71-89.
Kann, Siegfried. 1909. *De iteratis apud poetas antiquae et mediae comoediae Atticae*. dissertation, Giessen.
Kassel, Rudolf. 1954. *Quomodo quibus locis apud veteres scriptores graecos infantes atque parvuli pueri inducantur describantur commemorentur*. Meisenheim.
Kassel, Rudolf. 1991. *Kleine Schriften*. H.-G. Nesselrath, ed. Berlin and New York.
Kassel, Rudolf and Colin Austin, edd. 1983- . *Poetae Comici Graeci*, vol. II (Agathenor-Aristonymus); III.2 (Aristophanes, testimonia et fragmenta); IV (Aristophon-Crobylus); V (Damoxenus-Magnes); VII (Menecrates-Xenophon). [=*PCG*/K.- A.] Berlin and New York.
Kennedy, George A., ed. 1989. *The Cambridge History of Literary Criticism*. vol. 1: *Classical Criticism*. Cambridge.
Keuls, Eva. 1985. *The Reign of the Phallus*. New York.
Klima, Edward, Ursula Bellugi, et al. 1979. *The Signs of Language*. Cambridge, Mass.
Kock, Theodor 1880-1888. *Comicorum Atticorum Fragmenta*. vols. 1-3. Leipzig.
Kolb, Frank. 1979. "Polis und Theater." in Gustav Adolf Seeck, ed. *Das griechische Drama*. Darmstadt. 504-45.
Konstan, David and Matthew J. Dillon. 1981. "The Ideology of Aristophanes' Wealth." *AJP* 102.371-94.
Körte, Alfred. 1938. "Pherekrates." *Paulys Real Encyclopädie der classischen Altertumswissenschaft* 19.2.1985–91.
Koster, W. J. W., ed. 1975. *Scholia in Aristophanem*. Pars I, Fasc. IA: *Prolegomena de comoedia*. Groningen.
Kurke, Leslie. 1992. *The Traffic in Praise: Pindar and the Poetics of Social Economy*. Ithaca.
Lakoff, George. 1980. *Metaphors We Live By*. Chicago.
Landfester, Manfred. 1979. "Geschichte der griechischen Komödie." in Gustav Adolf Seeck, ed. *Das griechische Drama*. Darmstadt. 354-400.

Langerbeck, Hermann. 1963. "Die Vorstellung vom Schlaraffenland in der alten attischen Komödie." *Zeitschrift für Volkskunde* 59.192–204

Lawler, Lillian. 1964. *The Dance of the Ancient Greek Theater.* Iowa City.

Lefkowitz, Mary. 1988. "Who Sang Pindar's Victory Odes?" *AJP* 109.1-11.

Lefkowitz, Mary. 1991. *First-Person Fictions: Pindar's Poetic 'I'.* Oxford.

Leighton, Angela. 1992. *Victorian Women Poets: Writing Against the Heart.* New York.

Leo, Friedrich. 1895. *Plautinische Forschungen.* Berlin.

Leo, Friedrich. 1908. *Der Monolog im Drama. Ein Beitrag zur griechisch-römischen Poetik.* Abhandl. d.k. Ges. d. Wiss. zu Göttingen, philol.-hist. Kl. N.V. X.5. Berlin.

Lesky, Albin. 1966. *A History of Greek Literature.* J. Willis and C. de Heer, trr. New York.

Lévêque, Pierre. 1955. *Agathon.* Paris.

Lévy, Edmond. 1976. *Athènes devant la défaite de 404: Histoire d'une crise idéologique.* Paris.

Ley, G. 1993. "Monody, Choral Song, and Athenian Festival Performance." *Maia* 45.2.105-24.

Lombardo, Stanley, tr. 1993. *Hesiod: Works and Days and Theogony.* "Introduction" pp. 1-16 by Robert Lamberton. Indianapolis.

Long, Timothy. 1978. "Pherecrates' Savages: A footnote to the Greek Attitude on the Noble Savage." *CW* 71.381–82.

Long, Timothy. 1986. *Barbarians in Greek Comedy.* Carbondale.

Longo, Oddone. 1990. "The Theater of the *Polis.*" in Winkler and Zeitlin, *Nothing to do with Dionysos?* 12-19.

Luppe, W. 1972. "Die Zahl der Konkurrenten an den komischen Agonen zur Zeit des Peloponnesischen Krieges." *Philologus* 116.53-73.

MacDowell, Douglas M. 1971. *Aristophanes' Wasps, Edited with Introduction and Commentary by Douglas MacDowell.* Oxford.

MacDowell, Douglas M. 1989. *Andocides' On the Mysteries, Edited with Introduction, Commentary, and Appendixes by Douglas MacDowell.* Oxford.

MacDowell, Douglas M., ed. 1990. *Demosthenes: Against Meidias*. Oxford.
MacDowell, Douglas M., (forthcoming) *Aristophanes and Athens*. Oxford.
MacLeish, Kenneth. 1980. *The Theatre of Aristophanes*. New York.
Maidment, K. J. 1935. "The Later Comic Chorus." *CQ* 29.1-24.
Maitland, J. 1993. "Tripping the Light Fantastic: Treading the Gender Boundaries in Aristophanes' *Ecclesiazusae*." in Slater and Zimmerman. *Intertextualität* 212-22.
Mastromarco, G. 1975. "Guerra peloponnesiaca e agoni comici in Atene." *Belfagor* 30.469-73.
Maurach, Gregor. 1968. "Interpretationen zur Attischen Komödie." *Acta Classica* 11.9-12.
McBrown, P. G. 1992. "Menander, Fragments 745 and 746 K.-T.: Menander's Kolax and Parasites and Flatterers in Greek Comedy." *ZPE* 92.91–107
McEvilley, Thomas. 1970. "Development in the Lyrics of Aristophanes." *AJP* 91.257-76.
Meineke, Augustus. 1839. *Fragmenta Comicorum Graecorum*, vol. I: *Historia critica Comicorum Graecorum*; vol. II.1: *Fragmenta poetarum Comoediae antiquae*. Berlin.
Mensching, Eckart. 1964. "Zur Produktivität der alten Komödie." *Museum Helveticum* 21.15–49.
Merkelbach, Reinhold and Martin L. West. 1977. *Fragmenta Hesiodea*. Oxford.
Merriam, A. P. 1964. *The Anthropology of Music*. Evanston.
Mette. H.-J. 1965. "Der heutige Menander." *Lustrum* 10.5-211.
Mette, H.-J. 1977. *Urkunden dramatischer Aufführungen in Griechenland*. Berlin and New York.
Miller, Paul A. 1993. "Sappho 31 and Catullus 51: The Dialogism of Lyric." *Arethusa* 26.3.183-99.
Morgan, K. 1993. "Pindar the Professional and the Rhetoric of the κῶμος." *CP* 88.1.1-15.
Morson, Gary Saul and Caryl Emerson. 1989. *Rethinking Bakhtin: Extensions and Challenges*. Evanston, Illinois.
Morson, Gary Saul and Caryl Emerson. 1990. *Mikhail Bakhtin: Creation of a Prosaics*. Stanford.
Mossé, Claude. 1962. *La fin de la démocratie athénienne*. Paris.

Mossé, Claude. 1972. "La vie économique d'Athènes au IVe siécle: crise ou renouveau?" in F. Sartori, ed. *Praelectiones Patavinae*. Rome. 135-44.
Mueller, Janel. 1992. "Lesbian Erotics: The Utopian Trope of Donne's 'Sappho to Philaenis'." *Journal of Homosexuality* 23.1-2.103-34.
Nagy, Gregory. 1989. "Early Greek Views of Poets and Poetry." in Kennedy, *Classical Criticism* 1- 77.
Nagy, Gregory. 1990. *Pindar's Homer: the Lyric Possession of an Epic Past*. Baltimore and London.
Nauck, Augustus. 1889. *Tragicorum Graecorum fragmenta.*^{2} Leipzig.
Nesselrath, Heinz-Günther. 1990. *Die attische Mittlere Komödie: ihre Stellung in der antiken Literaturkritik und Literaturgeschichte*. Berlin and New York.
Norwood, Gilbert. 1931. *Greek Comedy*. London.
O'Higgins, Dolores. 1990. "Sappho's Splintered Tongue: Silence in Sappho 31 and Catullus 51." *AJP* 111.157-67.
Ober, Josiah. 1990. *Mass and Elite in Democratic Athens*. Princeton.
Olson, S. Douglas. 1989. "Cario and the New World of Aristophanes' *Plutus*." *TAPA* 119.193-99.
Oppé, A. P. 1897. *The New Comedy*. St. Andrews.
Page, D. L. 1941. *Select Papyri III: Literary Papyri, Poetry*. London and Cambridge, Mass.
Parker, L. P. E. 1991. "Eupolis or Dicaeopolis?" *JHS* 111.203-208.
Pelling, Christopher. 1990. *Characterization and Individuality in Greek Literature*. Oxford.
Perusino, Franca. 1987. *Dalla commedia antica alla commedia di mezzo*. Urbino.
Perusino, Franca. 1989. *Platonio, La commedia greca. Edizione critica, traduzione e commento*. Urbino.
Pečirka, Jan. 1976. "The Crisis of the Athenian Polis in the Fourth Century BC." *Eirene* 14.5-29.
Pianko, Gabriella. 1963. "Un comico contributo alla storia della musica greca, Chirone di Ferecrate." *Eos* 53.56–62.
Pickard-Cambridge, A. W. 1946. *The Theater of Dionysus at Athens*. Oxford.
Pickard-Cambridge, A. W. 1962. *Dithyramb, Tragedy and Comedy*. 2nd ed. Revised by T. B. L. Webster. Oxford.

Pickard-Cambridge, A. W. 1968. *The Dramatic Festivals of Athens.* 2nd ed. Revised by John Gould and D. M. Lewis. Oxford.
Pingiatoglou, Semeli. 1992. "Eine Komödiendarstellung auf einer Choenkanne des Benaki-Museums." in H. Froning, T. Holscher, and H. Mielsch, edd. *Kotinos. Festschrift E. Simon.* (Mainz). 292-300.
Platnauer, Maurice. 1964. *Aristophanes* Peace. Oxford.
Platter, Charles. 1993. "The Uninvited Guest: Aristophanes in Bakhtin's 'History of Laughter'." *Arethusa* 26.2.201-16.
Pohlenz, Max. 1920. "Die Anfänge der griechischen Poetik." *Nachrichten von der Gesellschaft der Wissenschaften zu Göttingen* 1920.142-78.
Pöhlmann, E. 1977. "Die Überlieferungswert der χοροῦ-Vermerke in Papyri und Handschriften." *Würzburger Jahrbücher für die Altertumswissenschaft* 3.69-81.
Pöhlmann, E. 1988. "Die Funktion des Chors in der Neuen Komödie." in *Beiträge zur antiken und neueren Musikgeschichte* . Frankfurt. 41-55.
Powell, Jim. 1992. "Afterwords: Sappho of Lesbos." *TriQuarterly* 86.244-58.
Pritchett, W. K. 1991. *The Greek State at War.* Part 5. Berkeley.
Pucci, Pietro. 1987. *Odysseus Polutropos: Intertextual Readings in the Odyssey and the Iliad.* Ithaca and London.
Race, W. H. 1982. *The Classical Priamel from Homer to Boethius.* Leiden.
Radt, Stefan. 1977. *Tragicorum Graecorum Fragmenta IV: Sophocles.* [*TrGF*]. Göttingen.
Rawlings, H. R. 1974. *A Semantic Study of Prophasis to 400 BC.* Wiesbaden.
Reckford, Kenneth. 1987. *Aristophanes' Old-and-New Comedy*, vol. I: *Six Essays in Perspective.* Chapel Hill.
Rehrenböck, G. 1985. *Pherekrates-Studien.* dissertation, Vienna.
Reinhardt, Udo. 1974. *Mythologische Beispiele in der Neuen Komödie.* vol 1: *Menander, Plautus, Terenz.* dissertation, Johannes Gutenberg University, Mainz.
Restani, Donatella. 1983. "Il *Chirone* di Ferecrate e la nuova musica greca." *Rivista Italiana di Musicologia* 18.139–92.
Rhodes, P. J. 1979/80. "The Athenian Democracy After 403 BC." *CJ* 75.305-23.

Rhodes, P. J. 1982. "Problems in Athenian Eisphora and Liturgies." *AJAH* 7.1-19.
Rogers, Benjamin Bickley. 1907. *The* Plutus *of Aristophanes*. London.
Rosen, R. M. 1988. *Old Comedy and the Iambographic Tradition*. Atlanta.
Rosen, Ralph. 1988. *Old Comedy and the Iambographic Tradition*. American Classical Studies 19. Atlanta.
Rosen, R. M. 1989. "Euboulos' *Ankylion* and the Game of Kottabos." *CQ* 39.2.355-59.
Rösler, Wolfgang. 1986. "Michail Bachtin und die Karnevals kultur im antiken Griechenland." *QUUC* 23.25-44.
Roux, R. 1976. "Un maître disparu de l'ancienne comédie. Le poète Cratès, jugé par Aristophane." *Revue de Philologie*. 50.256–65.
Runciman, W. G. 1990. "Doomed to Extinction: The Polis as an Evolutionary Dead End." in O. Murray and Simon Price, edd. *The Greek City from Homer to Alexander*. Oxford. 347-67.
Ruschenbusch, E. 1987. "Symmorieprobleme." *ZPE* 69.5-81.
Russell, D. A. and M. Winterbottom. 1972. *Ancient Literary Criticism: The Principal Texts in New Translations*. Oxford.
Russo, Carlo F. 1994. *Aristophanes: An Author for the Stage*. Kevin Wren tr. Routledge.
Rusten, Jeffrey *et al.*, trans (forthcoming). *The Birth of Comedy: Fragments of Greek Drama 520-250 BC*. Baltimore.
Sancho-Royo, A. 1983. "Analisis de los motivos de composicion del Ciclope de Filoxeno de Cithera." *Habis* 14.33-49.
Sandbach, F. H. 1970. "Menander's Manipulation of Language for Dramatic Purposes." *Entretiens Fondation Hardt* 16.113-43.
Sartori, K. 1893. *Das Kottabos-Spiel der alten Griechen*. Munich.
Schmid, Wilhelm. 1946. *Geschichte der griechische Literatur*. part 1. vol. 4. Munich.
Schneider, K. 1913. "Hetairai." *Paulys Real Encyclopädie der classischen Altertumswissenschaft* 8.2.1331-72.
Sealey, Raphael. 1993. *Demosthenes and His Time: A Study in Defeat*. New York and Oxford.

Segal, Charles. 1971. "The Two Worlds of Euripides' *Helen*." *TAPA* 102.553-614.
Segal, Erich. 1973. "The φύσις of Comedy." *HSCP* 77.129-36.
Seidensticker, Bernd. 1982. *Palintonos Harmonia. Studien zu komischen Elementen in der griechischen Tragödie.* Hypomnemata 72. Göttingen.
Sifakis, G. M. 1967. *Studies in the History of Hellenistic Drama.* London.
Sifakis, G. M. 1971. "Aristotle, *E.N.*, IV, 2, 1123a 19-24, and the Comic Chorus in the Fourth Century." *AJP* 92.410-32.
Sifakis, G. M. 1971. *Parabasis and Animal Choruses.* London.
Silk, Michael S. 1980. "Aristophanes as a Lyric Poet." *YCS* 26.99-151.
Silk, Michael S. 1990. "The People of Aristophanes." in Pelling, *Characterization and Individuality* 150-73.
Silk, Michael S. and J. P. Stern. 1981. *Nietzsche on Tragedy.* Cambridge.
Silk, Michael S. (forthcoming). *Aristophanes and the Definition of Comedy.* Oxford.
Slater, Niall W. 1985. *Plautus in Performance: The Theatre of the Mind.* Princeton.
Slater, Niall W. 1985. "Play and Playwright References in Middle and New Comedy." *Liverpool Classical Monthly* 10.103-5.
Slater, Niall W. 1987. "Transformations of Space in New Comedy." in James Redmond, ed. *Themes in Drama 9. The Theatrical Space,* Cambridge. 1-10.
Slater, Niall W. 1988. "Problems in the Hypotheses to Aristophanes' *Peace*." *ZPE* 74.43-57.
Slater, Niall W. 1991. "The Players Come Again": review of Frost, *Exits and Entrances. Arion* 1.3.195-201.
Slater, Niall W. 1992. "The Fabrication of Comic Illusion." Presented at the APA Annual Meeting, Dec. 29, 1992. Printed in this collection pp. 29-45.
Slater, Niall W. 1993. "Space, Character, and ἀπάτη: Transformation and Transvaluation in the *Acharnians*." in Alan Sommerstein, et al. ed., *Tragedy, Comedy, and the Polis: Papers from the Greek Drama Conference, Nottingham, 18-20 July 1990. Bari.* 397-415.

Slater, Niall W. and Bernhard Zimmerman edd. 1993. *Intertextualität in der griechisch-römischen Komödie. Drama* 2. Beiträge zum antiken Drama und seiner Rezeption. Stuttgart.

Slings, Simon R. 1991. *The Poet's "I" in Archaic Greek Lyric: Proceedings of a Symposium Held at the Vrije Universiteit Amsterdam.* Amsterdam.

Snell, Bruno and R. Kannicht, edd. 1986. *Tragicorum Graecorum Fragmenta I: Tragici minores.*² [*TrGF*]. Göttingen.

Sommerstein, Alan H. 1984. "Aristophanes and the Demon Poverty." *CQ* 34.323-33.

Sommerstein, Alan H. 1986. "The Decree of Syrakosios." *CQ* 36.101-8.

Sommerstein, Alan H. 1986. *The Comedies of Aristophanes.* vol. 1: *Acharnians.* Warminster.

Sommerstein, Alan H. 1987. *The Comedies of Aristophanes.* vol. 6:*Birds.* Warminster.

Sommerstein, Alan H. 1994. *The Comedies of Aristophanes.* vol. 8:*Thesmophoriazusae.* Warminster.

Sparkes B. 1960. "Kottabos: An After-Dinner Game." *Archaeology* 13.202-6.

de Ste. Croix, G. E. M. 1983. *The Class Struggle in the Ancient Greek World.* London.

Stemplinger, E. 1912. *Das Plagiat in der griechischen Literatur.* Leipzig and Berlin.

Stier, H. E. 1971. *Der Untergang der klassischen Demokratie.* Opladen.

Storey, I. C. 1988. "The Date of Kallias' Pedetai." *Hermes* 116.379–83.

Storey, I. C. 1990. "Dating and Re-dating Eupolis." *Phoenix* 44.1–30.

Strauss, Barry. 1987. *Athens after the Peloponnesian War. Class, Faction and Policy 403-386.* Ithaca.

Styan, J. L. 1975. *Drama, Stage and Audience.* Cambridge.

Süss, Wilhelm. 1954. "Scheinbare und wirkliche Inkongruenzen in den Dramen des Aristophanes." *RhM* 97.306-13.

Sutton, Dana F. 1980. *Self and Society in Aristophanes.* Washington, D.C.

Sutton, Dana F. 1983. "Dithyramb as Drama: Philoxenus of Cythera's Cyclops or Galatea." *QUCC* 42.37-43.

Sutton, Dana F. 1990. "Aristophanes and the Transition to Middle Comedy." *LCM* 15.81-95.
Taafe, Lauren K. 1993. *Aristophanes and Women*. London.
Taillardat, Jean. 1965. *Les images d'Aristophane*. 2nd ed. Paris.
Taplin, Oliver. 1986. "Fifth-Century Tragedy and Comedy: A Synkrisis." *JHS* 106.163-174.
Taplin, Oliver. 1987. "Classical Phallology, Iconographic Parody, and Potted Aristophanes." *Dioniso* 57.95-109.
Taplin, Oliver. 1987. "Phallology, *Phlyakes*, Iconography and Aristophanes." *PCPS* 213 (n.s. 33) 92-104.
Taplin, Oliver. 1991. "*Auletai and Auletrides* in Greek Comedy and Comic Vase-Paintings." *Quaderni Ticinesi di Numismatica e antichità classiche* [= *NumAntCl*] 20.31-48.
Taplin, Oliver. 1993. *Comic Angels and Other Approaches to Greek Drama through Vase-Paintings*. Oxford.
Thiercy, Pascal. 1987. "Il ruolo del pubblico nella commedia di Aristofane (Le rôle du public dans la comédie d'Aristophane)." *Dioniso* 57.169-85.
Townsend, Rhys F. 1986. "The Fourth-Century Skene of the Theater of Dionysus at Athens." *Hesperia* 55.421-38.
Trendall, A. D. 1991. "Farce and Tragedy in South Italian Vase-Painting." in T. Rasmussen and N. Spivey, edd. *Looking at Greek Vases*. Cambridge. 151-82.
Trendall, A. D. and T. B. L. Webster. 1971. *Illustrations of Greek Drama*. London.
Trenkner, Sophie. 1960. *Le style kai dans le récit attique oral*. Assen, Pays-Bas.
Vernant, J.-P. and P. Vidal-Naquet. 1990. *Myth and Tragedy in Ancient Greece*. Janet Lloyd, tr. New York.
Wall, Anthony and Clive Thompson. 1993. "Cleaning up Bakhtin's Carnival Act." *Diacritics* 23.2.47-70.
Webster, T. B. L. 1950. *Studies in Menander*. Manchester.
Webster, T. B. L. 1952. "Chronological Notes on Middle Comedy." *CQ* 2.13-26.
Webster, T. B. L. 1965. "The Poet and the Mask." in *Classical Drama and its Influence: Essays Presented to H. D. F. Kitto*. London.
Webster, T. B. L. 1970. *Studies in Later Greek Comedy*.^{2} (1st ed., 1953). Manchester.
Webster, T. B. L. 1970. *The Greek Chorus*. London.

Webster, T. B. L. 1974. *An Introduction to Menander.* Manchester.
Webster, T. B. L. and J. R. Green. 1978. *Monuments Illustrating Old and Middle Comedy.* 3rd ed. revised by J.R. Green. BICS Supplement 39. London.
Wehrli, Fritz. 1936. *Motivstudien zur Griechischen Komödie.* Zürich and Leipzig.
West, M. L. 1974. *Studies in Greek Elegy and Iambus.* Berlin and New York.
Whitehead, David. 1986. "Festival Liturgies in Thorikos." *ZPE* 62.213-20.
Whitehead, David. 1986. *The Demes of Attica: 508/7 - ca. 250 BC.* Princeton.
Whitman, Cedric. 1964. *Aristophanes and the Comic Hero.* Harvard.
Wiles, David. 1991. *The Masks of Menander: Sign and Meaning in Greek and Roman Performance.* Cambridge.
von Wilamowitz-Moellendorff, Ulrich. 1903. *Timotheos: Die Perser, aus einem Papyrus herausgegeben.* Leipzig.
von Wilamowitz-Moellendorf, Ulrich. 1931-32. *Der Glaube der Hellenen.* vols. 1-2. Berlin.
von Wilamowitz-Moellendorff, Ulrich. [1877] 1969. "Die Thukydideslegende." *Hermes.* 12:326-67. Reprinted in *Kleine Schriften* 3.1-40. Berlin.
Willems, Alphonse. 1919. *Aristophane. Traduction avec notes et commentaires critiques.* Paris and Brussels.
Winkler, John J. 1982. "Akko," *CP* 77.137-45.
Winkler, John and Froma Zeitlin, edd. 1990. *Nothing to Do With Dionysos? Athenian Drama in Its Social Context.* Princeton.
Xanthakis-Karamanos, G. 1980. *Studies in Fourth-Century Tragedy.* Athens.
Zeitlin, Froma. 1980. "The Closet of Masks: Role-Playing and Myth-Making in the *Orestes* of Euripides." *Ramus* 9.51-77.
Zeitlin, Froma. 1981. "Travesties of Gender and Genre in Aristophanes' *Thesmophoriazusae.*" in H.P. Foley, ed. *Reflections of Women in Antiquity.* New York. 169-217.
Zielinski, Thaddeus. 1885. *Die Gliederung der altattischen Komödie.* Leipzig.

Zimmermann, Bernhard. 1984. *Untersuchungen zur Form und dramatischen Technik der Aristophanischen Komödien.* vol. 1. Königstein.

Zimmermann, Bernhard. 1986. *Untersuchungen zur Form und dramatischen Technik der Aristophanischen Komödien.* vol. 2. Königstein.

Zimmermann, Bernhard. 1992. *Dithyrambos: Geschichte einer Gattung.* Hypomnemata Heft 98. Göttingen.

Zimmermann, Bernhard. 1993. "Comedy's Criticism of Music." in Slater and Zimmerman, *Intertextualität* 39–50.

Zonana, Joyce. 1990. "Swinburne's Sappho: The Muse As Sister-Goddess." *Victorian Poetry* 28.39-50.

Index Locorum

ADESPOTA COMICA (CGFP)
77: 18; **215:** 6 n.22, 7, 8 n.28, 14, 23-26, 24 n.62, 26 n.63, 177; **215.2-3:** 24 n.62; **215.4:** 24; **215.7:** 24; **215.8:** 23 n.57; **215.9:** 23 n.58, **215.11:** 23 n.58; **239:** 112, 112 n.61; **239.18:** 112 n.61; **241:** 112 n.61
AESCHINES, **1.157:** 40 n.32, 112, 179
AESCHYLUS, **fr.47a, 786-820** (Radt): 2 n.6; **fr.281a:** 157 n.63
ALEXIS (K.-A.), **fr.20:** 68; **fr.42:** 35, 37 n.26; **fr.43:** 36; **fr.44:** 71; **fr.77:** 36 n.25; **fr.113:** 36 n.25; **fr.145:** 71-73, 77-78; **fr.145.3-4:** 77; **fr.145.5:** 77; **fr.145.13:** 77; **fr.153:** 172-73; **fr.184:** 19, 36 n.25; **fr.239:** 39, 112; **fr.281.3-4:** 136; **fr.284:** 33 n.16
AMEIPSIAS, **fr.2:** 22 n.56
AMPHIS (K.-A.), **fr.1:** 69, 73; **fr.8:** 37 n. 26; **fr.17:** 69, 73, 76; **fr.17.4:** 37 n.26
ANAXANDRIDES (K.-A.)
test ad Panos Gonai: 5 n.14: **test.1-6:** 20 n.51; **test.5:** 20 n.51; **fr.4.3-4:** 32 n.11; **fr.46:** 20 n.51
ANAXILAS (K.-A.), **fr.13:** 39
ANDOCIDES, **1.12:** 149 n.41; 149 n.42
ANTIPHANES (K.-A.)
test.1: 20, 20 n.52; **test.2:** 20, 20 n.52; **fr.17:** 26 n.63, 76 n.49; **fr.19-20:** 8 n.28, 26 n.63; **fr.57:** 4 n.9, 20-22, 126; **fr.57.15:** 126; **fr.58:** 71; **fr.89:** 33 n.16; **fr.110:** 26 n.63; **fr.157:** 70-71, 73, 76; **fr.157.4:** 76; **fr.157.9:** 76; **fr.157.12:** 76; **fr.189:** 37-38, 66 n.30, 69 n.36

APOLLODORUS, **1.7.1:** 67 n.32
ARAROS (K.-A.), **test. ad Panos Gonai:** 6 n.17; **test.1:** 19 n.48; **test.3:** 19, 19 n.48; **test.4:** 19; **fr.13:** 3 n.8, 19; **fr.13-15:** 6 n.17, 19; **fr.14:** 19, 19 n.49; **fr.15:** 19
ARCHIPPUS (K.-A.), **fr.27:** 115 n.72; **fr.48:** 149 n.39
ARISTOPHANES
Acharnians, **1-18:** 59 n.21; **1-36:** 58-59, 89-90; **1-42:** 58, 156; **3:** 60; **4:** 60; **6:** 75, 75 n.47, 86; **6-8:** 93; **8:** 60, 93; **9:** 60; **9-16:** 93; **9-18:** 75; **11:** 37 n.25; **12:** 60; **15:** 60; **16:** 149 n.35, 165; **19-22:** 59; **19-42:** 75; **24:** 60; **27:** 60, 93; **30:** 60; **31:** 60; **35:** 61; **38:** 60; **41:** 60; **140:** 37 n.25; **151:** 60; **300-301:** 86; **377-382:** 50, 82, 83 n.61; **496-508:** 88 n.75; **500-506:** 82, 83 n.61; **501-503:** 50; **502-505:** 82; **716:** 149 n.39; **866:** 149 n.35; **1150-1161:** 106 n.31
Birds, **11:** 149; **31:** 149; **92:** 85; **142:** 155; **227-262:** 164 n.81; **429-430:** 60; **462-610:** 84; **753-768:** 93; **753-797:** 88 n.75; **764:** 149; **785-800:** 93; **904-959:** 166; Σ **1294:** 149 n.38; **1372-1409:** 77 n.53; **1373-1409:** 166; **1378-1385:** 166; **1403-1404:** 148; **1527:** 149; **1565-1692:** 11
Clouds, **260:** 60; **510-626:** 50; **522-523:** 181; **523:** 31 n.6; **575-577:** 163 n.79; **963-972:** 166; **968:** 155, 156 n.62; **1003:** 151; **1214:** 72 n.41; **1371-1372:** 166

ARISTOPHANES (cont.)
Ecclesiazusae, **577**: 163 n.79; **646-648**: 171 n.93
Frogs, **1-2**: 80 n.55; **1-32**: 77 n.50; **1-100**: 93; **16-18**: 80 n.55; **21**: 72 n.41; **21-23**: 72-73; **51**: 54 n.14, 84 n.64; **52-54**: 80 n.55; **285-308**: 11; **338-339**: 155 n.58; Σ **404**: 108 n.38; **479-493**: 11; **730**: 148, n.32; **1327**: 155 n.58; **1422**: 149 n.39
Knights, **526-36**: 127 n.20; **589**: 109 n.46; **1378-1380**: 60; **1400-1401**: 159 n.68
Lysistrata, **89**: 60; **158**: 140, 142 n.9; **200**: 159 n.67; **530**: 160 n.28; **770**: 74 n.43; **838**: 132 n.34; **1004**: 132 n.34
Peace, **43-48**: 47, 80, 93; **50-55**: 88 n.75; **135-136**: 62; **236-288**: 11; **700-703**: 127 n.20; **781-790**: 149; **829**: 164-65; **851**: 149 n.35; **864**: 149 n.37
Thesmophoriazusae, **52-53**: 167; **67-68**: 167; **100**: 151, 167; **120-122**: 167; **121**: 167; **167**: 168; **170**: 37 n.25; **383-432**: 144
Wasps, **44-46**: 149 n.39; **54**: 79; **54-67**: 85; **56-66**: 79; **71-77**: 79-80; **74-87**: 79; **74-87**: 88 n.75; **85**: 80; **136**: 80; **401**: 150; **1052**: 163 n.79; **1501ff.**: 149 n.37; **1525**: 142 n.9
Wealth, Σ **179**: 132; **288**: 170; **290**: 170 n.90; **290-291**: 170; Σ **298**: 170 n.91; **290-321**: 153, 167; **302-306**: 171; **304-305**: 171; **316-317**: 171
Fragments (K.-A.), **fr.191-204**: 11 n.35; **fr.205**: 149 n.39; **fr.231**: 22 n.56; **fr.239**: 144 n.17; **fr.244**: 149 n.39; **fr.346**: 115 n.73; **fr.347**: 142 n.9; **fr.364**: 159 n.67; **fr.422**: 149 n.40; **fr.556**: 149 n.39; **fr.953**: 146

ARISTOPHON (K.-A.), **fr. 11**: 65, 67, 68 n.34
ARISTOTLE
Ath. Pol., **47.4**: 102; **56.3**: 107 n.37
Eth. Nic., **1128a22**: 119
Poetics, **1448a17ff.**: 10; **1449a9**: 84; **1449a14-15**: ii; **1449a32-34**: 10; **1449b5-9**: 96 n.86, 141; **1449b7-9**: 121 n.6; **1449b8-9**: 115; **1451b9**: 48; **1451b18-23**: 167; **1456a27-32**: 167; **1456a32**: 111 n.53
Politics, **3.3 1276b4**: 109; **5.8 1309a17**: 107
ATHENAEUS, **1.6e ff.**: 168; **8.364a**: 142 n.11; **9.368b**: 142 n.11; **9.373f-374b**: 31; **12.534b ff.**: 149 n.39; **13.559b-c**: 66 n.31; **13.590f**: 4 n.12, 159 n.68; **13.591a**: 4 n.12; **14.653f**: 142 n.11; **15.665b-668f**: 22 n.56; **63d-64f**: 135; **110d**: 124 n.12
CALLIAS (K.-A.), **fr.12**: 22 n.56
CALLIMACHUS
Hymn to Artemis, **4-28**: 1 n.3
Hymn to Delos, **55-274**: 1 n.3
CEPHISODORUS (K.-A.)
fr.5: 22 n.56
CRATINUS (K.-A.), **test. ad Odysses**: 115, 128 n.28; **fr.32**: 142 n.9, 149 n.38; **fr.37**: 150 n.43; **fr.114-127**: 11 n.35; **fr.124**: 22 n.56, 125; **fr.150**: 17 n.45; **fr.150.2-5**: 130 n.32; **fr.247**: 144 n.17; **fr.248**: 144 n.17; **fr.254**: 144 n.17
DEMETRIUS I (K.-A.), **test.1**: 18; **test.2**: 18; **test. ad Dionysou Gonai**: 5 n.14.
DEMOSTHENES, **1.19**: 103 n.15; **18.180**: 40 n.32; **21.13-18**: 106; **21.14**: 106; **21.16**: 107 n.36; **24.98**: 102; **39.17**: 101 n.10;
DIOGENES LAERTIUS, **V 83**: 18
DIONYSUS THRAX, Σ **XVIIIa** (Koster), **test.16** (K.-A.): 122: n.7
EPHIPPUS (K.-A.), **fr.15.3-4**: 33 n.16

EPICRATES (K.-A.), **fr.5.4-9**: 33 n.16
EPIGENES (K.-A.), **fr.4**: 159 n.67
ERATOSTHENES (Str.), **fr.46**: 143 n.14
EUBULUS (K.-A.), **fr.2**: 112 n.56, 112; **fr.6**: 136; **fr.7**: 112; **fr.15**: 22 n.56, 126; **fr.20**: 150 n.43; **fr.41**: 68; **fr.42**: 159 n.67; **fr.60-63**: 11 n.35; **fr.67.4**: 33; **fr.75**: 133; **fr.89**: 17 n.45; **fr.102-103**: 39, 112; **fr.109.1-2**: 33 n.16; **fr.122**: 33 n.16
EUPOLIS (K.-A.), **fr.95**: 22 n.56; **fr.399**: 22 n.56
EURIPIDES
  Helen, **1301-1368**: 111 n.54
  Hippolytus, **616-624**: 67 n.32
  Medea, **471**: 67 n.31
  fr.7 (Mette): 67 n.31; **fr.537** (Mette): 67 n.31; **fr.720** (N²): 60; **fr.1341** (Mette): 76 n.31
EUSTATHIUS, **1834.15**: 31
EVANTHIUS (XXV 1 Koster)
  De Fabula, **p. 125.78-85**: 99 n.1; **p. 124.58**: 2 n.6
HERMIPPUS (K.-A.), **fr.2**: 3 n.8, 13; **fr.2-6**: 7 n.25; **fr.3**: 13; **fr.48**: 22 n.56
HERODOTUS, **4.2**: 71 n.37
HESIOD
  Theogony, **53-60**: 16 n.42
  Works and Days, **259-264**: 157 n.63
  fr.268: 67 n.32, **fr.143ff.** (Merkelbach-West): 143 n.15
HIPPONAX, **84.17**: 155 n.58
HOMER
  Homeric Hymns,
  To Aphrodite (VI) 2-18: 1 n.1; **15-18**: 3-4; **17-18**: 4
  To Apollo (III) 14-18: 1 n.1; **25-139**: 1 n.1; **303-354**: 1 n.1
  To Athena (XXVIII) 4-16: 1 n.1
  To Dionysus (I) 6ff.: 5 n.15; **6-8**: 1 n.1
  To Helius (XXXI) 2-7: 1 n.1

To Hermes (IV) 3-end: 1 n.1, 1 n.2; **235ff.**: 7; **327ff.**: 7
To Hermes (XVIII) 3-9: 1 n.1;
To Pan (XIX) 28-47: 1 n.1; **30-47**: 6; **38**: 6 n.19
To Selene (XXXII) 14-16: 1 n.1
Illiad, **1.518-523**: 5 n.15; **1.536-570**: 5, 10; **1.540-543**: 5 n.15; **1.551-559**: 5 n.15
Odyssey, **8**: 10; **9.394**: 170
HYGINUS, **fab.142**: 67 n.32
INSCRIPTIONES GRAECAE
  I² **187**: 106 n.32
  I³ **254**: 106 n.32
  II/III² **2325**: 40 n.32
  II² **18**: 148 n.33; **1611.9**: 103 n.16; **1613.302**: 103 n.16; **1627.269**: 103 n.16; **2318**: 108; **3028**: 148 n.31, 149 n.33; **3095**: 108 n.43; **3096**: 108 n.43; **3098**: 108 n.43; **2325.131**: 18
INSCRIPTIONES GRAECAE URBIS ROMAE, **218**: 20 n.51
ISAEUS, **5.36**: 106 n.31
ISOCRATES, **8.14**: 179; **16.6**: 149 n.42
LUCIAN
  Dialogues of the Gods, **2 [22]**: 1 n.4, 6; **11 [7]**: 1 n.4; **12 [9]**: 1 n.4, 5; **13 [8]**: 1 n.4, 7; **18 [16]**: 1 n.4
  Dialogues of the Sea Gods, **9 [10]**: 1 n.4
LYSIAS
  1.33: 176 n.77; **20.21**: 148 n.33; **fr.53**: 148 n.33
MENANDER
  Aspis, **97-98**: 74 n.43; **299ff.**: 30 n.4
  Dyscolus, **153-159**: 62; **153-168**: 58, 61-62, 74-75, 74 n.45, 78; **154**: 63; **154-172**: 63; **158**: 65 n.29; **160-161**: 63; **173-176**: 63; **173-179**: 63; **176**: 63; **230-232**: 39 n.30, 110; **283-286**: 30 n.5; **690-758**: 30 n.4; **758**: 30 n.4; **880**: 30
  Georgus, **22-23**: 74 n.43

MENANDER (cont.)
  Perikeiromene, **779-827:** 62 n.24
  Samia, **1-57:** 71 n.39; **269:** 30 n.3;
    725: 30 n.3
  fr. 198: 67 n.33; **fr.718:** 65-67
NICOCHARES (K.-A.), **fr.4:** 171
    n.92, **fr.13:** 22 n.56
NICOPHON (K.-A.), **test. 4:** 18;
    fr.1-5: 4 n.9, 18
NONNUS, **13.148:** 15 n.40
OVID
  Metamorphoses, **3.259ff.:** 5 n.15;
    3.310-315: 5 n.15
P. KÖLN (=*TrGF* II [Kannicht-Snell]
    217) **242A:** 42-45, 42 n.40;
    242A.19: 44; **242A.20:** 44, 44 n.42;
    242A.23: 44; **242A.25:** 44
P. OXY., **3540:** 114 n.70
PAUSANIAS, **10.4.4:** 67 n.32
PHERECRATES (K.-A.), **test.2a:** 140;
    fr.6: 149, 149 n.36, 154, 166; **fr.7:**
    150 n.43; **fr.11:** 149, 149 n.38;
    fr.15: 149; **fr.31:** 151, 154; **fr.37:**
    150; **fr.47:** 154; **fr.64:** 149; **fr.75:**
    159-60; **fr.76:** 159; **fr.76.3:** 148 n.28;
    fr.84: 163-64; **fr.113:** 143 n.14, 154;
    fr.114: 154; **fr.116:** 143 n.14; **fr.119:**
    144; n.16; **fr.122:** 144 n.16; **fr.125:**
    144 n.16; **fr. 138:** 154; **fr.143:** 149;
    fr.152: 159 n.67; **fr.155:** v-vi, 77
    n.53, 145 n.21, 139-64, 173-74, 179;
    fr.155.1-3: 143, 147 n.25; **fr.155.2:**
    157; **fr.155.3:** 157; **fr.155.4-5:** 155,
    156; **fr.155.7:** 157; **fr.155.8-13:** 147;
    fr.155.9-13: 151; **fr.155.10:** 150;
    fr.155.11-12: 147 n.26, 153;
    fr.155.14: 153, 155; **fr.155.14-18:**
    147; **fr.155.15:** 150; **fr.155.18:** 158;
    fr.155.19-20: 150; **fr.155.19-25:** 147;
    fr.155.21: 148; **fr.155.22-23:** 158;
    fr.155.23: 151; **fr.155.23-25:** 153; **fr.
    155.26-28:** 140 n.4, 142; **fr.155.28:**
    156; **fr.156:** 143; **fr.157-158:** 145;
    fr.159: 144; **fr.161:** 145; **fr.162:** 143-
    45; **fr.164:** 149; **fr.168:** 145 n.21
PHILEMON (K.-A.), **fr.114:** 33 n.16

PHILISCUS (K.-A.), **test. ad
    Aretemidos kai Apollonos
    Goanai:** 8 n.26; **test. ad Panos
    Gonai:** 6 n.17; **test.1:** 3 n.9, 7 n.24,
    14 n.37; **test.*2:** 22
PHILOXENUS, **fr.838** (PMG): 134-35
PHILYLLIUS (K.-A.), **fr.22:** 171 n.92
PLATO
  Laws, **626d:** 148 n.29; **653a ff.:** 154;
    653d-673a: 152; **700a-701b:** 153;
    701a: 105 n.27; **795a-812e:** 152;
    935e: 179
  Protagoras, **327d:** 140 n.5
  Republic, **3.391c:** 143 n.15; **398c-
    399d:** 152; **398e:** 155
PLATO COMICUS (K.-A.)
  test.18: 122 n.8; **fr.46f.:** 22 n.56;
    fr.46.1-2: 125; **fr.46.4-5:** 125; **fr.47:**
    125; **fr.65:** 171 n.92; **fr.71:** 22 n.56,
    125; **fr.71.10-11:** 126; **fr.89:** 124;
    fr.89-94: 124; **fr.90:** 124; **fr.92:** 124
    n.12; **fr.93:** 124, 124 n.14; **fr.143:**
    155 n.58; **fr.188:** 132-33; **fr.188.1-4:**
    132; **fr.188.6:** 135; **fr.189:** 133-35;
    fr.189.4: 134; **fr.189.9:** 135;
    fr.189.10: 135; **fr.189.20:** 135;
    fr.207: 144 n.17
PLATONIUS (I Koster)
  *On the Different (Periods) of
    Comedies,* **3.13-4.30:** 12-13 n.36;
    4.20-22: 99 n.1, 105 n.28;
    4.29ff.: 127; **4.36:** 99 n.1; **5.42-
    47:** 3 n.7; **5.49-5.52:** 13 n.36;
    5.51-52: 128 n.28
PLAUTUS
  Amphitryo, **142-145:** 124;
    474-475: 124
  Poenulus, **578-614:** 113
  Rudens, **290-323:** 113
PLUTARCH
  *Synkrisis of Aristophanes and
    Menander (Moralia),* **853a-854d:**
    51-56, 51 n.11; 62 n.24
[PLUTARCH]
  De Musica (Moralia), **1141d:**
    78 n.53; **1141d-1142a:** 145-47

POLYZELUS (K.-A.), **test. ad Aphrodites Gonai:** 4 n.9; **test. ad Panos Gonai:** 5 n.14; **test.4:** 18 n.46; **fr.6-7:** 5 n.14; **fr.8-11:** 8 n.27; **fr.9:** 15-17, 23; **fr.11:** 17
PROLEGOMENA DE COMOEDIA **8.27** (III Koster): 140 n.3; **8.30** (III Koster): 140; **9.44-10.45** (III Koster): 81, 81 n.58-59, 84; **13.10ff.** (V Koster): 99 n.1
SOPHOCLES
Oedipus, **629:** 60
fr.314 (Radt): 10 n.34
STRATON (K.-A.), **fr.1:** 33 n.16
SUDA, φ **357:** 7 n.24, 14 n.37
SUSARION (K.-A.), **test.8:** 57
TERENCE
Eunuch, **292ff.:** 4 n.11

THEOPOMPUS (K.-A.), **fr.5:** 171 n.92; **fr.166:** 103 n.16
TIMESITHEUS (Snell), **I 214:** 7 n.22
TIMOCLES (K.-A.), **fr.6.8-19:** 34-35; **fr.27:** 109
TIMOTHEUS, **fr.788** (PMG): 148 n.27; **fr.791.29:** 148
XENARCHUS (K.-A.), **fr.1.4-6:** 136; **fr.4.6:** 33; **fr.14:** 71, 71 n.38
XENOPHON
Cyropaedia, **1.1.2:** 143 n.15; **1.1.5:** 143 n.15
Memorabilia, **3.11.4:** 162
Oeconomicus, **7.3:** 106 n.29
Symposium, **8.23:** 143 n.15
[XENOPHON], **3.4:** 106 n.32

DATE DUE

NOV 24 1997